# Capitalism:
# The New Segregation

Lewis Eldridge

## ACKNOWLEDGEMENTS

I am who I am because of the following individuals of whom I'm eternally grateful, just for whom they are and the impact they've had on my life, even unaware:

**<u>All praises go to Jesus who is the Christ, our Lord and our Savior</u>!**

*My Wife*: Dena Denise Eldridge

*My Parents*: Reverend Booker Douglas & Johnnie Mae Eldridge

*My Father in the Ministry*: The late Dr. E.E. Stafford

*My Undergraduate Pastor & Friend*: Moreh Marvin E. Davis

*My Pastor and Friend*: Dr. Kevin E. Stafford

| | |
|---|---|
| Dr. Angulus Wilson | Al Haymon |
| Dr. Anthony Bennett | Angela Perry |
| Dr. Charles Morris | Ben Eiland |
| Dr. Claybon Lea Jr. | Darren Smith |
| Dr. Cornell West | Douglas Eslinger |
| Dr. Emil Thomas | LaRonda Lauderdale |
| Dr. James Cone | Liz Gutierrez |
| Dr. Marc Lamont Hill | Patrick Hill |
| Dr. Melvin Von Wade | Richard Beal |
| Dr. Richard Wolff | Roslyn Brock |
| Dr. Rodney S. Croom | Salahudin Akbar |
| Dr. Ticey Brown | Tory Erickson |
| The late Dr. T.M. Chambers Jr. | Tracey Bracey |
| Dwayne Odom | Trisha Stafford-Odom |

Special thanks to the *NAACP;*

Special thanks to: "*Celebrity Net Worth.com*" as my primary net worth source;

Special thanks to *Forbes Magazine;*

Special thanks to: *Celebritystacks.com; GetNetWorth.com; How-Rich.org; The-Net-Worth.com,* and *"The Richest.com.*
All required permissions on file at *Justine1964Publishing;*

Special thanks to my publisher, Maureka Davis!

**Dedicated to my biological mother, *Justine Woodard*, who birthed & gave me physical life**

**as my Heavenly Father gave me spiritual life.**

**I love and miss you ever so dearly, more & more, as each day progresses!**

# NET WORTH
## RESOURCES

| # | PERMISSION | RESOURCE |
|---|---|---|
| 1 | On File @ Justine1964Publishing | CelebrityNetWorth.com |
| 2 | N/A | Celebritystacks.com |
| 3 | On File @ Justine1964Publishing | GetNetWorth.com |
| 4 | N/A | How-Rich.org |
| 5 | N/A | The-Net-Worth.com |
| 6 | On File @ Justine1964Publishing | The Richest.com |

# TABLE OF CONTENTS

The setting was unique, innovative, and impressive. The greatest upwardly mobile minds of the African-American ethnicity sitting at a 100-seat board table in the center of a banquet hall while the greatest seasoned minds of wisdom and experience sitting around the perimeter of the room. Those who made up the room's nucleus came from all academic career backgrounds and accomplishments ranging from the most prestigious career industries of medicine and law to politics, university professors, pastors, CEO's, MBA's, entrepreneurs, cutting-edge and trend-setting success stories from every dimension of influential lifestyles. On May 26-29, 2005, I was honored to have received an invitation, attended, participated, and sat at the table with some of the greatest African-American minds of my generation.

The summit was well organized. With the younger accomplished invitees in the middle of this very large hall decorated with high vaulted ceilings and the *NAACP's* current leadership and senior statesmen/stateswomen around the perimeter, a critical question faced this great organization and was presented directly to the centered nucleus. As the *NAACP* was nearing its centennial celebration within the next five years (*NAACP Centennial Celebration: 2010*), the secondary question that brought these advanced thinkers together, "Why was the total current membership, at that time, only 300,000?"

With the goal of identifying and developing the next generation of leaders, the *NAACP* held its first annual

*NAACP Leadership 500 Summit* at the Sandestin Golf and Beach Resort in Destin, Fla., May 26-29, 2005. The Summit themed "Reaching in and Pulling Back," was the brainchild of *NAACP National Board of Directors* Vice Chairman Roslyn Brock, and was designed to attract professionals and entrepreneurs 30-50 years of age.[1]

However, the ultimate question and primary purpose of the meeting was, "Of the total membership size, why were those who were younger than 50 years of age only a very small composite encompassing a single digit enrollment percentage of active and involved members?" The question was highly relevant as the primary host presented the question in such a manner that it invoked and required both a cognitive and emotional response. Paraphrasing the symposium's chairperson, Rosalyn Brock, who posed the ultimate question, "If those around the wall made the sacrifices for you all to sit in the seats you now occupy based on infinite educational opportunities and unlimited career possibilities as well as the current achievements of both, what prevents you from giving back to the organization that facilitated these realities?"

Many offered thought provoking answers lending to creative dialogue and debate of the highest scholasticism. However, it was Dr. Marc Lamont Hill (former Professor of *African-American Studies* at *Temple University*, *Columbia University*, and now, Professor of *African-American Studies* at *Morehouse College*, Atlanta, GA., and one of the foremost

---

[1] *NAACP*. http://action.naacp.org/page/-/annual%20reports/2005ar.pdf (accessed May 29, 2005).

authorities in the field of *African-American Studies* in our time) who confounded the room with a question, a diagnosis, and an impressive reality. Dr. Hill asked, "What is your 'Mission Statement'? In this question, it was implied that if the original 'Mission Statement' of the organization was racial equality, although still a reality, it is not something that is as blatantly affecting younger generations as it was for elder where the need for active membership involvement is evident to those who did not experience the struggle. Therefore, a re-assessment of the 'Mission Statement' was encouraged.

Yet, he blew my wig back when he said that racial division is still an awful reality in modern America, but the primary division is no longer 'racial', its "economic". The greatest division in America is between the "haves" and "have-nots". Consequently, if those of Generations "X" and "Y" can see how they can achieve economic equality, they will be more inclined to consider membership.

The Mission Statement for the *NAACP* was/is powerful, efficient, and effective:

**2005 *NAACP* Mission Statement:** "The goal of eliminating race prejudice and removing all barriers of racial discrimination through democratic processes."[2]

**2016 *NAACP* Mission Statement:** "The mission of the *National Association for the Advancement of Colored People* is to ensure the political, educational, social, and economic equality of rights of all persons and to eliminate race-based discrimination."[3]

---

[2] *NAACP.* http://action.naacp.org/page/-/annual%20reports/2005ar.pdf (accessed May 29, 2005).
[3] *NAACP.* http://action.naacp.org/page/-/annual%20reports/_NAACP_2013AR_WebFNL.pdf (accessed November 1, 2013)

Dr. Hill's recommendation was given strong consideration as the 'Mission Statement' changed during the intermediate decade. As a result, many thanks go to Dr. Marc Lamont Hill. Many thanks to the *NAACP* for the work of this historical organization for more than a century and for the wisdom to include and combine the greatest "up and coming" African-American thinkers with those who paved the way towards generational achievement for all cultures, ethnicities, and people groups. It is the element of "economic equality" that has established the foundation for this particular work.

## INTRODUCTION

*Inequality* provides the total net worth for the entire African-American people as a culture to be a mere $2t compared to America's overall net worth of $77t. These figures quickly and clearly show that African-American's have not achieved economic equality, as their ethnicity's entire net worth is only 3% of America's overall general net worth. As well, *Inequality* and the *Huffington Post* reports that 35% of the African-American population has zero or negative net worth. Both sources have established that 56% of the total cumulative African-American net worth, are owned by the top 1% with complete capitalistic assimilation projected to occur in 2026 when 98% of the entire African-American culture's net worth will be owned by the top 1% of all African-Americans.

At present, the total African-American population is very near 40 million total persons. For the sake of simplistic statistical mathematics leading to an inevitable conclusion, 10% is 4 million, making the top 1% of the entire ethnicity, 400,000. It must be noted and emphasized that this book and its content is fact based. As a result, the charts, contained within the *Appendix*, are critical components towards understanding and making the thematic point that the top 1%, 400,000 African-Americans, will soon own and 98% of the entire culture's wealth. I was highly tempted to name 4,000 of the wealthiest African-Americans thereby listing .01%. However, the 2,000 plus listed were adequate enough data to establish a foundation towards making the point and following the trend of economic segregation's inevitability. Certainly, I hope that all would read, find interesting, and useful, the book's material. However, if one only viewed the charts, I believe the point would still be made.

The wealthiest 400,000, the top 1%, will soon own 98% of the entire culture's wealth. The top two wealthiest African-American individuals currently own $4B of the culture's entire $2t of net worth according to *Appendix: Charts XIX and XX*. The wealthiest top 40 African-Americans currently own $20B according to *Appendix: Chart XIX*. The richest top 2,000 African-Americans currently own $45B according to *Appendix: Chart XX*. These are all named, listed, and documented in the "Charts" of the "Appendix".

Four periods define African-American history, slavery, segregation, stagnation, and the current era of capitalism. Does slavery still exist? Of course! Just not in blatant overt realities! No longer is there the existence of a slave master who legally owns "other people" as property. This has long been determined to be illegal. People, regardless of color and ethnicity, are still bigots based on deep-seeded hate that will continue within the heart of humanity as long as greed, supremacy, and the need to experience the feelings of superiority remains apart of the human existence. Unfortunately, African-Americans are in no wise exempt as bitterness, resentment, and the practices of reverse discrimination continue to fuel generationally rippled hatred. Does slavery still exist? Emphatically, one can conclude that enslavement has effectively replaced slavery. Since enslavement can be something that is imposed, either self-inflicted, or systemically perpetuated, it can assume infinite forms. Although slavery is cruel and inhumane, with the possible passionate personal disagreements of those who experienced such atrocities, it cannot be as disconcerting as enslavement.

The increase in mortality rates due to gang violence, criminality, and chemical addiction overdoses is imposed as guns are not manufactured in the ghetto nor is there any coca or poppy fields in the projects of urban American cities. These deaths are also self-inflicted as there are no requirements to be gang affiliated or a drug dealer, much less an addict. Simultaneously, they are systemic, as the influential fragile minds of adolescents will always succumb to the power of juvenile peer pressure.

While enslavement has replaced slavery in highly sophisticated complexities, the stagnation of the African-American has served as the foundation and critical component to the ultimate segregation, capitalism! Likewise, segregation does not have to always appear in the form of physical separatism but in other more sophisticated forms. If the next step after slavery, segregation, and stagnation was to flood the African-American ethnicity with billions of dollars, however, only to an elite few (i.e., a top 1%), there had to be a limitation on the quantity of the elitist class, thus, the rationale for population controls. This is a highly sophisticated form of segregation rudimentary to capitalism. Consider all those who died, were and are literally imprisoned, or enslaved by addiction that would have been talented athletes or entertainers and thus, possibilities of being and/or expanding that top 1% of the elite class. As a result, active population controls have oppressed, stagnated the African-American people, and reared its ugly head in indirect practices. Within the concept of population controls lies the protection of the status-quo establishment while simultaneously preparing for the execution and reality of capitalistic segregation.

The core of capitalism requires that the proletariat support the bourgeoisie. Within the realm of a culture's own self-destruction, would one African-American sell drugs to another in their quest towards a capitalistic end resulting in a rich class, i.e., "the dealers", and a poor class, i.e., the "crack-head"? Likewise, does not the working class purchase the music, the sneakers, and economically support the entertainment of actors, actresses, and athletes thus perpetuating the latter's riches, the former's poverty, and legitimizing the myth that African-Americans are nothing more than consumers opposed to manufacturers, as this will always and only yield nothing more than pseudo-wealth.

Within the simplicity of capitalistic polarization between the rich and poor lie the elements of hope and despair. Concurrently, in order for capitalism to work, the kin cousins of hope and despair must coexist. Does the African-American need to be fed hope but experience despair in order to sustain the exclusivity of the bourgeoisie class? Must the African-American believe that wealth is always at their reach for this concept to be effective? Has the purest entity to any culture, i.e., faith, been so

14

corrupted by greed and celebrity personalities that capitalistic ideologies have infiltrated Christianity with false hopes of imminent prosperity? Has the African-American been provided false hopes towards celebrity with the dynamic of direct role modeling serving as a bonus, gridlocking the pursuit towards entertainment and consequently limiting aspirations towards the more prestigious careers? Will adults assume unreasonable debt while their children aspire to be these icons no matter what the cost?

While America and Europe offers the greatest comforts of life, are they living beyond their means, thus, the downsides of capitalism, deficit and debt? This is evident, by not just America, but practically every westernized country has exceeded an 80% *Debt-to-GDP* (*Gross Domestic Product*) ratio. This is highly problematic as well as intensified for America, as it is still an adolescent in years of existence as a country compared to its European capitalistic neighbors. To further add complexity to America's age is the fact that it has only taken one generation, two decades, twenty years since its half century *Cold War* victory to literally borrow 104% of its *GDP*. If $19t has not solved America's problems but has yielded more homelessness, helplessness, and hopelessness, capitalism cannot be the best economic system. If capitalism has caused such a serious imbalance in wealth whereby the richest 1% owns 99% of the entire country's wealth, this system has proven to only benefit a few, divides a people into a rich and poor class, and presents the ultimate segregation. As this is the realistic outcome for America, what would make the African-American believe that they would not experience the same result? Rich and poor is not equality. The greatest fear of all is that the African-American as individuals or collectively as an ethnicity, culture, or people group could care less about this very realistic dynamic and consequently do nothing to reverse these trends. As a result, **Capitalism is The New Segregation!**

## Chapter One

## THE CONSTRUCTS OF A DEMOCRACY
### (1860-1960)

In a democracy, how does any given ethnicity maintain a majority especially when a key component of a developed country as defined by *United Nations Developed Country Policy* is to reproduce no more than 2.1 children per household?[4] If unchecked, it is automatic that the most reproducing people group, race, or ethnicity would eventually become the overwhelmingly majority. While European-based Americans hold to this standard, it is apparent that African-Americans have never consciously or unconsciously upheld this practice. It is indisputable, that Hispanic Americans are by far the fastest growing people group within the *United States of America (USA)*.

Of course, the Chinese and those from India and Japan are significantly more globally populous than Americans are. However, within America, whites have been able to maintain a 59% voting majority within the *USA* since it's founding in spite of low birth rates, high mortality, controlled immigration, and other reproductive factors. How has this been possible especially in relationship to African-Americans who clearly have more children than their white counterparts as indicated by *Appendix: Chart #IV*? Is this intentional, in order to maintain a democratic voting majority and accordingly continue, to make and enforce the laws

---

[4]*United Nations.* "World Population Policies 2011: Economic and Social Affairs." http://www.un.org/en/development/desa/population/publications/pdf/policy/WPP2011/wpp2011.pdf, pg.7 (accessed 2013).

that all live by? Alternatively, is this just another one of those paranoid conspiracy theories? There is one infallible way to determine. Let us examine the facts.

In 1790, when the first census was taken, African-Americans numbered about 760,000, approximately 20% of the population (*Appendix: Chart #III*). In 1860, at the start of the *Civil War*, the African-American population increased to 4.4 million, but the percentage rate dropped to a little over 13% of the overall country's population (*Appendix: Chart #III*). In order to escape the oppression of Jim Crow, African-Americans bailed north from 1890 to 1970 in what history has termed, *The Great Migration,* in search for better living conditions and employment opportunities. This trend is currently in reverse with African-Americans moving back south to the *Bible Belt*.

There are two different periods in American history when it appears that intentional elements were interwoven like a spider's web into African-American history; in 1865 during the *Emancipation Proclamation* and in 1965 during the Rosa Parks incident that contributed to an African-American revolution when Dr. Martin Luther King Jr., led a non-violent movement towards equality. How ironic it is that these two events occurred exactly one hundred years apart? During both periods, African-Americans were robbed of their voting rights and privileges as home-born working citizens of this great nation.

In a system where the boss of the *USA* is not the President, the *Senate*, the *House of Representatives*, or the *U.S. Supreme*

*Court* but the people of this great nation, how does a specific populous maintain a majority? In a system and country that is governed by the "Rule of Law", how does a single ethnic group maintain a majority? Not only does a democracy require a maintained majority of a given ethnic group but limitations on those who can participate in the law making process whether they are disqualified by criminality, immigration controls, politics or included because of socio-economic or political influence.

A democracy is one of the many "ocracies" (*Appendix: Chart #VII*) within political science. The suffix comes from the Greek word "archon" which means "to rule". By adding any given prefix, it defines who rules. After processing all of these forms of government, it reminds me of words spoken by Winston Churchill in his speech to the *House of Commons* on 11 November 1947, "Democracy is the worst form of government except for all those others that have been tried."[5]

Since "Demo" means people, then "Democracy" by definition means, "Ruled by the People". How do the people rule? They rule by their voice and by their vote! *The First Amendment* of the *United States Constitution* allows any citizen the privilege of saying, endorsing, criticizing, or protesting any process of the government, another citizen, any concept, or philosophy.

> Congress shall make no law respecting an establishment of religion, or prohibiting the free exercise thereof; or

---

[5] Barnes, Matt. Capitalism: *The Worst Economic System, Except for All the Others.* University of Pittsburg: The Pitt News. http://pittnews.com/article/5424/opinions/capitalism-the-worst-economic-system-except-for-all-the-others/ (accessed August 26, 2014).

abridging the freedom of speech, or of the press; or the right of the people peaceably to assemble, and to petition the Government for a redress of grievances.[6]

This is one of the principal advantages of capitalism over communism. While communism is an imperfect system of government because of corruption, the media and the citizens of the *USA* will exercise their *First Amendment* right to expose corruption through dramatic high profile scandals. The publicity of the matter serves as self-protection in itself.

In a democratic country such as the *United States of America*, it is by the very definition of the word, "democracy", a society "ruled by the people", primarily, and "ruled by vote", secondarily. How then have the African-American people been unable to become the majority race, ethnicity, and people when they clearly have a higher reproduction rate than their European-American counterparts? The quintessential question is, "In a democracy, a country governed by the people via voting rights, how does any given people group especially the original, host, and primary linguistic ethnicity maintain a voting majority in the face of other mass reproducing internal ethnic groups?

Countries have been recently placed into two categories, "Developed" and "Developing". These are evolutionary terms from the former language of "First", "Second", and "Third-World"

---

[6] "The Charters of Freedom." Government Archives.
http://www.archives.gov/exhibits/charters/bill_of_rights_transcript.html (accessed: 1776).

countries. *Developing Countries* have been defined by certain criteria with 2.1 children per family as a primary criterion.

> Developed countries usually have a much lower fertility rate due to greater wealth, education, and urbanization. Mortality rates are low, birth control is understood and easily accessible, and costs are often deemed very high because of education, clothing, feeding, and social amenities...In undeveloped countries on the other hand, families desire children for their labour and as caregivers for their parents in old age. Fertility rates are also higher due to the lack of access to contraceptives; generally lower levels of female education, and lower rates of female employment in industry.[7]

If white or European-Americans have been able to successfully maintain these criteria while African-Americans have far exceeded these reproductive standards, how then is the former able to maintain a significant majority? The most recent figures supplied by the *United States Census Bureau* dictates that colonial America has been able to maintain a 53% majority (*Appendix: Chart #II*) while reproducing at a rate three times less than their African-American counterpart and much less than their fellow Hispanic progressive countrymen.

> The total fertility rate in the *United States* after *World War II* peaked at about 3.8 children per woman in the late 1950s and by 1999 was at 2 children. This means that an imaginary woman (defined in the introduction) who fast-forwarded through her life in the late 1950s would have been expected to have about four children, whereas an imaginary woman who fast-forwarded through her life in

---

[7] Sanyal, Sanyeev. "The End of Population Growth." Project Syndicate. http://www.project-syndicate.org/commentary/the-end-of-population-growth (accessed October 30, 2011).

1999 would have been expected to have only about two children in her lifetime. The fertility rate of the total U.S. population is at around the replacement level of about 2.1 children per woman. However, the fertility of the population of the *United States* is below replacement among those native born, and above replacement among immigrant families, most of who come to the U.S. from countries with higher fertility than that of the U.S.[8]

As America was built on a political premise, like any other democracy, so also was it built on an economic system, capitalism, where the host or dominant ethnicity would maintain an economic majority even if the continuity of this way of life requires active labor for the capitalist, consumer spending back to the capitalist of the same product produced by the laborer, and tax controls upon the laborer to the government who also are the same capitalist. This is triple dipping. Within a complete legal agreement, the employee sells their labor to the employer at a cost that permits the employer to make a profit while the employee is compensated at a rate that may permit them enough to break even for the basic necessities of life. When the employee needs a good or service whether produced directly by them or another citizen, they take of their limited compensation and barters it for the good or service needed, to either the same or different employer. The employers are the capitalist who are required to take directly from the

---

[8] Hill, Laura E., l and Johnson, Hans P. "How Fertility Changes Across Immigrant Generations." Public Policy Institute of California, Research Brief #58. http://www.ppic.org/content/pubs/rb/RB_402LHRB.pdf (accessed April 2002).

employee's compensation a tax paid to the government even before the employee receives compensation for labor rendered. This tax is designed to pay for the government's expenses specifically relating to monopolistic services, such as the military, highways, and foreign affairs. Although the government should make a profit as the employer, they instead incur a deficit causing them to borrow. Whom do they borrow from? The employer! This is actually quadruple dipping that perpetuates a new and improved segregation, capitalism, and classism that causes a huge schism between the rich and poor.

Richard Wolff, the leading objective authority on the subject matter of "capitalism", in one his many publications on the subject matter, *Democracy at Work: A Cure for Capitalism (2012)*, covers the entire spectrum of capitalism from its inception, dynamics, benefits, problems, and inevitable demise because of its inherent flaws.

> Capitalism has had an extraordinary run in the world – and nowhere more so than in the *United States*. Its celebrants demand, and capitalism as a system deserves, significant credit for catapulting *Britain's* former secondary colony, the *United States*, to its status as a global economic, political, and cultural superpower in two hundred years.... The former colony turned to immigration and imperialism as key means to further its ascendancy. Yet they also contributed to economic dependency on an evolving globalization of capitalism.... A capitalist system is, then, one in which a mass of people – productive workers – interact with nature to fashion both means of production (tools, equipment, and raw materials) and final products for human consumption. They produce a total output larger than the portion of that output (wages) given back to them.

The wage portion sustains the productive workers; it provides their consumption and secures their continued productive labor. The difference between their total output and their wage portion is called the "surplus," and it accrues to a different group of people, the employers of productive laborers: capitalist.... The productive laborers – those who produce the surplus – use the wages paid to them by the capitalists to buy the goods and services they consume and to pay personal taxes.[9]

[9] Wolff, Richard. *Democracy at Work: A Cure for Capitalism*. Chicago, IL: Haymarket Books, 2012; 17,22.

## Chapter Two

## THE ABSENTEE SLAVE MASTER

### (1960-1970)

The Slave Master is visualized by the African-American youth and remembered by the African-American senior citizen as sitting on a horse watching the whipping of the 'Field Negro' while simultaneously laying back in a living room rocking chair barking orders to the "House Negro". During these realities, he intentionally executed three priorities.

First, the Slave Master had and held an economic priority to protect his property. This is, by far, the worst aspect of slavery, i.e., to realize that one is not there own but literally and physically owned by another. While a violation of the constitutional rights, which is held so near, and dear, the slave master believed it to be morally correct because it was legally correct. The inability for anyone to make their own decisions is degrading in a democracy where freedom and justice for all stands at the very premise of its constitution, creeds, and philosophy.

Of all my personal beliefs, individual liberty is second in importance immediately after my theological beliefs as it relates to salvation. If I make a wrong decision, I suffer the consequences. If I make the right decision, I reap the benefits. However, what I deem critically important is that, it is my decision to make.

Second, the Slave Master had and held an economic priority, to protect the bottom line of his profit-and-loss statement. What better way to do this than to control his labor cost? What better labor cost, or any expense for that matter, than, 'free'. With

25

productivity high and labor low (or "no", i.e., slavery), his profits soared.

Third, how can an individual reside and work within a certain democratic community, however, have absolutely no voting rights? This stands at the very heart of the matter within politics, for "politics", by definition, is the process that determines "policy" or the very laws we live by. There was a time when African-Americans were deemed as property under the corruptible genius of the 'Willie Lynch Laws'. This period required an ever-present slave master whether in the house, field, or ship. Many attempted to reverse this injustice. There is little argument that Garveyism would have allowed African-Americans to create their own society by returning to Africa and develop their own political climate, culture, and country. The antithetical logic of Carter G. Woodson won out from two perspectives, leaving the African-American fighting injustice and praying for equality. Not only was Woodsonism the preferred option and inevitable reality over Garveyism, it also has surfaced through capitalism as preference over the Washingtonian Doctrine (i.e., "Booker T") of educating the masses opposed to the top ten percent as Woodson proposed. It was the realities of Booker T. Washington, W.E.B. Dubois, Malcolm X, Martin Luther King Jr., Jesse Jackson, Joseph Lowery, Al Sharpton, Spike Lee, Dr. E.E. Stafford, and many others who sought solutions.

The African-American population, by year since 1790 (*Appendix: Chart #III*), shows a positive rate of growth of the

26

African-American people producing the ultimate question, "How can the influence of slavery continue in the absence of a slave master and during a period of toleration?" [10]

Consequently, the critical question is, "Does slavery still exist and if so, in what form? Is it "Neo-Slavery", non-blatant, and biological, as in warfare, with the intent to stagnant an ethnic population that would increase in growth so fast that it would threaten the host population's majority? Do these questions suggest or imply reverse discrimination or a conspiracy theory?

I believe in a society and world of diverse cultures; a mosaic of all people groups who speak different languages, live different lifestyles; a co-existence of a cultural matrix. I would not want to live in a world, society, country, city, or neighborhood where there was only one culture! However, as discussed in Chapter Fifteen of this book entitled, *Classism of African-Americans via Capitalism*, there has to be equality, not superiority or inferiority, not a better than, not a greater than, nor a less than society. Therefore, one, as I, am able to exam certain facts and raise various questions without it neither being nor implying reverse discrimination. The facts are undeniable and real and must at some point be challenged by someone.

There was a time when the Slave Master's PRESENCE was needed in order to maintain these three objectives; first,

---

[10] Gibson, Campbell and Jung, Kay. "Historical Census Statistics On Population Totals By Race, 1790 to 1990, and By Hispanic Origin, 1970 to 1990, For Large Cities And Other Urban Places In The United States." United States Census Bureau (accessed 2016). https://www.census.gov/population/www/documentation/twps0076/twps0076.html. (accessed February 2005).

property interest that happen to be human; second, free labor; third, control of the law, with the law being defined as the rules and morality of life or the protection of democracy. The Slave Master was needed in order to keep the slaves in line, enforce a spirit of slave inferiority, and maintain a perpetual reminder of master superiority.

This entire literary chapter is to establish the foundation that the Slave Master's presence is no longer needed in a capitalistic culture and has been replaced by other more sophisticated abstract entities. The ever-present horseman has been replaced by internal "Clashing", "Criminality", and "Chemical Dependency" perpetuated by "Capitalism" that promotes internal competition, destroys the family structure, and perpetuates a severe decline of the African-American "Community", as well as, the discord of cultural unity. Nevertheless, the African-American must cognitively embrace much of the blame that cannot be cast onto another race or ethnicity nor solely be assigned to any organized secret conspiracy. Much has been brought onto the African-American people through their own mentalities and behaviors.

No longer is the horseman needed but has been replaced by other elements far more superior and far more powerful than a single man on a horse. While a horseman is a single man who must experience shift changes, bathroom breaks, and human error, there are abstract entities that are far more effective and able to span multiple locations and generations. As in warfare, does one need to be at the place of battle during wartime? In modern warfare, do boots have to be on the ground or can war be won from afar via a naval carrier in the *Gulf*, a satellite in space, or a biological, chemical, or technological agent imported by the very population seeking to be controlled?

No longer is the horseman needed who was always out-numbered yet understood that mentality dominance would compensate for any numerical imparities. This concept is as old as Exodus within the scriptures. When a Pharaoh who knew not Joseph arose and realized that the Hebrew people had amassed to over 600,000, he readily recognized that if they continued at their current rate of reproduction, they would out-number the indigenous Egyptians and naturally position themselves to make the rules, subject the natives, and usurp authority.[11] Therefore, let us make them get their own brick and mortar and thus fulfill one of the fundamental laws of Sun Tzu, "All warfare is based on deception.[12] No longer is the horseman needed when as unto "Neo-Colonialism", we can have "Neo-Slavery".

---

[11] Exodus 1:7-13 (KJV).

[12] Tzu, Sun. "The Art of War". Minneapolis, MN: Filiquarian; (accessed November 7, 2007).

## Chapter Three
## POPULATION CONTROLS OF AFRICAN-AMERICANS VIA CLASHING
### (1970-1980)

How ironic it is that that the unholy kin cousins of guns and competition initiated slavery and these same dualistic dynamics serves as perpetual absentee slave masters. The westernized European exploiters provided guns to the Africans in exchanged for slaves. If they failed to trade, the Europeans would sell guns to their native enemies who would, in turn, enslave the former.

> In the fifteenth and sixteenth centuries, new and dynamic forces, which were to affect Africa vitally, emerged from this Mediterranean combination of economic cooperation with political and military warfare. Africa north of the Sahara ultimately became much more of a dead frontier land than before. Other parts of the continent, however, were introduced to the new European demand for African slaves, and received in return from both Europeans and Turks a new weapon, the firearm that was ultimately to lead to considerably upset in the balance of power in many parts of Africa.[13]

It was a catch-twenty-two, enslave or risk becoming a slave.

> Invariably, the Europeans bought their slaves from African kings or merchants. This explains the early concentration of European slave traders on the Gold Coast, for it was there that the Africans taste for European imports – cloth, hardware and metals, spirits and firearms was probably better established than elsewhere, while the African traders who were already accustomed to supplying the Europeans with gold were willing to supply slaves too when the demand for those developed. The persistent growth of the demand led to the extension of the trade, principally

---

[13] Oliver, Roland and Fage, J.D. *A Short History of Africa.* New York: Penguin Group, Sixth Edition, 1988; 94-95.

eastward, towards the Niger Delta and beyond, rather than towards the less economically developed and more thinly populated western coasts. The early slave trade was largely a catch-as-catch-can affair, but after c.1650, as the demand for slaves increased, and as Europeans provided increasing quantities of firearms in exchange, it became a big business organized in their own interest by a series of large new kingdoms that developed close to the Guinea coast.[14]

This dynamic has been a reality of the African-American community since the 1970's with the advent of gangs in Los Angeles. Other cities, such as New York and Chicago used guns to protect their drug trade and economic interest. Thomas Lee Wright, writer of the movie, *New Jack City*, via the character Neno Brown played by Wesley Snipes, said it better than I ever could in his geo-political tirade, "There ain't no oozes made in Harlem." The guns were made in Europe and sold or traded in Africa in exchange for slaves. All enslavement has seldom been outwardly and overtly forced by an external enemy but inwardly exploited by plain natural survival instincts and perpetuated by internal greed and betrayal.

While African-American slavery began with the element of guns, it continues over five hundred years later in the streets of America's largest urban cities as a source of continued, internalized, blatant, and overt enslavement. Since guns are not made in the ghettos of American cities, there continues to be a combination of internal and external forces that contribute to the African-American demise via clashing, guns, and violence. *Smith*

---

[14] Oliver and Fage, pg.102.

*and Wesson*, the most famous of all gun manufacturers is based out of Springfield, Massachusetts and proudly advertises that they have been making guns since 1852. Made in Massachusetts and Maine, yet shipped, sold, and used in the ghettos of our largest cities, this is yet another classic tacit of enslavement that does not require the presence of a human slave master.

Both of these experiences, although five hundred years apart, led to the greatest of all enslavement, death, however now, largely through gang violence. The similarities are undeniable; Conquer or be conquered. Gang or drug lords establish their individual territories. Herein lay the seeds of the capitalistic elements of superiority and inferiority, true separatism and internal segregation. As I grew up in the heart of most renowned gang in all of *South Central Los Angeles*, the *Rollin 60's Crips* based largely out of the streets, 60th – 69$^{th}$, between Crenshaw and Western, the concept of one gang being superior and more revered than another served as the premise of gang dynamics. Once the gang has gained the status of dominance, the gang member embraces the mentality of superiority, popularity, and ultimately, identity and self-esteem in being feared. Consequently, some of the fundamental roots of capitalism's negative attributes are evident as peer pressure within adolescent fragile minds is both present and unavoidable; conquer or be conquered. The sad reality is the existence of a "better than" opposed to an equality outcome. Erick Erickson, in his *Eight Stages of Human Development* suggest, during the ages 5-12 the child is faced with the "Basic Virtue" of "Competency" and will either experience "Industry" or "Inferiority" based on each child's ability to master the latest innovation in comparison to their peers.[15] As a result, the element of competition is engrained and programmed within the child long before the harsh realities of economic capitalism are experienced. Willie Lynch, within the wisdom of his corruptible genius wrote,

> A brief discourse in offspring development will shed light on the key to sound economic principles. Pay little attention to the generation of original breaking, but concentrate on future generations.[16]

Concurrent to the initiation of slavery, once the gang has gained the status of dominance, the goal for each gang member is the mentality of superiority. Is the element of humanity's innate programming of "industry versus inferiority" engrained within children and exploited with the harsh realities of competitive capitalism? The fellow that would ride upon a lady in a Phantom or Mercedes with the intent of establishing a relationship is an idiot as this is the essence and epitome of classism. It is the paraphrased equivalent of saying, 'I have the money that places me in a certain economic class that qualifies me for consideration of your love, intimacy, affection, and relationship.' What is sad is that this reality is one that occurs daily as a common mentality within the African-American culture existing from both genders. The male who engages such practice is unwittingly classist. The woman,

---

[15] Leod, Saul. "Erick Erickson". Simply Psychology. http://www.simplypsychology.org/Erick-Erikson.html (accessed 2008, updated 2013).

[16] Lynch, Willie, *The Willie Lynch Letter and the Making of a Slave*. New York, NY: Classic Books America; 2009.

who bites on it, reduces her standard, thus class, from lady to opportunist. This is classism in its finest.

Black-On-Black crime dictates that African-American homicides within the *United States* from 1970 to 2010 as reported by the *Center for Disease Control* in Atlanta, GA states that within the last 50 years of the twentieth century, 418,500 Black men, women, and children have lost their lives to gun violence. The *United States Justice Department* concur consistency with the *Center for Disease Control* related to Black homicide rates.[17] *The Census Bureau*, a division of the *United States Commerce Department* is also in accord.[18]

Jail or the grave was the inevitable result of guns within a hostile culture as African-Americans would simultaneously be both victims and victimizers of direct oppression. In a democracy, how do you maintain a majority population in the face of a mass reproducing internal ethnic group such as the African-American people? One way is to remove the competitive population from society. Another is to ensure a high mortality rate of the counter race. Third is to ensure a lower mortality rate of the host. Fourth, is to take the vote of any race presenting competition (discussed in

---

[17] Cooper, Alexia and Smith, Erica L. "Homicide Trends in the United States, 1980-2008: Annual Rates for 2009 and 2010." U.S. Department of Justice: Office of Justice Programs: Bureau of Justice Statistics. http://bjs.gov/content/pub/pdf/htus8008.pdf (accessed November 2011).

[18] Rastogi, Sonya, Johnson, Tallase D., Hoeffel, Elizabeth M., and Drewery Jr., Malcolm P. "The Black Population 2010." U.S. Department of Commerce: Economics and Statistics Administration" United States Census Bureau. http://www.census.gov/prod/cen2010/briefs/c2010br-06.pdf (accessed September 2011).

the chapter termed, *Classism of African- American via Corruption*).

How many years officially determine a generation? To know this, provides the multiplication of a people. In developed nations, the average familial generational length is in the high 20s and has even reached 30 years in some nations. Conversely, a generation's length has changed little and remains in the low 20s in less developed nations. As a result of the homicide figures from any of the statistical organizations heretofore charted, it would not appear that the population of the African-American people would be significantly affected. However, when one begins to exam the possibilities of what could have been if those who lost their lives to death via guns and homicide would have reproduced at the average rate of a developed country, then African-Americans would have closed the democratic voting gap between the White majority populous and the Black-threatening minority to a 50.2%, White, and 13.4%, Black, respectively.

Projected Lost: 418,500
Reproduction Rate (Appendix: Chart #6): 2.36
Generations: 2.5
Time Frame: 50 years (or 2.5 generations; Cold War Era)
Potential African-American Quantitative Gain: 2,469,150
2010 African-American Population via USA Census (Appendix: Chart #6): 38,929,319
Potential African-American Quantitative Result: 41,398,469
Total USA Population (Appendix: Charts #1 & #2): 308,745,531
2010 African-American Percentage (Appendix: Chart #2): 12.6%
Potential African-American Percentage Result: 13.4%
2010 White Percentage (Appendix: Chart #2): 53%
Potential White Percentage Result: 50.2%

## Chapter Four
### POPULATION CONTROLS OF AFRICAN-AMERICANS VIA CHEMICAL DEPENDENCY
### (1980-1990)

In all of my research, experience, and exposure, I have never witnessed anything that has enslaved a people like substance abuse. Drugs have been proven to attack the complete person, deteriorating the body, mind, soul, and personality of an individual quicker than any other physical entity ever beheld. As the year's progress, the drug epidemic has become worst especially as drugs move from natural to synthetic derivatives. Alcohol comes from natural <u>FRUIT</u>. Heroin, morphine, and other opiates come from the poppy <u>PLANT</u>. Powder, freebase, and crack cocaine comes from the coco <u>LEAF</u>. Marijuana is crumpled from <u>BUDS</u> in the Indonesian villages, Columbian tropics, or Humboldt County fields of Northern California. Yet, the new drugs on the block are made with <u>CHEMICALS</u> in black market basements leading to the quickest demise of the body and human psyche in the form of methamphetamines or their street equivalent names, "speed" or "crystal", ecstasy, spice, etc. Even the aforementioned drugs are being cut and stepped on so many times for economic or capitalistic reasons that they are unrecognizable and possibly only 5% raw material. According to one of my former supervisors, Tracey Bracey, one of the most unique and effective personalities within the field of substance abuse treatment services states, "There ain't no more dope in dope". Another former supervisor of mine, Dr. Darryl Inaba wrote, in his book, *Uppers, Downers, All-Arounders*, "This increase in the number of street chemist means

37

that it is hard to halt the supply and difficult for users to know what they are getting until they snort it or shoot it into a vein."[19]

It is not a wonder or a coincidence that the ultimate biological agent is something that affects the pleasure center of the brain for a people that are emotionally centered and cultured. The height of the African-American experience is to feel good. Of course, everyone, regardless of culture, ethnicity, or nationality wants to feel good physically, emotionally, and intellectually.

However, because the African-American has to 'feel good' throughout performance based expressions that will move them to an emotional high, serves as evidence of limbic brain activity for an entire culture. The same holds true for the African-American culture as a whole based on their primary *GDP* products and services, i.e., emotionally based entertainment. African-Americans equate music as the 'healing of the soul'. As a result, the dopamine levels secreted by the brain within chemical dependency are the same enzymes that provide the optimal feeling for the believer and the audience of entertainment-based activities inclusive of sports, music, television, comedy, sex, and spiritual activities. Consequently, African-Americans, as well as Africans, can easily be labeled as the "Limbic People".

The same individual(s) who considered placing drugs into the African-American culture is the same person(s) who looked at the origin of these dynamics and concluded that not only would

---

[19] Inaba, Dr. Darryl. *Uppers, Downers, All-Arounders 5th Edition*. Ashland, Oregon: CNS Publication, 2000; 101.

this culture gravitate to mind altering substances for various reasons but noticed the emotional dynamics of the African who serve as the ancestors of the African-American people. These emotional trends were intuitive and also transplanted by certain African derivatives through Animism, Voodoo, and other ritualistic activities, such as palm reading and soothsaying. Dr. Darryl Inaba, in the pioneer wisdom of his book entitled, *Uppers, Downers, All-Arounders*, placed drugs into three classifications, stimulants, depressants, and hallucinogens. Most African-Americans either want to feel good through sexual stimulus caused by a stimulant, depressed because they are unable to achieve their ideal lifestyle due to either past trauma or the lack of material resources, or hallucinogens in order to remove themselves from all sense of reality.

It is unquestionable that drugs are a biological agent intentionally designed to execute practical and realistic outcomes, population control. Three periods of slavery or enslavement are noted throughout African-American history; (1) *The Pre-Civil War Age* (2) *The Civil Rights Era*, and (3) *The Period of Chemical/Biological Agents*. In evaluating these three periods of slavery or enslavement, the latter, that of biological agents, such as drugs and alcohol may be the worst having contributed to increased crime, mortality, health problems, and ethnic divisions. It is the ultimate *Absentee Slave Master* as the African-American is enslaved without the presence of an illegal slave master nor is the person any longer declared as property, but is unable to escape this oppression without the power of a miracle or miraculous God. No one is so naive as to not know that drugs have been apart of the African-American culture since Vietnam beginning with morphine, escalating to heroin, and powder cocaine being the preference of the rich and famous with alcohol and marijuana having pre-existing origins. Therefore, population controls do not appear to have served as the original priority of the cultural epidemic. The escape from reality is the culprit for this societal ill and always will, as hopelessness and the realities of trauma and tragedy will always exist.

As ironic as the unholy kin cousins of guns and competition initiated slavery, the same holds true today in modernity that the ungodly kin cousins of drugs and competition have done equal, if not worst damage to entire generations and cultures. As stated in the previous chapter, all enslavement is not always outwardly forced by an external enemy but inwardly exploited by just plain old internal greed and betrayal. As guns were not made by the enslaved African, but supplied for self-enslavement, so also are drugs. As there are no poppy fields or acres of coca plants within American ghettos, drugs had to also be provided to the African-American.

One African-American will sell drugs to another in their quest towards a capitalistic end perpetuating division by pitting one against another, creating classism's ultimate polarization, superiority and inferiority, where one is termed a "crack head" and the other a "dealer". The former lends itself to a poverty class while the latter, a rich class, albeit illegal. The drug dealer will drive around in expensive cars courtesy of the addict while the latter will spend their last, literally to the point of a demeaning existence. Conceptually, this is yet again another example of the proletariat supporting the bourgeoisie class. Herein is classism expressed in its finest, a rich and poor class, within a totally illegal industry and sub-culture.

Therefore, it must be noted that all those jailed for drug offenses are not drug users or abusers but also include those convicted on the criminal charge of possession for sales. In other words, they seek to fulfill capitalistic ideologies and lifestyles through illegal means and to experience the same need for immediate gratification materialistically as the addict does through chemical dependency and stimulation. This provides the ultimate transition into the coming chapter, *Population Controls of African-Americans via Criminality*. Likewise, the rationale for the increase in PED's (Performance Enhancing Drugs) lie at the very bases of capitalistic ideologies, competition. In order to remain competitive and ensure an upper edge, the abuse of PED's has become an epidemic and overwhelming temptation in the African-American's top industry that produces their greatest amount of wealth, athleticism. This merely provides another concrete fact and example of capitalism's cultural infiltration and the ethnicity's acculturation.

This concept of chemical agents lending to population controls specifically placing 'quality of life' limitations within the

African-American people is perfectly exemplified in the increase of their cultural mortality due to food pesticides. When African-Americans raised their own livestock and crops in the country, their cultural life span was much longer. Because African-Americans successfully removed themselves from the cotton fields and consequently the wealth of the earth, their consumption of produce and meat from the supermarket has increased their ethnic mortality rate. The question was once raised by an African-American woman in a soul food restaurant, "How is it that our fore-parents lived longer than the modern African-American, yet, ate the same food that has been currently deemed to be unhealthy, contributes to high blood pressure, and known to cause clogged arteries through elevated bad cholesterol?" Some 'Soul Food" is unquestionably unhealthy. Nonetheless, consumed in moderation, it is not terminal. However, when African-Americans were raising their own livestock and crops, they knew exactly what they were eating and feeding their families. Now, crops are saturated with pesticides and chickens are plumbed full of steroids diminishing all American's life spans, especially African-Americans who are the largest consumers of these foods. These are not new concepts as syphilis, the *Tuskegee Airman* scenario, HIV, and other chemical and biological agents have always been used as population controls upon Africans and African-Americans alike.

Statistical figures have been given in the previous chapters as to the possibility and loss of population growth threatening a host majority within a democracy in direct relationship of African-

American mass reproduction. If the figures in the next chapter are true, placing 1,000,000 blacks incarcerated over time and the figures below are also accurate, we can surmise that 225,000 African-Americans have been incarcerated for drug related offenses thus diminishing the voting populous.

All Inmates: 19.5%
White Inmates: 15.4%
Hispanic Inmates: 21.3%
African-American Inmates: 22.5%[20]

Projected Lost: 225,000
Reproduction Rate (Appendix: Chart #6): 2.36
Generations: 2.5
Time Frame: 50 years (or 2.5 generations; Cold War Era)
Potential African-American Quantitative Gain: 1,327,500
Potential African-American Quantitative, Previous Chapter: 41,398,469
Total USA Population (Appendix: Charts #1 & #2): 308,745,531
2010 African-American Percentage (Appendix: Chart #2): 12.6%
Potential African-American Quantitative Result: 42,725,969
Potential African-American Percentage Result: 13.8%
2010 White Percentage (Appendix: Chart #2): 53%
Potential White Percentage Result: 51.8%

---

[20] West Ph.D., Dr. Heather C. "Prison Inmates at Midyear 2009 - Statistical Tables." U.S. Department of Justice: Office of Justice Programs: Bureau of Justice Statistics. http://www.bjs.gov/content/pub/pdf/pim09st.pdf (accessed June 2010).

## Chapter Five

## POPULATION CONTROLS OF AFRICAN-AMERICANS VIA CRIMINALITY
### (1990-2000)

No state is able to better express the relationship of "Corrections" and "Capitalism" like my home state of California. California has more prisoners than not only any other state in the union but more than any country in the world with the exception of nine others.[21] One report placed these dynamics in simple concise language stating, "Between 1986 and 2006, California's prison population soared from approximately 60,000 inmates to an all-time high of 173,479 inmates."[22] Another report provided more details stating,

> Prior to realignment, the state's prison population had been rising for decades. In the 1980s and 1990s, California built more prisons. But construction could not keep pace with the prison population growth, and the state could not afford to keep building more prisons. In October 2006, the prison population reached its all-time peak of 173,479 inmates. The following month, the department began paying to house inmates in private prisons in other states.[23]

Worst still, the *State of California* has the largest economic budget than most global countries with Corrections being a larger annual expenditure than most country's total yearly revenues. Because California has been forced to make difficult decisions in

---

[21] "Highest to Lowest - Prison Population Total." World Prison Brief: Institute for Criminal Policy Research. http://www.prisonstudies.org/highest-to-lowest/prison-population-total?field_region_taxonomy_tid=All (accessed April 2016).

[22] "The Future of California Corrections." California Department of Corrections and Rehabilitations. http://www.cdcr.ca.gov/2012plan/docs/plan/complete.pdf, pg. Introduction 4 (accessed 2016)..

[23] "The Future of California Corrections." California Department of Corrections and Rehabilitations. http://www.cdcr.ca.gov/2012plan/docs/plan/complete.pdf, pg. Population Projections 10 (accessed 2016).

order to balance its state's budget, the *California Department of Corrections and Rehabilitation (CDCR)* was arguably most affected. Many actions, both in legal case precedence and ballot proposition initiatives have been made in order to achieve economic idealism.

It is always termed and spoken of as to how much each inmate "cost to house". This automatically suggests there is a revenue source and stream that is pooled from in order to satisfy these expenditures. Therefore, if there is an existing expense, by default, there must also be an existing income. Since the values of governments are determined by *GDP*, does an inmate fall under the classification of a "good" or "service", (or possibly, both)? Sadly, it is the former for the inmate. The inmate is the equivalent of an economic "good" which makes him or her, a "product". As discussed in the chapter on *The Absentee Slave Master*, the harshest reality for the slave is the feeling and mentality that one is not their own but the "property" of another. As a result, would the common prison system be an exalted legal extension of the plantation where inmates are synonymous to slaves?

As Governor Wilson was looking at a projected $2.5B in annual state revenues, but facing an $8.5B deficit, what would he do?[24] Governor Pete Wilson passed the *Three Strikes Law* increasing revenue for the *State of California* that provided satisfaction to the *California Legislature*, its budget, and registered

---

[24] "An Overview of the Governor's 1993-94 Budget." California's Legislative Analyst Office: Budget Brief. http://www.lao.ca.gov/1993/Overview_Gov_Budget_170_0193.pdf (accessed January 1993).

voters as a huge revenue source only to be veiled behind the curtain of being tough on crime. It justified tax increases that created the needed revenue. It was like unto a governmental economic stimulus package increasingly adding over $6B in revenue over the next decade. More revenue for the state, an increase in jobs and employment opportunities, a satisfied legislature, and elated voters who held jobs formerly non-existent, became the immediate perception and reality. Everyone was happy, at least, for the moment. However, as consistent to all capitalistic systems, greed becomes the fuel that always mobilizes the vehicle to the same destination and outcome, excess. Nothing exceeds like excess! As more and more inmates flooded California prisons and more and more revenues and incomes resulted, likewise, more and more expenses came equally and excessively with each prisoner. Let us examine the math:

In 1979-80, Corrections equaled 3% of state's expenditures.
In 2008-09, Corrections equaled 11% of state's expenditures.

The outcome was inevitable, overcrowding. Consequently, this led the *State of California* to *The Realignment Act of 2011*.

> The state's 33 prisons currently house about 119,600 inmates — 17.2 percent below the September 30, 2011 (pre-realignment) level of 144,456. In fact, the prison population is now roughly the same size as in 1994-95, when it ranged from about 115,000 to just over 121,000. Yet, even as the number of prisoners has dropped since realignment, the cost per inmate – adjusted for inflation – has continued to climb and is substantially higher than in the mid-1990s, as we show in our recent report on state corrections spending. California is expected to spend about

$60,000 for each inmate in 2013-14 — 82.3 percent higher than in 1994-95, when the state spent slightly less than $33,000 per inmate, after adjusting for inflation.[25]

Let us examine the math:

1994 Governor Pete Wilson's Three Strike Law: 115,000 x $33,000 = $3.8B
2014 Governor Jerry Brown's Capitalistic Inheritance: 144,456 x $60,000 = $8.7B

Overcrowding rippled and began straining other state expenses in spite of the obvious $5B increase in revenue where expenses inevitably exceeded revenues, termed as a "deficit" requiring action termed 'budgeting'. Although Governor Jerry Brown inherited serious debt and deficit from the *Three Strikes Law* written into law on March 7, 1994 by its pioneer, former Governor Pete Wilson, the "Lawrence Precedent" offered Brown a solution.

> When Brown took office in 2011, the federal courts were already banging on the state to reduce inhumane overcrowding in its prisons. The *California Supreme Court* had made it tougher in 2008 to deny parole to inmates considered relatively less dangerous. New laws allowed for the shifting of qualifying low-level offenders to county jails and oversight while Brown and the parole board took aim at the 33,000 parole-eligible lifers among the 165,000 prisoners.[26]

A profound change is underway in California's criminal justice system. Inmates serving life sentences with the possibility

[25] Graves, Scott. "Fewer State Prisons, Higher Cost Per Inmate." California Budget and Policy Center. http://calbudgetcenter.org/blog/fewer-state-prisoners-higher-cost-per-inmate/ (accessed April 7, 2013).
[26] Broder, Ken. "Record Number of Prison Lifers Released, but Few Return." All Gov California. http://www.allgov.com/usa/ca/news/top-stories/record-number-of-prison-lifers-released-but-few-return-141230?news=855226 (accessed December 30, 2014).

of parole are being released in record numbers. Since 2009, nearly 2,300 lifers have been paroled. That's more than three times the number paroled in the previous 17 years combined.[27]

Overcrowded prison conditions culminated in a 2011 ruling by the *United States Supreme Court* ordering the *California Department of Corrections and Rehabilitation* to reduce its prison population by tens of thousands of inmates by June 2013. Sandra Davis Lawrence, an African-American woman, in the case, *Sandra Davis LAWRENCE on Habeas Corpus. No. S154018* on August 21, 2008 decided by *Supreme Court of California* did not just change the law but set legal precedent, African-American history, and provided new and improved capitalistic ideologies. Consequently, it met the goal of the *California Legislature* to relieve its burdened budget by corrections. In the ruling, the justices said there was "overwhelming" evidence in Lawrence's rehabilitation while in prison which demonstrated her suitability for parole. [28]

> In 1971, Sandra Davis Lawrence (petitioner) murdered her lover's wife, Rubye Williams.... After the jury returned a guilty verdict on a charge of first-degree    murder,    the trial court imposed a sentence of life imprisonment-the statutory penalty for murders committed prior to November 8, 1978-and set a minimum eligible parole date of November 29, 1990. In August 2005, after numerous hearings before the Board of Parole Hearings (the Board), that entity for the fourth time found petitioner suitable for parole and set a parole date. In finding petitioner suitable

---

[27] Walker, Brenda. "California Releases Thousands of Lifers from Prison." V DARE. http://uscpcjp.com/meet-our-clients/sandra-davis-lawrence/ (accessed August 9, 2014).
[28] Ibid.

for parole, the Board emphasized the presence of multiple statutory factors favoring suitability, including petitioner's exemplary record of rehabilitation, her acceptance of responsibility for the crime, her realistic parole plans, and her close ties to her family, who would offer her support in reintegrating into the community. [29]

Many, followed suit using "suitability" as their liberation from a life sentence preventing parole boards the ability to draw a nexus between post conviction behavior and the committed offense. Since Californians accepted the liberalism of offenders back into society, it provided economic ideations for the *California Legislature* to relieve its overwhelming budget through more voting ballot initiative. Proposition ballot initiatives, such as *Proposition 36 (P36)*, *Proposition 63*, *AB109*, and *Proposition 47* have all served to assist an economic end. *P36* serves as an excellent example of capitalistic extremism. *P36* provided convicted drug offenders the option of incarceration or treatment.

For the drug dealer, i.e., the individual seeking wealth through illegal means immediately adapted and made the necessary adjustments in order to become an eligible benefactor to these proposition initiatives. *P36* essentially stated that one who possessed a certain limited quantity of drugs determined whether the charge would be a mere 'possession' opposed to a 'possession for sales' charge where the penalty is much more severe for the latter. Therefore, drug dealers would only hold on their person

---

[29] "Sandra Davis Lawrence." Post Conviction Justice Project: University of Southern California. http://uscpcjp.com/meet-our-clients/sandra-davis-lawrence/ (accessed 2016).

quantities indicative of use and place their product of sales in trees and gas meters, collect their money, and point the buyer to the respective area. If searched by the police or entrapped by an undercover agent, the dealer could always claim possession for personal use, as no other drugs were found on their person complicating the burden of proof by the prosecution to prove sales opposed to use. This flooded addiction treatment centers with dealers complicating the treatment process. Worst of all, it perpetuated classism, rich and poor, better and worse, dealer and crack-head dynamics. Nevertheless, it met the goal of the *California Legislature* to relieve its burdened economic budget through corrections.

On the other hand, *P63* enabled mental health disordered persons the option of treatment opposed to incarceration. Consequently, it met the goal of the *California Legislature* to relieve its burdened budget by corrections. *Proposition 47*, the ballot initiative passed by California voters on November 4, 2014, reduced/reduces certain drug possession felonies to misdemeanors. It also requires misdemeanor sentencing for petty theft, receiving stolen property and forging/writing bad checks when the amount involved is $950 or less.[30] In the official statement from "CA.gov", *The Cornerstone of California's Solution to Reduce Overcrowding, Costs, and Recidivism*, proposition initiative *AB109*

---

[30] "What You Need to Know About Proposition 47." California Department of Corrections and Rehabilitations. http://www.cdcr.ca.gov/news/Proposition_47.html (accessed 2016).

51

allows "non-violent", "non-serious", and "non-sex offenders" to serve their sentence in county jails instead of state prisons.[31]

The concept is as simple as a flow chart. Sober living is more reasonable than treatment. Treatment is more reasonable than county jail time. County jail time is more reasonable than state prison time. Private prisons are cheaper than state prisons. However, other state prison cost is far cheaper to house California prisoners than the natives. Therefore, every reduction of incarceration, level of care in treatment, and sober living environment, fulfills a capitalistic end.

California set precedent again by contracting private prisons with localized counties and cities and thereby stimulating local economies with jobs and employment opportunities. However, nothing remotely compares to the ability for the *State of California* to contract with other states and house their long-term prisoners for the better portion of their judicial sentence. Arizona, Mississippi, and Oklahoma immediately jumped on board. The official website of the *CDCR* identified the contracted states, the exact venue information for each location, and states verbatim, "CBU" ("Contract Bed Units") is a unit within the *Division of Adult Institutions* whose mission is to transfer inmates out of state

---

[31] "The Cornerstone of California's Solution to Reduce Overcrowding, Costs, and Recidivism." California Department of Corrections and Rehabilitations. http://www.cdcr.ca.gov/realignment/ (accessed 2016).

for the purpose of temporarily alleviating overcrowding within existing institutions."[32]

Consequently, the *State of California* can infinitely increase their *GDP* through unlimited arrest, convictions, and the negotiating of their expenses, fulfilling every component of capitalism, supply and demand, superiority and inferiority or better than and less than dynamics.

> In 2008-09, the department comprised over 11 percent of the state's budget, and until last year, managed the largest state prison system in the country... To fund such an expansion, the state would have needed to sell up to $7.5 billion in lease revenue bonds.[33]

By 2011, California faced a $26.6 billion General Fund budget deficit, in part because the department's budget had grown from $5 billion to over $9 billion in a decade.[34]

Faced with the possibility of bankruptcy, out-of-control debt and deficit, and the need to balance the states' budget, the *California Legislature* debated and implemented measures to solve their economic crisis.

> Combining the actual budget savings with the avoided expenditures that would have been required without realignment, over a ten-year span the state will have saved and avoided over $30 billion in General Fund costs.[35]

---

[32] "Out of State Prison Facilities." California Department of Corrections and Rehabilitations. http://www.cdcr.ca.gov/Visitors/CA_Out_Of_State_Facilities.html (accessed 2016).

[33] "The Future of California Corrections." California Department of Corrections and Rehabilitations. http://www.cdcr.ca.gov/2012plan/docs/plan/complete.pdf, pg.15 (accessed 2016).

[34] "The Future of California Corrections." California Department of Corrections and Rehabilitations. http://www.cdcr.ca.gov/2012plan/docs/plan/complete.pdf, pg. Introduction 1 (accessed 2016).

[35] "The Future of California Corrections." California Department of Corrections and Rehabilitations. http://www.cdcr.ca.gov/2012plan/docs/plan/complete.pdf, pg. Introduction 3 (accessed 2016).

They used ballot initiatives, contracted with private prisons, and established relationships with other states to take their prisoners for a more reasonable rate than it cost them to house. The buying and selling of prisoners, looks suspiciously like a new Jim Crow and neo-slavery practices.

> The department began sending inmates out- of-state when overcrowding was at its worst in 2007. Currently, there are more than 9,500 inmates outside of California…. Returning these inmates to California will stop the flow of taxpayer dollars to other states, and is expected to save the state $318 million annually.[36]

The prisoner is owned and consequently sold and contracted as a slave. Not very different from professional sports, specifically the *National Basketball Association (NBA)* and *National Football Association (NFL)* where professional athletes have made public interview statements that they discovered that they had been traded on *ESPN*. Failing to embrace the decency and courtesy of a face-to-face conversation, because each athlete via contract is deemed as property, teams have the legal right to buy, sell, and trade without notice as though they are slaves. How is this any different from the practices during the height of slavery?

Additionally, African-American's within the criminal justice population have limited the ethnicity's voting power, thus, much less competition in a democratic society. Louise D. Palmer in her article, on the *Number of Blacks in Prison Nears 1 Million*,

---

[36] "Out of State Prison Facilities." California Department of Corrections and Rehabilitations. http://www.cdcr.ca.gov/2012plan/docs/plan/complete.pdf, pg. Introduction 7 (accessed 2016).

"We're incarcerating an entire generation of people." Come the new millennium, the number of African American adults behind bars will hit the million marks for the first time, according to an analysis of Justice Department statistics. That represents nearly an eightfold increase from three decades ago (1970), when there were only 133,226 blacks in prison..." These numbers are staggering," said Laurie Levensen, a former federal prosecutor and associate dean of *Loyola Law School* in Los Angeles. "We're incarcerating an entire generation of people." Why blacks contribute about half of all prison inmates when they are only 13 percent of the U.S. population is subject to much speculation...Over the past five decades, the disparity between races has widened dramatically as minorities have replaced whites in the prison population, according to the center. In 1950, whites made up about 65 percent of all state and federal inmates, white minorities made up 35 percent. Today, the opposite is true, with 35 percent of the prison population made up of whites. "The face of crime to white Americans is now that of a black man," said David Bostis, senior political analyst at the Center for Political and Economic Studies, a think tank that specializes in black community issues.[37]

No one is so naive as to not know that crime has been apart of the African-American culture since the *Era of Prohibition* when blacks, such as Bumpy Johnson, Stephanie St. Clair, and other Harlem gangsters, capitalized on the alcohol industry, nightlife, and prostitution. Therefore, population controls did not serve as the priority of this cultural epidemic. Economics, power, and

---

[37] Worthen M.Div., Carlton. "Slavery is Legal in America."
http://carltonworthen.blogspot.com/2010_09_01_archive.html (Accessed September 10, 2010).
Palmer, Louise D. The Boston Globe. This article includes information from the Seattle Post-Intelligencer Staff. This article appeared in the Seattle Post-Intelligencer, Pages A-1 & A-4.
http://ronmull.tripod.com/racism.html (accessed March 2, 1999).

competition has to own this societal ill and will always, as long as capitalism exists.

Second, criminality decreases the African-American voting pool by disqualification. In other words, a felon's right to vote is taken where the law does not allow them to register to vote, nor permit them to participate in the democratic process.

> Another concern is the mass disenfranchisement of African Americans.... By 2000, roughly one in 10 black men will be in prison – a statistic with major social implications because prisoners don't have jobs, pay taxes or care for their children at home. And because many states bar felons from voting, at least one in seven black men will have lost the right to vote. "It means 10 percent of (black men) are not productive," said Massachusetts state Rep. Byron Rushing, a Boston Democrat. "Not only are their talents not available for development of the community, but the community spends a large amount of time dealing with their absence...". According to an October 1998 report by The Sentencing Project, a Washington-based legal research and services organization, in a dozen states, 30 percent to 40 percent of the next generation of black men will permanently lose the right to vote if current trends continue. In nine states, one in four black men can never vote again because they were convicted of a felony. This loss of voting rights nationwide not only highlights the eroding political power base of blacks, but it also calls into question the notion of democracy in America, Shelton said.[38]

Third, Black-On-Black Crime has increased the African-American mortality rate significantly, thus, decreasing the voting pool. Again, when one begins to exam the possibilities of what

---

[38] Palmer, Louise D. The Boston Globe. This article includes information from the Seattle Post-Intelligencer Staff. This article appeared in the Seattle Post-Intelligencer, Pages A-1 & A-4. http://ronmull.tripod.com/racism.html (accessed March 2, 1999).

could have been if those who lost their lives to death via clashing, chemical dependencies, and corrections at the average rate of a developed country, then African-Americans would have closed the democratic voting gap between the White majority populous and the Black-threatening minority to a 48.9% to 16.7%.

As well, it must be equally noted that if the African-American population continued to grow at the rate of 6% every 50 years, the projections noted in the (*Appendix: Chart #V*), *Projections Noted Through 2060*, would bring the African-American population to 27%, up the same 7% from the previous half century. At the current projections noted in (*Appendix: Chart #V*), Hispanics and African-Americans combine to make up 44% of the total population, still a minority behind a 69% White majority. Without population controls and with natural fertility rates, Whites would be out-projected by Hispanics and African-Americans, 57%-55%, thus, compromising the American democracy.

Projected Lost: 1,000,000
Reproduction Rate (Appendix: Chart #6): 2.36
Generations: 2.5
Time Frame: 50 years (or 2.5 generations; Cold War Era)
Potential African-American Quantitative Gain: 8,975,000
Potential African-American Quantitative, Previous Chapter: 42,725,969
Total USA Population (Appendix: Charts #1 & #2): 308,745,531
2010 African-American Percentage (Appendix: Chart #2): 12.6%
Potential African-American Quantitative Result: 51,700,969
Potential African-American Percentage Result: 16.7%
2010 White Percentage (Appendix: Chart #2): 53%
Potential White Percentage Result: 48.9%

## Chapter Six

**POPULATION CONTROLS OF AFRICAN-AMERICANS VIA PRO-CREATION COMPLEXITIES**

**(1990-2000)**

Since Flip Wilson who played the character of "Geraldine" in the 1970 sitcom, *The Flip Wilson Show*, best known by the famous quote, "Don't let me get *Killer*" who was her imaginary boyfriend, African-Americans males have embraced the role of alternative genders towards celebrity, fame, and fortune. Since that time, nearly all *A-List* high profile African-American actors have assumed a feminine character association. The following African-American actors have all played female roles in sitcoms and movies:

1. Flip Wilson played, "Geraldine" — (*The Flip Wilson Show*: 1970)

2. Arsenio Hall played an, "Extremely Ugly Woman" — (*Coming to America*: 1988)

3. Jaime Foxx played, "Wanda" — (*In Living Color*: 1990-94)

4. Damon Wayans played a, "Gay Critic" — (*In Living Color*: 1990-94)

5. David Alan Grier played a, "Gay Critic" - (*In Living Color*: 1990-94)

6. Martin Lawrence played, — "Sheneneh Jenkins" - (*Martin*: 1992-97)

7. Will Smith played, "Paul" - (*Six Degrees of Separation*: 1993)

8. Wesley Snipes played, "Noxemma" - (*To Wong Foo*: 1995)

9. Chris Tucker played "Ruby Rhod" — (*The Fifth Element*: 1997)

10. Eddie Murphy played, "Mrs. Klump" — (*Nutty Professor*: 2000)

11. Ving Rhames played, Holiday Heart - (*Holiday Heart*: 2000)

12. Martin Lawrence played, "Big Momma" — (*Big Momma's House*: 2000, 2006, & 2011)

13. Miguel Nunez Jr., played, "Juwanna Mann" — (*Juwanna Mann*: 2002)

14. Tyler Perry played, "Madea" — (*Madea*: 2002-2015)

15. Shawn Wayans played, "Kevin Copeland" — (*White Chicks*: 2004)

16. Shawn Wayans played, "Marcus Copeland" — (*White Chicks*: 2004)

17. Brandon T. Jackson played, "Charmaine" - (*Big Momma's House*: 2011)

18. DeAndre Jordan played, "An Old Lady" — (Farmer's Insurance Commercial; 2016)

It has been stated by many in barbershops and beauty salons that these are intentional long-term subliminal messages intended to promote and instill a homosexual agenda within the African-American culture. Others have embraced the belief that there is a prerequisite agreement within the (tabooed, "never talked about") *Illuminati* before one can begin their acting career, conceive stardom, or propel into true celebrity. Therefore, if this is true, it cannot be accidental.

At the same time, if true, what is the purpose? What is the benefit to those who conceived the concept, approach the actors, and ensure the execution of the practice? There is no way possible for this subject matter to be raised and not be aggressively criticized as homophobic, stereotypical, and discriminatory. However, is it possible that it can be none of these, yet, merely another population control whether facilitated by conspirators, coincidental, or nothing more than just another expression of film artistry. Nevertheless, if the practice of African-American male actors consistently playing female roles is a population control, it makes perfect sense as it relates to the mastery of subliminal messages being slowly ingrained and indoctrinated into the cultural psyche of African-Americans especially for the highly influential, fragile, and developing adolescent mindset. As a child is naturally drawn to the colors of animated figures enabling them to find cartoons upon retrieving a remote control without any adult assistance as well as the attention spans of westernized television watchers having been limited to 4-6 seconds based on each scene of commercials, sports events, sitcoms, and movies ever changing every 4-6 seconds, subliminally, subconsciously, and intentionally altering attention spans, consequently, all these are programming viewers towards immediate gratification. Likewise, the same subliminal dynamics are occurring by having African-American male actors embrace female television roles.

This is not an attempt to address the morality of homosexuality, trans-genders, cross-dressing, sexual orientation, sexual preference, or sexual identity. Therefore, our approach is not towards moral judgment but how this dynamic affects and limits a cultural population. Those who believe this dynamic to be an *Illuminati* requirement, equates a moral rationale suggesting that one must "sell their soul" and show their willingness to do anything in exchange for riches. Regardless of what side of the moral spectrum one assumes, a factual reality is that a homosexual relationship is incapable of procreating naturally. If reproduction will occur within an intimate, marital, partnership, or common-law homosexual relationship, it will have to be through an unnatural, faux, or via the voluntary or involuntary infringement upon another of the opposite sex. Simply put, if two women co-exist within an intimate relationship and desire children or a family, one of them will have either to engage in a sexual encounter with a man or experience in vitro fertilization. Likewise, for two men to engage in an intimate relationship and desire children would require for one them to have a sexual experience with a woman requesting that the woman bear their child or allow in vitro fertilization for the sake of their own parental goals and desires. The perpetual reality of African-American actors playing female roles limits the reproduction of the entire culture, thus, reducing the quantitative progression of the ethnic population and perpetuates the unnatural procreation of the same. As well, it multiples the seed planting of de-traditionalized family dynamics. Conclusively, an unnatural reality requires natural processes to sustain its way of life. Unlike our ability to quantify the limitations of certain population controls in the previous chapters, it is significantly difficult to measure, formulate, or establish a barometer on how many reproductions do not occur based on gay lifestyles due to these complications or how many do not even consider reproduction due to pro-creation complexities.

For those who argue the connection between African-American actors playing female roles lending to population controls, the obvious high amount of African-American male actors playing homosexual characters contributes to indisputable conclusions and considerations. The emphasis here is not moral but the fact that alternative lifestyles brings complexities to pro-creation and thus limits cultural population increases. Examine the list for yourself:

1. Forest Whitaker — (*The Crying Game*: 1992)

2. Roger Guenveur Smith — (*Poetic Justice*: 1993)

3. Will Smith — (*Six Degrees of Separation*: 1993)

4. Ving Rhames — (*Pulp Fiction*: 1994)

5. Wesley Snipes — (*To Wong Foo*: 1995)

6. Harry J. Lennix — (*Get on the Bus*: 1996)

7. Isaiah Washington — (*Get on the Bus*: 1996)

8. Ving Rhames — (*Holiday Heart*: 2000)

9. Nelsan Ellis — *(True Blood*: 2000-4)

10. Matthew Saint Patrick — (*Six Feet Under*: 2001)

11. Seth Gilliam — (*Punks*: 2001)

12. Michael Boatman — (*Spin City*: 2002)

13. Michael Kenneth William — (*The Wire*: 2002)

14. Jeffery Wright — (*Angels in America*: 2003)

15. Anthony Mackie — (*Brother to Brother*: 2004)

16. Brian White — (*The Family Stone*: 2005)

17. Chiwetel Ejiofor — (*Kinky Boots*: 2005)

18. Jesse L. Martin — (*Rent*: 2005)

19. Kenneth Hamilton Cobb — (*Noah's Arc*: 2006)

20. Rockmond Dunbar — (*Dirty Laundry*: 2006)

21. Taye Diggs — (*Will and Grace*: 2006)

22. Calvin Owens — (*Greek*: 2007)

23. Darrin Henson — (*Life Support*: 2007)

24. Evan Ross — (*Life Support*: 2007)

25. Leon — *(Cover*: 2007)

26. Terrell Tilford — (*The DL Chronicle*: 2007)

27. Blair Underwood — (*In Treatment*: 2008)

28. Haaz Sleiman — (*Nurse Jackie*: 2009)

29. Omari Hardwick — (*For Colored Girls*: 2010)

30. Harrold Perrineau — (*Romeo and Juliet*: 2013)

31. Jussie Smollett — (*Empire*: 2014-present)

32. Viola Davis — (*How To Get Away With Murder?*(2014 — present))

# DECREASE THE POPULATION!

The purpose for Population Controls does not appear to be based out of the need towards damaging a race although this may be a bonus if intentionally facilitated by conspirators. The priority appears to be the limitation of fertility rates among those who would exceed and jeopardize the average figures of developing countries especially the colonial and majority people group.

While protecting the democracy within a system governed by the "rule of vote" from the general population, population controls also assist the mathematics of limiting the top 1% as the total population is held in check. In simple terms, the greater the population, the greater the highest 1% will expand compromising the exclusivity of the elitist crowd. If the total population is 1300 citizens, the elite, if 1%, will be 13 people. These 13 will monopolize the power, laws, and economics. If the next step in the process was to flood the African-American ethnicity with billions of dollars, however, only to an elite few (i.e., a top 1%), there had to be a limitation on the quantity of the elitist class, thus, the rationale for population controls. This is a highly sophisticated form of segregation foundational to capitalism. Consider all those who died and are either literally imprisoned or enslaved through addiction who would have been talented athletes or entertainers. Within the concept of population controls lies the protection of the establishment and democracy while simultaneously preparing for the execution and reality of capitalistic segregation. There is, has to be, and will always be, the exclusivity to the elitist class.

While victory celebrations were occurring in bars and pubs all across the real estate of westernized countries after fifty long years of *Cold War* intensity, the world was radically changing before our very eyes. Simultaneously, there was a perception of capitalistic conquest based on three dominant factors. First, the falling communistic governments towards capitalistic and democratic alternatives were overwhelmingly blinding. Second, the economic policy changes of the Clinton Administration leading to the first balanced budget in half a century set the stage for the greatest economic growth since the *Industrial Age*. Third, although President William Jefferson Clinton can and should be given credit for the prosperity of the *United States of America*, the fact still remains that President Clinton also rode the wave of Bill Gates and Steve Jobs of *Microsoft* and *Apple*, respectively, who led the world into the *Information Age*, the pseudo-rise of the dot-com *NASDAQ* technological stocks, and wealth that had never been witnessed in the history of the *USA,* far exceeding the per-capita comparisons of the *Industrial Age*, albeit, barring that of a newly found route to wealth, i.e., borrowing!

African-Americans made the remarkable, however, simultaneously dangerous discovery of borrowing their way to wealth. As Reagan initiated the trend of borrowing, African-Americans followed suit with the rest of America. While America celebrated, it was rarely noticed that an African-American wealthy class was being established right before their very eyes.

The entire African-American culture became overwhelmed with the historical events that consumed their complete attention. The Rodney King case was decided on March 3, 1991. Clarence Thomas was nominated to the *United States Supreme Court* on March 23, 1991 amid the Anita Hill misfortunate and scandal. Magic Johnson made the announcement of his HIV status on November 7, 1991. The O.J. Simpson case, the most popular and watched criminal case in American and world history, was decided on June 12, 1994. Minister Louis Farrakhan made history by leading one million African-American men in unity to the *District of Columbia* on October 17, 1995, termed, *The Million Man March*. The fatality of Tupac Shakur on September 13, 1996 and the Notorious B.I.G. on March 9, 1997 unfortunately occurred. While a continued belief that racism was the enemy successfully and artistically communicated by Spike Lee and others, African-Americans were assuming capitalism into their nature and culture. Consumed by racism and a chase for wealth, African-Americans never noticed that they were being socially divided by capitalistic ideologies especially when on November 4, 2008, the first African-American, was voted into the highest office in the land, *President of the United States of America* in the person of Senator Barack Obama of Illinois.

Concurrently, an evolutionary process of the wealthiest 1% of all African-Americans was unconsciously and unknowingly acquiring 56% of all combined African-American wealth. During the same 20 years, 1989-2009, exactly one generation, while the U.S. experienced the degradation of toxic leveraged debt leading to the housing market crash, a global economic crisis, and the *Great Recession*, African-Americans experienced the rise of the celebrity class which established and demonstrated complete assimilation, acculturation, and the polarization of internal ethnic and cultural capitalism, i.e., the rich and the poor class.

Ultimately, there has been a paradigm shift within the African-American culture where first generation millionaires, largely through entertainment, which has always been the catalyst of success for this people group, has become trend setters, leaders, and coveted by the average African-American. As the wealthiest 1% of the American population owns 99% of the United States' total cumulative wealth, likewise, the wealthiest 1% of all African-Americans owns 56% of all combined African American wealth occurring within the same two decades of capitalistic victory celebrations concurrent with the degradation of toxic leveraged debt after the end of the *Cold War* in 1991.

> One of the most striking developments over the past quarter century is the  dramatic shift of taxable incomes toward the wealthiest people…. Overall, the top tenth of 1 percent more than tripled their share of cash income to about 9 percent, while the top one-hundredth of 1 percent – or fewer than 15,000 taxpayers – quadrupled their share to 3.8 percent of all taxable income.[39]

---

[39] Morris, Charles. *The Two Million Dollar MeltDown*. New York, NY: Pubic Affairs; 2008; 152-153.

It is these elements and practices that have led to the rise of the celebrity class within the African-American ethnicity promoting assimilation, acculturation, the extremism and polarization of cultural capitalism, the rich and the poor, and a new and improved segregation. Meritocracy, plutocracy, and oligarchy are the political cultural sub-systems within the macro-general systems of democracy and capitalism. Division is the ultimate end and demise. Hope is the key element. I hope to live to see the day when someone develops this foundation of first generation African-American capitalistic work into a second-generation research and its historical realistic outcomes.

During the *Cold War* and prior to 1989, I doubt very seriously if there were 400 African-American millionaires inclusive of the most lucrative of all African-American markets, music, film, and athletics. The *NY Times* publicized this reality on June 25, 1991 when Magic Johnson signed a $25M at $1M/year for 25 years and by the Boston Globe on May 23, 2010 in their article, *Some Athletes Were Legendary but Felt Their Salaries Weren't.*

A clear shift in paradigm occurred while America's focus was centered on global dominance, empirical celebrations, and the comforts of financial materialism. Cornell West, who serves as the leading African-American academic pioneer on capitalism, concurred with Dr. Richard Wolff. In an interview with Dr. Wolff, Dr. West responded to the facilitator who asked if Karl Marx's theory of 19th century industrialized Europe is relevant to African-Americans:

> I think it's very relevant. Karl Marx was one of the greatest prophetic figures of the 19th century because he had an analysis of capitalism that kept track of the precious humanity of working people and poor people. No can deny under global capitalism that it's been an escalation of oligarchic and plutocratic; no one can deny that big bank and big corporations are not dominating government. No one can deny the working people are not benefitting from the way hedge funds folks are, Wall Street folks are. In that sense, so that wealth and equality and all that goes with it, one has to come to terms with it. Marx's analysis is probably one of the most indispensable forms to make sense of a financial monopoly in our day.[40]

The captivating sounds from such musical groups as *Cameo, Con Funk Shun, Earth, Wind, & Fire, Funkadelic, Gladys Knight and The Pips, LTD, Midnight Star, Ohio Players, Parliament, Rose Royce, SOS Band, The Bar-Kays, The Deele, The Emotions, The Four Tops, The Gap Band, The Isley Brothers, The Manhattans, The Mary Jane Girls, The O' Jays, The Stylistics,* and *The Temptations*, along with the solo voices of Al Green Bobby Womack, Lou Rawls, Luther Vandross, Marvin Gaye, and Teddy Pendergrass and the angelic melodies of Aretha Franklin, Diana Ross, Gladys Knight, and Tina Turner have taken second stage in monetary profit to a transitioning *Age & Era of Hip Hop*. This was clearly evident with the release of such sounds as Dr. Dre's, *The*

---

[40] Billinghurst, David. "Richard Wolff and Cornel West Talking About What's Wrong With Capitalism." You Tube. https://www.youtube.com/watch?v=gEOYVA0R1Tc (accessed July 28, 2015).

*Chronic*, Snoop Dogg's, *Doggystyle*, Tupac's, *All Eyez on Me*, and The Notorious B.I.G, *Ready to Die*. In *Appendix: Chart #XX*, a clear distinction was made between African-American general music, largely R&B, and the artistry of rap or *Hip Hop*. Although both musical genres, 'General' versus "*Hip Hop*/Rap" when combined at $12B in total net-worth, athleticism is the clear industry leader exceeding $20B. What the data clearly shows is that *Hip Hop* and rap is increasing so fast that it will exceed all other types of African-American musical genres. The critical component in making the distinction between *Hip Hop* and other music types is the influence that the former is having on succeeding cultural generations. In other words, African-American infants, adolescents, teenagers, and youth aspire towards wealth through this method. This statement is not made from a perspective of judgment or condescension towards the rapper or the art form of rapping. I do not believe that any career is better than another although the word "prestige" is ascribed to professions with the societal belief that a doctor or lawyer is more of a prestigious profession than a mechanic or plumber. Strange it is however, that $100K a year physician or attorney which is the equivalent of $48 per hour, is the same labor rate as the mechanic who services their luxury car and the plumber who customizes the décor of their kitchen and bathroom. The right career and profession for each person is the one that fulfills their individualized purpose and brings one into a realm of peace and serenity. As defined by a former boss of mine, Michael Brenner, "one will never to have

72

work if they're doing something they love to do." Nonetheless, it is a matter of fact that if a mass percentage of young people fork towards the road of a certain career path, it will decrease the traffic towards certain other professional career paths and gridlock alternate destinies. In short, the more rappers within the African-American culture, the less African-American doctors and lawyers will exist. African-American Executives have been best defined with these words:

> The "Fortune 500" is a list of the 500 largest companies in the United States as compiled by Fortune Magazine. Only 15 black executives have ever made it to the Chairman    or CEO position of a "Fortune 500" listed company. Of these 15 executives, there are currently 5 active. In 1987, Dr. Clifton R. Wharton, Jr. became Chairman and CEO of *TIAA-CREF* — distinguishing him as the first black CEO of a "Fortune 500" company. Franklin Raines became the second black person to lead a "Fortune 500" company, when he became CEO of *Fannie Mae* in 1999. On July 1, 2009, Ursula Burns became the first black woman to head a "Fortune 500" company. There is currently no black majority owned company in the "Fortune 500" rankings. (Updated January 29, 2015).[41]

These dates provide significant evidence of the paradigm shift not only through the classic entertainment industries that have apparently defined the African-American culture as well as the growing educated elitist professionals.

Certain African-American names must be placed into infamy upon every film director who ever uttered the words, "Take

---

[41] "African American Chairman & CEO's of Fortune 500 Companies." Black Profiles. http://www.blackentrepreneurprofile.com/fortune-500-ceos/ (accessed: January, 29, 2015).

One, Take Two, etc."; Moms Mabley, Cab Calloway, Lena Horne, Nipsey Russell, Esther Rolle, Dorothy Dandridge, Cicely Tyson, Sammy Davis Jr., Harry Belafonte, Maya Angelou, and Ben Vereen. African-American television shows were fairly known during the *Cold War Era* however limited to such shows as *Sanford and Son*: (1972-77); *Good Times*: (1974-79); *The Jeffersons*: (1975-85); *The Fresh Prince*: (1985-94); *Amen*: (1986-91); *A Different World*: (1987-93); and the all-successful *Cosby Show*: (1984-92). Talk Shows were limited to *The Oprah Winfrey Show*: (1986-2011) along with *The Montel Williams Show*: (1991-2008) who represented African-Americans during daytime television while *The Arsenio Hall Show*: (1989-94) set cultural precedent during late night.

Although there were many more African-American comedians, Richard Pryor, Paul Mooney, Redd Foxx, Eddie Murphy, and Bill Cosby cornered the laughing market as its cultural pioneers. The transitional *Cold War Era* brought forth such successful sitcoms as, *In Living Color* (1990-94).

Sports were dominated by many African-American household names. However offensive, the infamous comment made by Jimmy "The Greek" Snyder during an interview in 1988 when he said, "the black is a better athlete to begin with because he's been bred to be that way ... [They] jump higher and run

74

faster",[42] has to be objectively and academically assessed, free from sensitivity, offensiveness, and racism, as athleticism as a matter of fact, is by far the highest monetary industry for the African-American culture, producing more than $20B of cumulative net worth. While film was first, music was always the number one contributor to the African-American's cultural net-worth until the 1990's when athleticism began its climb to ethnic ascendancy during the post-*Cold War Era*.

> During the 1980s and 1990s, the situation changed dramatically. In 1991, for example, *Sports Illustrated* noted that Eric Dickerson of football's Indianapolis Colts had just signed a $10.65 million dollar contract over a four-year period, making him one of the highest paid players in football. In 1990, the twelve highest paid players in *National Basketball Association* were all Black.[43]

Although the athlete does not have the physical freedom restrictions as the inmate, the mere fact that the athlete is bound by the terms of a contract that allows the creator of the contract to buy, sell, or trade the player without input from the player sounds strangely similar to the terms and processes that governed the economics of slavery. If as an athlete, one "can be traded" without input, negotiations, nor even the courtesy of a conversation, equates as an athlete with the exact same dynamics of slave. It is not a wonder why it is termed as a "trade" especially after many

---

[42] Page, Clarence. "Thanks For Being Honest, Jimmy 'The Greek'-too Honest." Chicago Tribune. http://articles.chicagotribune.com/1988-01-20/news/8803230751_1_thighs-black-professional-sports (accessed January 20, 1988).

[43] King, Peter . "Why Is This Man Smiling?" Sports Illustrated (accessed Aug. 12, 1991), pp. 13-14.

hearing of their own trade on *ESPN* without the courtesy of prior notice is tantamount to being like unto property. The word, "trade" is a foundational term of economics where commodities are traded on stock markets floors all over the world.

Although this reality might offend a great many people, especially the economically successful, the athlete is no different than the inmate in that they are property veiled behind the curtain of the less offensive term "contract" and seven, eight, and nine figure wealth. As the classic case on the shores of the South Carolina slave trading dock, the man who held the greatest physique capable of mass field production, likewise, is the case with the professional athlete. Those, who are able via physical ability, enhanced if natural, to rebound, tackle, run, and athletically perform, goes to the highest price bidder or the more politically correct term, "receives the best contract". It can be said to be the post-modern plantation system or that which leads to an economic end just as bad as the physical reality of the plantation, i.e., superiority and inferiority. Like wise are the contracts within the music industry as defined by the late great legend, Prince, who stated,

> "Record contracts are just like — I'm gonna say the word – slavery...I would tell any young artist... don't sign." Prince also voiced his disapproval about how record labels turn artists into "indentured servitude," since the artists have

little control or insight over how labels take their music and profit off it online.[44]

Jackie Robinson, Roy Campanella, Satchel Paige, Willie Mays, Hank Aaron, Frank Robinson, Vida Blue, Reggie Jackson, Joe Morgan, Dave Parker, and Willie Stargell were the pioneers of African-American baseball. The post-*Cold War Era* brought us such Hall of Fame *Major League Baseball* (*MLB*) names as Bobby Bonds, Rickey Henderson, Frank Thomas, Mo Vaughn, Kenny Griffey, and Barry Bonds. As is the case with the *NBA* and the *NFL*, pay compensations as well as collective bargaining contracts became radically different in such a sudden and subtle manner never noticed by high profile publicity unlike current day negotiations.

Wilt Chamberlain and Bill Russell were the prominent African-American names in basketball with Earvin "Magic" Johnson and Kareem Abdul-Jabbar being the icons of transition. None of these players was paid much and has made more money in endorsements and investments than in salary. Endorsements were needed to supplement salaries and served to begin the capitalistic assimilation. Many others were household names that is owed mention, inclusive of Julius ("Dr. J") Erving, George ("The Ice Man") Gervin, Moses Malone, Isaiah Thomas, Dominique Wilkins, Hakeem Olajuwon, Patrick Ewing, Karl Malone, Charles Barkley, and of course, Michael Jordan.

---

[44] Kreps, Daniel. "Prince Warns Young Artists: Record Contracts Are 'Slavery'." Rolling Stone. http://www.rollingstone.com/music/news/prince-warns-young-artists-record-contracts-are-slavery-20150809#ixzz476VdNN4j (accessed August 9, 2015).

Jim Brown, Deacon Jones, Gale Sayers, "Mean" Joe Greene, O.J. Simpson, Gene Upshaw, Franco Harris, Art Shell, Drew Pearson, Jack Tatum, Terry Metcalf, Lynn Swan, Cliff Branch, the late Walter Payton, Earl Campbell, Ahmad Rashad, Tony Dorsett, Franco Harris, Mel Blount, Donnie Shell, James Lofton, John Stallworth, Kellen Winslow, Lawrence Taylor, Ronnie Lott, Ed "Too Tall" Jones, Ozzie Newsome, Everson Walls, Marcus Allen, Eric Dickerson, Mike Singletary, Art Monk, Henry Ellard, Freeman McNeil, Ron Brown, Wes Chandler, Jerry Rice, Dexter Manley, Reggie White, Bruce Smith, Charles White, Herschel Walker, Tim Brown, Warren Moon, Drew Hill, Eric Martin, Sterling Sharpe, Barry Sanders, Rod Woodson, Eric Allen, Thurman Thomas, Tim McDonald, Derrick Thomas, Randall Cunningham, Andre Rison, Bo Jackson, Emmitt Smith, and Michael Earvin served as the African-American pioneers within professional football. Based on this extensive list of *NFL* Hall of Famers, football appears to have the widest gateway into wealth out of all of the athletic sports.

Boxing champions were obvious with Muhammad Ali, Joe Frazier, George Foreman, Ken Norton, Larry Holmes, and Leon Spinks being the African-American *Cold War* greats. Evander Holyfield, Mike Tyson, Pernell Whitaker, Sugar Ray Leonard, Marvin Hagler, Larry Hearns, Riddick Bowe, Roy Jones Jr., Sugar Shane Mosley, and Floyd Mayweather took inflated wealth to unconceivable levels.

Tennis was nearly a cultural monopoly with Arthur Ashe being the sole African-American name of an entire era until the William's sisters, Serena Williams, soon to be the best ever in the *Women's Tennis Association* (*WTA*) by total majors, records held, and overall dominance with her older sister, Venus Williams, a near second. Because of these aforementioned pioneers, James Blake, Donald Young, Madison Keys, and Sloan Stephens have entered the millionaire club of American tennis players.

Whether television, comedy, or sports, all of the aforementioned pioneers and legends based upon cumulative income, albeit inflationary, would very well, possibly, and most likely, not exceed an eight-figure salary combined. They are pioneers and legends but did not make up the First Generation of African-American Wealth opposed to African-American pioneering and popularity. They paved the way but did not experience riches, let alone wealth opposed to worldly comforts. The tide has since turned. As segregation succeeded slavery literally in history, it has also done so through neo-sophisticated forms. As the slave master is absentee in post-modernity, segregation is equally abstract. No longer is segregation blatant and overt evident in having to sit in the back of the bus, drink from separate water fountains, or use rear entrances. Segregation is now subtle and subliminal. Segregation is now ethnically internal through capitalistic classism.

## Chapter Eight
## THE ABSENTEE SEGREGATIONIST
### (1990-present)

Segregation existed for the primary purpose of maintaining a clear geographic separation between Whites and Blacks. While the intentional distancing and perpetual refusal towards co-existence is undeniable, that purpose has to be considered as priority. During this era, three realities appeared to serve as priority.[45]

First, the Blacks could not receive education at the same rate as Whites, thereby, facilitating and perpetuating knowledge, employment, career, and "standard of living" inferiority. Second, Blacks could not inter-marry, thereby, ensuring pure blood, the assurance of a master race, and the inferiority of a sub-standard race. Third, Blacks could not vote, thereby, ensuring the protection of the establishment, democracy, and the laws, policy, and politics within the elitist class.

The critical question is, "Does segregation still exist and if so, in what form? Is it "Neo-Segregation", non-blatant, subtle, and subliminal with the intent to stagnant an ethnic population that would increase in growth so fast that it would threaten the host population's majority? How can the spirit of segregation continue in the absence of blatant laws that prohibited the co-existence of two principal ethnicities? Do these questions suggest or imply reverse discrimination or a conspiracy theory? However, as

---

[45] Alchin, Linda. "Jim Crow Laws." Americana Historama. http://www.american-historama.org/1866-1881-reconstruction-era/jim-crow-laws.htm (accessed April 2016).

discussed in chapter fifteen of this book entitled, *Classism of African-Americans via Capitalism*, there should be equality, not superiority or inferiority, not a better than, not a greater than, nor a less than. Therefore, one, as I, am able to exam certain facts and raise various questions without it neither being nor implying reverse discrimination or the existence of a conspiracy. The facts are undeniable and real and must at some point be challenged by someone.

There was a time when *Jim Crow Laws* were needed in order to maintain the aforementioned three objectives; first, "standard of living" superiority; second, racial superiority; third, political superiority. Accordingly, segregation was needed in order to maintain economic superiority, enforce the spirit of ethnic inferiority, and maintain dominance over the establishment.

This entire literary chapter is to establish the foundation that no longer is *Jim Crow Laws* needed but has been replaced by other more sophisticated abstract entities. Nevertheless, the African-American must cognitively embrace much of the blame that cannot be cast onto another race or ethnicity nor solely be assigned to any organized secret conspiracy. Much has been brought onto the African-American people through their own mentalities and behaviors.

No longer are *Jim Crow Laws* needed that were blatantly racial. No longer are *Jim Crow Laws* needed that were clearly inhumane while veiled behind legality. Within the realm of contemporary means, remove of the laws, since they are illegal and implement methods that will accomplish the same outcomes, this is not to suggest a conspiracy theory or an intentional strategy nor is it to eliminate the existence of one. No longer are *Jim Crow Laws* needed when as unto "Neo-Colonialism", we now have "Neo-Segregation" via internal and ethnic classism.

## Chapter Nine
### CLASSISM OF AFRICAN-AMERICANS VIA CELEBRITY
#### (1990-present)

The billionaire landscape has changed over the past decade largely due to one dominant entity, "divorce". Robert Johnson was the world's first African-American billionaire due to the founding of *Black Entertainment Television*, better known as *"BET"*, his ownership of the *Charlotte Bobcats*, as well as other lucrative investments only to have him compromise his historical economic status as the first seven-figure African-American wealthy achiever and his current net worth reduced in half after a life changing divorce. Consequently, Sheila Johnson, Bob's ex-wife, lives a $700M standard of living apart from Robert. Since the time of their divorce, Bob has only been able to add an additional $50M to his net worth based on existing investments.[46]

Oprah Winfrey was the second and only African-American to attain, sustain, and maintain billionaire status and wealth because of her unique gift as being "America's Greatest Sociologist" as well as the "Queen of Day-Time Television". Today, according to Forbes last quarterly report, Oprah is nearing $4B of total net worth making her currently, the wealthiest African-American, as well as the wealthiest African-American in African-American history.[47]

---

[46] Mars, Errol L. "Robert L. Johnson." Black Profiles.
http://www.blackentrepreneurprofile.com/profile-full/article/robert-l-johnson/ (accessed 2016).
[47] "#569 Oprah Winfrey." Forbes. http://www.forbes.com/profile/oprah-winfrey/ (accessed April 7, 2016).

Michael Jordan, the third to reach the billionaire club, only to suffer the same fate as Robert Johnson where divorce compromised his net worth delaying him from the ranks of the ten figure club complements of his ex-wife, Juanita Jordan, who assumed $168M of his wealth as she was not only his wife before wealth and during his athletic dominance but also co-founded and served as Chairman of their philanthropic foundation, *Michael and Juanita Jordan Endowment Fund* throughout this entire time. Michael Jordan has since regained his former net worth and serves as the only of two African-Americans within the billionaire club based on his acquisition of the now, *Charlotte Hornets*, Robert Johnson's former *NBA* team ownership, his extremely profitable endorsements, wise investments, being the three-figure trend setting face of his *Nike* tennis shoes, i.e., "Jordan's", as well as his video game residuals.[48] Jordan has been projected to increase his net worth of $4.5B by 2020.[49]

Tiger Woods became the fourth African-American to near billionaire status only to sustain the pattern of delaying him from the ranks of the exclusive high society billionaire club complements of divorce due to repetitive infidelity. Tiger immediately sent his endorsement investors scurrying to maintain their marketing integrity. Tiger's on-the-course struggles appeared

---

[48] Tadena, Nathalie and Zhou, Momo. Divorce Has a Hefty Price Tag for Celebrities, Billionaires. ABC News. http://abcnews.go.com/Business/divorce-hefty-price-tag-celebrities-billionaires/story?id=8363063 (accessed August 20, 2009).

[49] Jules, Marvin. "If All Goes To Plan, By 2020 Michael Jordan's Annual Nike Royalty Check Will Be RIDICULOUS!" Celebrity Net Worth. http://www.celebritynetworth.com/articles/billionaire-news/wont-believe-much-money-michael-jordan-may-make-royalties-year-2020/ (accessed October 22, 2015).

to have little effect on his return to former economic heights due largely to his former $70M a year annual profits from the video golfing game bearing his name, *Tiger Woods PGA TOUR 14 – Xbox 360*, that served as a steady source of income for Woods in route up to the ten figure club.[50] Although Rory McIlroy has become the new face of *EA PGA Tour 15 Xbox 360*, Woods has an ever increasing net worth currently at $700M, significantly up from where it was at the point of his divorce.

Dr. Dre revealed his genius as a businessman, and rare modern day African-American innovator and manufacturer through his *Dre-Beats*. Selling the rights to *Apple* for $2.6B, although the terms of the deal were not a one-time payment, but $400M in stock options. This deal was adequate enough to add to his already existing quarter-billion dollar portfolio placing him at a current net worth of $800M that positions him to becoming the third existing billionaire after Oprah and Jordan in very short order.[51]

On the other hand, the same contributing factor, divorce, which led to the demise of the previously named African-American billionaires have equally contributed to the richest African-American married couple in Hollywood in the persons of Jay-Z and Beyoncé whose combined wealth exceeds $1.1B. While

---

[50] Sands, Darren. "As He Soars, Sales of Tiger Woods PGA Tour 14 Steady." Black Enterprise. http://www.blackenterprise.com/lifestyle/tiger-woods-pga-tour-14-sales-steady-videogame/ (accessed May 14, 2013).

[51] Lazarowitz, Elizabeth and Siemaszko, Corky. "Dr. Dre Sells Beats Electronics to Apple for $3 Billion." NY Daily News. http://www.nydailynews.com/entertainment/dr-dre-sells-beats-apple-3-billion-article-1.1808975 (accessed May 29, 2014).

their combined African-American net worth has exceeded that of Will Smith and Jada Pickett-Smith at $220M, Dwayne Wade and Gabrielle Union at $107M, Carmelo and Lala Anthony at $70M, and T.I., and Tiny Harris at $43M, it falls significantly short of the ridiculously wealthy Francois Henri-Penault and Salma Hayek whose combined wealth exceeds $15B or even the modest life styles of the rich and famous marital couple, Steven Spielberg and Kate Capshaw who occupy the number two position on the wealthy celebrity couple's list at a mere $3B.[52]

Although there are significant numbers of African-Americans who exceed a half billion dollars in their net worth portfolios, however, none as fast as Tyler Perry whose talents and innovative approaches of captivating audiences, as he intricately weaves the everyday realities and plights of the ethnicity's upper middle class, professionally, prestigious careered through both artistic and realistic characters, successfully went viral. His unique style caught the attention of the general American audience as Kevin Hart has equally done within the industry of comedy. Sean (Diddy) Combs has never lost the same hunger that led to his current $700M current net worth with a projected transition into billionaire status coming before the end of the second decade of the 21th century. Earvin (Magic Johnson) Johnson is projected to propel into the African-American billionaire club suffering minor set backs as he needed to restructure and temporarily stagnant the

---

[52] Warner, Brian. "The Richest Celebrity Couples In The World – 2013." Celebrity Net Worth. http://www.celebritynetworth.com/articles/entertainment-articles/the-richest-celebrity-couples-in-the-world-2013/ (accessed June 4, 2013).

growth of his economic portfolio in his acquisition of the *Los Angeles Dodgers*, the largest acquisition in sport's history at $2.15B. This is obviously the sacrifice of short-term riches towards long-term wealth. Floyd Mayweather, as the new king of economic athletic success, combined with his alliance with Warren Buffet and Al Haymon, has moved him to be able to dine at the same table with other African-American half-billionaires.

Extra ink must be spilled for Floyd Mayweather as his ability to make economic athletic history receiving $360M in 36 minutes, $10M a minute, is mind-blowing, historical, and impressive from someone whose greatest critics have sought to attack him based on their perceived literacy of him. However, kudos to Floyd who has clearly shown that one can make history and achieve the highest per hour employment compensation in African-American history regardless of academic achievement. Equally, true for LeBron James who literally froze an entire sport, the *NBA*, free agency, collective bargaining, agents, and marquee players by taking his resume for a spin on the open market testing his talent worth as a free agent in 2014. His influential power so impacted the sport of basketball causing the *League*, as well as owners, to develop rules preventing any one player from enveloping that level of power to gridlock free agency thereafter. LeBron's actions literally changed a sport and its approach towards the salary cap and collective bargaining. Likewise, Tiger Woods changed an entire sport, golf, through his dominance as being the only athlete to change the "field of play" of any athletic venue, specifically relating to "Tiger-Proofing", a well-known reality in order to level the playing field for others to compete in the sport.[53]

Among active African-American athletes, Tiger Woods at $700M leads *PGA* competition. LeBron James $300M heads all *NBA* players. Alex Rodriguez is the economic *MLB* front-runner with his $300M of earned net worth. Serena Williams' $140M is the *WTA* earnings leader. Julius Peppers & Terrell Suggs are first in personal net worth of *NFL* players at $40M. Bernard Hopkins at $40M stands at the financial helm in the sport of boxing with Roy Jones Jr., and Shane Mosley at $35M each following.

Relating to music, James Brown, the "God-Father of Soul" died at a net worth of $100M only surpassed by the late greats, Jimmie Hendrix at $175M, the legend and true "Prince of Music", Prince, at $300M, and the "King of Pop", Michael Jackson $600M upon their respective transitions. Of active musicians is Lionel Richie at $200M. Following Richie are more old school names that currently hold high net worth such as Billy Paul at $145M, Stevie Wonder at $110M, and Smokey Robinson at $100M. Usher, at $180M, is believed by many to be the 'heir apparent' to the "King of Pop" based upon his overall musical IQ as a singer, performer, and businessman. Possibility and opportunity still avails itself for Usher to fill the rather larger and practically immortal shoes of Michael Jackson. Master P at $250M, Lil Wayne at $140M, Kayne West at $135M, Snoop Lion at $135M, and Ice Cube at $120M

---

[53] Harig, Bob. "'Tiger-proofing' Augusta Took A Toll On All." ESPN. http://espn.go.com/golf/masters11/columns/story?columnist=harig_bob&page=110329-RTTMasters (accessed April 1, 2011).

continue to seize opportunity and develop creative artistry lending to increased wealth in the most aggressive industry of the African-American culture, *Hip Hop*, all following the aforementioned Dre, Diddy, and Jay-Z.

Highest personal net worth among <u>actors</u> is Bill Cosby at $400M, Will Smith at $260M, with Samuel L. Jackson at $170M, Denzel Washington $140M, Morgan Freeman at $90M, and Jaime Foxx at $85M, all following Tyler Perry at $450M. It should be noted that Samuel L. Jackson held the number one position of selected roles in the highest grossing movies at $4.6B than any other actor in Hollywood, regardless of ethnicity, until toppled by Harrison Ford in January 2016.[54]

Byron Allen leads all African-American <u>comedians</u> at $300M with Martin Lawrence being both talented and an under-valued frugal manager of his $110M career earnings with Steve Harvey, at the very height of his career, most likely to soon exceed them both from his current $100M net worth.

Jeh Johnson, former *Secretary of Homeland Security*, (2013 – present), <u>leading all African-American politicians</u> in personal net worth at $51.5M. Christopher Paul, net worth of $10M, is the wealthiest African-American <u>male author</u>. Creflo Dollar of Atlanta has the highest net worth among African-American <u>Pastors</u> with a net worth of $27M, Bishop T.D. Jakes of Dallas, second, at $18M, although all follow Bishop Charles Blake of Los Angeles in

---

[54] "Harrison Ford Reclaims Title of Highest Grossing Actor." The Telegraph. http://www.telegraph.co.uk/film/movie-news/harrison-ford-highest-grossing-actor/ (accessed January 16, 2016).

membership, at 20,000 congregants on roll, with an unknown and undeclared net worth and income.

The following ladies hold extraordinary wealth and is listed for quick viewing purposes according to descending net worth's: **(1)** Oprah Winfrey: $3.2B, **(2)** Sheila Johnson: $700M, **(3)** Janice Bryant Howroyd: $610M, **(4)** Mariah Carey: $520M, **(5)** Beyoncé Knowles: $450M, **(6)** Diana Ross: $250M, **(7)** Tina Turner: $250M, **(8)** Juanita Jordan: $170M, **(9)** Rihanna: $170M, **(10)** Serena Williams ($140M), **(11)** Janet Jackson: $125M, and completing the list at those exceeding nine figure net worth personal values, at exactly, $100M is **(12)** Baroness Monica von Neumann.

These females, who lead each one of their respective African-American popular industry, highlighting the "Queen of African-American Wealth", in the person of Oprah Winfrey's $3.2B net worth, is quite impressive. Shelia Johnson leads non-celebrity executive wealth at $700M. Mariah Carey leads all African-American women in net worth acquired via music at $520M. Juanita Jordan leads all African-American models with a net worth of $170M with Tyra Banks coming in second for those who argue that the total net worth of Juanita Jordan comes from sources other than the primary income of modeling. Rihanna serves as the African-American *Hip Hop* Princess at $170M. Serena Williams leads all African-American female athletes at $140M. Halle Berry leads all African-American actresses at an ever growing net worth of $80M. Nicki Minaj appears to be the

"Queen of Hip Hop" at a daily increasing net worth of $80M while I maintain a personal bias to Aretha Franklin being the "Queen of Soul", the late great Whitney Houston, a.k.a., "The Voice", as the "Queen of R&B", with Mary J. Blige being the "Princess of R&B". Terry McMillian leads all female African-American authors with a net worth of $40M. Alexis Herman, former *Secretary of Labor* during the Clinton Administration appears to lead African-American female politicians with a net worth of $20M. Monique leads all African-American women as a primary comedian with a current net worth of $13M. Juanita Bynum and Yolanda Adams with respective net worth's of, $10M and $5M, lead female gospel artist with both needing to be named, as Bynum is both a singer and proclaimer opposed to Adams who is solely a singer.

The "Age of Reality Shows" is contributing to an extraordinary amount of seven figure African-American millionaires who would not have experienced this level of wealth or standard of living without the existence of this era. The "Judge Shows", existing out of the *People's Court* and Judge Wapner has led to a minimum of three African-American multi-millionaire judges, Judge Joe Brown at $66M, Judge Greg Mathis at $20M, and Judge Kevin Ross at $10M. Bert, the bailiff of Judge Judy, is the atypical example of an African-American who held a routine job as a bailiff and U.S. Marshall to the lifestyles of the 'Rich and Famous" as he was invited by Judge Judy to be her bailiff once receiving the job as Wapner's successor. This serves as a prime example of a plethora of seven figure Reality Show celebrities from mere commoners with the "Medically Based Reality Shows" appearing to lend to the most and fastest degree to wealth considering *Sisters in Law* as offering considerable competition for reality show supremacy based on the common knowledge that medicine and law has always been long perceived to be the two most prestigious careers.

Simply because African-Americans are a meritocracy and a plutocracy, an "ethnocracy" if you will, this is by no means an indictment or intended to suggests nor cast a negative shadow over those who have been either blessed through inheritance, gifted through artistry, or worked hard and smart to gain their wealth. It should be noted, commended, and celebrated that their talents have afforded them luxury. Nevertheless, the reality still remains that there is a huge schism between the "haves" and "have not's" based on celebrity.

If the ultimate theme is the assimilation of the African-American culture into capitalism and capitalistic ideologies with the danger of acculturating into a failed system, the ultimate question, of how will this occur, is paramount. An inquisitive quagmire presented itself during data collection. Several names of individuals who made the African-American millionaire club appear to automatically be linked to certain key industries. This linkage is inextricable. In other words, when you hear the name Don King, it is immediately ascribed to boxing. However, Don King has never had a professional fight. When you hear the name of Stephen A. Smith, it is instantly linked to sports. However, Mr. Smith is not a professional athlete. When you hear the name James Brown ("sportscaster"), the *NFL* naturally comes to mind although Mr. Brown has never played professional football. Consequently, a presentation of the facts relating to route to wealth becomes skewed when these linkages are ascribed. At the same time, to not place them with their popular industry opposed to primary career is tantamount to misplacement as to industrious route to success. Therefore, certain African-Americans need to be added to the innovation list along with the great black inventors in history.

The following names are applicable to this quagmire, alphabetized: Al Haymon ($15M), Bryant Gumbel ($18M), Cari Champion ($2M), Chris Brossard ($5M), Greg Gumbel ($16M), James Brown ($10M), Jamelle Hill ($1M), Lisa Salters ($2M),

Michael Smith ($2M), Michael Wilborn ($12M), Pam Oliver ($1M), Sage Stelle ($1.5M), and Steven A. Smith ($10M) relating to sports. Ben Tankard, Wayman Tisdale, Russell Simmons ($340M), Berry Gordy ($345M), and Quincy Jones are applicable to music. Al Haymon is a businessman that graduated from *Harvard University* with an MBA who happens to be a boxing manager and promoter. Bryant Gumbel of *Bates College*, Cari Champion of *UCLA*, Chris Broussard of *Oberlin College*, Greg Gumbel of Loras College, James Brown, another *Harvard* graduate, Jemele Hill of *Michigan State University*, Lisa Salters of *Penn State University*, Michael Wilborn of *Northwestern University*, Michael Smith of *Loyola University*, Pam Oliver of *Florida A&M University*, Sage Steele of *Indiana University*, and Steven A. Smith of *Winston-Salem University*, are all outstanding par-excellence' journalist in the field of sport's journalism. The late great, Stuart Scott ($15M), who belongs in a class by himself as one of the greatest trend setters of any industry, specifically, sport's journalism, was a graduate of *UNC, Chapel Hill*. Therefore, these individuals should be placed in the category of executives as they made their riches as successful journalist opposed to athletes and would thus transfer a total of $474.5M (nearly $.5B), inclusive of Sport's Agents later identified, from the industries of "Athletics" to "Executives". Without making this distinction, one would be led to believe that the only and/or best way to success for the African-American is through athletics or in the larger context, entertainment that is already a long-lasting and existing stigma of the culture itself. Consequently, college does matter and make the entire world's difference. Ben Tankard and Wayman Tisdale played football but are also known for being successful jazz musicians.

However, the ultimate dilemma comes in the comparison of Berry Gordy to Quincy Jones. Although Berry Gordy's name is infinitely tied to music, as a writer and producer, Gordy is, above all things, a businessman. He is not a musician. On the other hand, the same can be said about Quincy Jones with the exception that Mr. Jones is both a businessman and musician. Without these examples, it limits the possibilities of influentially minded children seeking success through means other than entertainment if they are not privy to this information.

Jay-Z is the most successful *Hip-Hop* artist of our time having performed, written, and produced music. However, his interest in *Roc Nation* makes him one of the most successful businessmen within the African-American culture. As Jews are well known to heavily dominate sport's agency, *Roc Nation* has done an amazing job in creating viable competition within a difficult industry causing others to follow suit. Rich Paul is one of the most successful African-American sport's agents as he has the biggest client in sports, in the person of LeBron James. Paul, with a net worth of $10M, would be set for life if he merely maintained a client list of one, when that client (Lebron James) is so powerful that he can gridlock an entire sport and free agency, as he did in delaying his announcement to return to Cleveland in 2014. No owners, no agents, no players were willing to make a move until James made his decision public. Paul works for *Klutch Sport's Group*, based out of Cleveland and serves as the one of the most successful executives among African-Americans. Eugene Parker, probably second only to the aforementioned Rich Paul, with a current net worth of $8M and a client base inclusive of Deion Sanders and Rod Woodson, works out of a firm in Fort Wayne, Indiana called *Maximum Sports Management*. Bill Duffy, founder, owner, and CEO of *BDA Sport's Management* with offices in Los Angeles, San Francisco, and Chicago, has a client base that includes Klay Thompson and Rajon Rondo. Bill Strickland, CEO of *Stealth Sports*, services clients such as Joakim Noah, Rasheed Wallace, and Allan Houston. Eric Goodwin and Aaron Goodwin, of *Goodwin Sport's Management Company* based out of Seattle, has a client list inclusive of Gary Payton, Chris Webber, Damian Lilliard, Matt Barnes, Nate Robinson, and Tina Thompson. Kimberly Holland has let America know that no ethnicity or gender will prevent success within any industry, as she is the most famous African-American female sport's agent and owner, operating *Icon Management* out of Atlanta with a clientele of largely sport's Olympians.

R. Donahue Pebbles, Janice Bryan Howroyd, Quinto Primo III Daymond John, John W. Thompson, Herman J. Russell, Ronald A. Williams, Albert Haynes, Kenneth I Chenault, and Monica von Neumann are the nine figure executives who acquired riches through means either than entertainment. R. Donahue Pebbles, with a net worth of $700M, is the most successful real estate tycoon within the African-American culture. Janice Bryant Howroyd is the second wealthiest non-celebrity African-American woman who made her $620M fortune as founder and operating CEO of *ACT-1 Group*, an employment agency. Quinto Primo III, to possess a net worth of $300M, as the second wealthiest African-American real estate manager, is not bad at all. Daymond John is founder, president, and CEO of *FUBU*, producing him a net worth of a ($250M) quarter of a billion dollars. John W. Thompson acquired his $250M fortune as former *Chairman of Microsoft*, vice-president of *IBM*, and CEO of *Symantec*. The late Herman J. Russell earned the right to permanently tattoo his name into the African-American history books as he transitioned from this world with a $200M net worth having achieved his wealth through the periods of segregation as a uniquely gifted property developer. Ronald A. Williams, another successful African-American CEO of *Aetna*, has produced $170M in total net worth. Kenneth Chenault became the third CEO (after Dr. Clinton Wharton in 1987 and Franklin Raines of *Fannie Mae* in 1999) of a *Fortune 500* company, *American Express*, yielding him a $125M net worth and fortune. Finally, Monica von Neumann, better known as Baroness Monica von Neumann, is the third wealthiest African-American non-celebrity female with a $100M fortune after her marriage to the great Baron of Switzerland in addition to her own entrepreneurial innovations.

The Baroness is the last of twelve African-American women in the nine figure exclusive club. Shondra Rhimes has earned a $60M net worth as the creator, producer, and writer of *Grey's Anatomy*. Cynthia Stafford, currently possessing a net worth of $40M derived her riches from a $112M lottery ticket with further investments and business ventures thereafter. Rosalind G. Brewer earned a $25M net worth as President and CEO of *Sam's Club*, a sub-division of *Wal-Mart*. Finally, Ursula Burns accomplished not only a $15M net worth, but also, made history being the first African-American woman to run a *Fortune 500* company as President and CEO of *Xerox*.

Richard Dean Parson leads the male eight-figure non-celebrity executives who is the retired CEO of *Time Warner* with a net worth of $99M. Following Parsons is Stanley O'Neal, former CEO of *Merrill Lynch*, the second wealthiest eight-figure non-celebrity male who has $70M of personal net worth. Christopher Gardner's name certainly is worth mention as he is the true character behind the popular and touching movie, *The Pursuit of Happyness*, starring Will Smith and his real life son, Jaden, portraying the message that "anyone can do anything they set their mind to" has provided Gardner with a $60M net worth as the most successful African-American stock broker who had no original plans towards this career path but was provided training and opportunity by *E.F. Hutton* and *Dean Witter Reynolds*. Jeh Johnson's name must be inked into the pages of African-American history, *Secretary of Homeland Security*, (2013 – present), leading all African-American politicians in personal net worth at $51.5M. Armstrong Williams, political commentator and radio host has a net worth of $50M. Charles E. Phillips, CEO of *Infor*, a software company, has a net worth of $34M. Dr. Ben Carson, a neurosurgeon and former Republican Presidential Candidate, has a net worth of $30M. Creflo Dollar, of Atlanta, has the highest net worth among African-American pastors with a net worth of $27M. Al Rooker, originally "Weather Reporter" turned morning wake-up television personality, has $20M in net worth. Daniel Simmone, his a.k.a., "Danny Simmons", brother of Russell Simmons and Joseph Simmons, Rev. Run, is a painter with a net worth of $20M. Donald Thompson continues the list of non-celebrity African-American male millionaires as CEO of *McDonald's* with a current net worth of $20M. Ralo Wonder is CEO of *Wonderboy Group Entertainment* who dabbles in marketing, publishing, and NASCAR with a net worth of $20M. Rodney O'Neal is President & CEO of *Delphi Automotive* who has a net worth of $14.2. Roger W. Ferguson Jr. is the former *Vice Chairman of the Federal Reserve* during the Clinton and Bush II administrations with a net worth of $12.5M. Alec Monopoly, also known as Alec Andon, is the painter and face of the famous *Monopoly Game* with a net worth of $12M. Franklin Raines is the former *Chairman of Fannie Mae & Director of Office of Management and Budget* (*OMB*) during the Clinton Administration. With a net worth of $10M, Charles Payne is a *Fox Economic Contributor*. Fred Mwangaguhunga developed a net worth of $10M as a corporate attorney & founder of the website *Media Take Out*. Jean-Michel Basquiat incurred $10M in net worth as probably the most popular graffiti artist in the world. Christopher Paul, net worth of $10M, is the wealthiest African-American male author who acquired his wealth by writing 'children books'. His first copyright was in 1996. Rushion McDonald has a net worth of $10M as a former *IBM* executive and now believed to be the brains behind one of the fastest growing African-American personalities, in the person of Steve Harvey as his personal manager. Shaun Thompson has a net worth of $10M as he provides professional training services to the stars. Kenneth C. Frazier is only one of two seven figure African-American non-celebrity males named with a net worth of $8.3M, who must be included by shear accomplishments as Chairman and CEO of the pharmaceutical company, *Merck & Co.* Finally, completing the list of males who made millions due to cognitive brilliance is the former CEO of *Darden Restaurants*, Clarence Otis Jr. with a net worth of $7.6M. The aforementioned men are gender specific examples of African-Americans who have established wealth through means other than entertainment.

These facts show two things. First, African-Americans have, are, and can be successful outside of the entertainment field. It confounds the mind and baffles the influential to not understand the personalities behind the celebrities. It limits the potentials and diminishes the possibilities for these individuals to not be named and known for their achievements. Yet, to know, expands the horizon and removes any limits or boundaries while opens a window that success can be achieved through infinite dimensions. Second, with only twelve African-American women exceeding nine figure net worth with the obvious caveat that the wealthiest African-American being a woman, in the person of Oprah, and another nine, exceeding eight figure net worth, gender equality, within the African-American culture, is still in progress and yet unaccomplished. The conclusions of ethnic cultural capitalism within the African-American people is not difficult to prove as I have been able to list slightly more than half of the "Top Wealthiest 1/100%", "4,000", exactly, "2099", attributing to $45B of cumulative net worth. It must be noted that no list is totally comprehensive. However, African-American millionaires via business ventures, accomplishment, achievements, and success are probably the least comprehensive and inexhaustible list.

## Chapter Eleven
## CLASSISM OF AFRICAN-AMERICANS VIA CLASSISM
### (1990-present)

Obviously, there are many pros and cons to capitalistic ideologies. As stated by Winston Churchill in his speech to the *House of Commons* on 11 November 1947, "Democracy is the worst form of government except for all those others that have been tried. Likewise, it is also true with capitalism."[55] At the end of the day, they both, democracy and capitalism, appear to be political and economic experiments indicative of the hypothetical scenario that if Jeb Bush would have occupied the *Oval Office* in succession to his father, President George H.W. Bush Sr., and his brother, President George W. Bush, would America be able to continue its identification as a democracy or would it have become a dynasty, aristocracy, or an oligarchy? Accordingly, if *Main Street* continues the need to bail out *Wall Street*, is it still capitalism, socialism, or some unofficial hybrid of both?

Is a meritocracy and plutocracy still a democracy or is it an oligarchy? *Appendix: Chart #XX* is evidence that African-Americans have completely assimilated, acculturated, and embraced the capitalistic ideology where the top 1% of the African-American population currently possesses 56% of all African-American wealth. African-Americans are unquestionably both a meritocracy and plutocracy within a democracy based on

---

[55] Barnes, Matt. Capitalism: The Worst Economic System, Except for All the Others. University of Pittsburg: The Pitt News. http://pittnews.com/article/5424/opinions/capitalism-the-worst-economic-system-except-for-all-the-others/ (accessed August 26, 2014).

the fact that the majority of their wealth has been acquired through celebrity and entertainment. Equally, there are growing signs of an aristocracy within the African-American plutocracy in multiple ways. First, those named in the *Appendix Charts* of this book are largely of first generation wealth where their riches have already created a second and third generation of cultural wealth. In other words, many first generation African-American millionaires have children who have already acquired millionaire status through their own individualized gifts, separate, apart, and distinct from their parents along with their own personal dedication and hard work. Second, for most second-generation millionaires, it is very difficult to separate themselves from their last name, parental affiliation, and direct or indirect assistance from parental influential support. I hope to live long enough to see the sequel to this work, as I hope and know that someone will thoroughly research the economic cultural landscape of second and third-generation African-American wealth especially when the current wealthiest 1% moves from owning 56% to 98% of the entire culture's wealth in projected single decade, 2026. The stage has already been set by endless names of second-generation wealth with Laila Ali, Ken Griffey Jr., Ken Norton Jr., Kobe Bryant, and Jaden and Willow Smith possibly being the most popular. These names were intentionally chosen as they cover the majority industries of the meritocracy; boxing from boxing, baseball from baseball, football from boxing, basketball from basketball, actor from actor/actress, and singer from actor/actress, respectively.

However, the reality show, *Growing Up Hip Hop*, is a prime example of those poised and set to replace, challenge, and exceed the meritocratic success of their pioneer parents. Romeo Miller, son of the 4th wealthiest *Hip Hop Artist* (Master P), Angela Simmons, daughter of Rev. Run and niece of Russell Simmons, Damon Dash, son of Rock-A-Fella, Kristina DeBarge, daughter of James DeBarge, Egypt Chriss, daughter of the Sandra "Pepa" Denton of *Salt-N-Pepa*, TJ Mizell, and son of the late Jam Master Jay of *Run DMC* make up the cast of *Growing Up Hip Hop*.[56]

There are those whom I am aware, such as Imani Boyette who is also destined for greatness as a second-generation descendant who has achieved greatness based on her own talent opposed to professional basket pedigree and her maiden name(s) as the new first round *WNBA* draftee of the *Chicago Sky*. Her brother is JaVale McGee, *NBA* super star. Her mother is Pamela McGee, former *WNBA* star, *Olympian* gold achiever, as well as two-time *NCAA Women's Basketball Champion*. Her father is the renowned Baptist pastor, Dr. Kevin E. Stafford and former collegiate 3-point state shooting leader. Her aunt is Trisha Stafford-Odom, women's professional basketball internationale', former *WBNA* great, accomplished women's collegiate basketball recruiting specialist for *UCLA, Duke, & UNC*, former *Head Coach* of *Women's Basketball, Concordia University* and now, *First Assistant of Women's Basketball* at the *University of Houston*. Incidentally,

---

[56] Colby C. "New Reality Show Spotlights Kids of Hip Hop Greats." Uptown. http://uptownmagazine.com/2015/07/meet-cast-growing-up-hip-hop/ (accessed July 8, 2015).

Pam McGee is the quintessential example of second-generation wealth as she made history when her daughter Imani was drafted into the *WNBA* as being the first mother to have children to reach the *WNBA* and *NBA* as well as being active players within both professional organizations simultaneously. The list of second-generation wealth is so endless and ripe that I dare not even attempt to begin mentioning names in fear of embarrassing the highest standards of academia through omission. Therefore, I pray that someone will capture this growing aristocracy and oligarchy within this existing plutocracy and publish the 'Second Generation of African-American Wealth'. These will be they who will move the African-American people from the top 1% currently owning 56% of the total cultural wealth to the inevitable day in 2026 when the top 1% will own 98% of the African-American cumulative wealth indicative of true capitalistic assimilation.

Caveats abound around acquired wealth via name and/or affiliation opposed to active industry derivatives. During research and data collection, I encountered several interesting and intriguing dilemmas and dynamics of *Classism within Plutocratic African-American Classism*. First, it appears natural to only view the transition of wealth from a vertical perspective meaning, from parent to child or via, the "old fashion way", inheritance.

Second, although this has and probably always will be true throughout history, not limited to time or culture, however, due to the most unfortunate of all experiences, a parent outliving a child, there is an unusually high amount of wealth moving vertically up opposed to gravitationally down within the African-American culture. Katherine Jackson, the matriarch of the Jackson family, the late Afeni Shakur, the mother of the late Tupac Shakur, and T'yanna Wallace, the mother of the Notorious B.I.G., all having net worth of $50M. This paragraph is so closely linked and intertwined with the chapter labeled, *African-American Population Control via Clashing*, based on the fact that African-American children are departing this world too soon.

Third, although not a new dynamic, however, there is a very obvious and evident growing oligarchy out of a plutocratic African-African core, albeit, from a horizontal opposed to vertical perspective. Marriage is the single greatest transition of wealth horizontally within the family unit, especially through divorce and unfortunately death. Cookie Johnson ($50M), wife of Magic Johnson, Camille Cosby ($20M), the ex-wife of Bill Cosby, Jackie Christie ($10M), the wife of *NBA* star, Doug Christie, and widower Chaz Ebert, wife of the greatest film critic of all times, Roger Ebert, has a net worth of $9M.

Nevertheless, the existence of sibling wealth through either aristocratic or meritocratic means is creating a fresh oligarchy. This dynamic is as old as the *Jackson Five* with Michael (RIP), at $600M, Janet at $175M, LaToya at $4M, Rebbie at $2.5M, and Jermain, Jackie, Marlon, and Tito all at $1M each lending to a combined family income of nearly $1B, when the matriarch is added. The Wayans Brothers have been creating familial wealth for almost 40 years with Keenan ($65M), Marlon ($40M), Shawn

($30M), Damon ($5M), and Mike ($2.5M) totaling a cumulative sibling wealth of $142.5M. Russell Simmons ($340M), Joseph Simmons (Rev. Run), ($70M), and their other brother, Danny Simmons ($20M), a professional painter has created a sibling wealth of ($430M). A litany of siblings in all forms of entertainment can be named from Eddie Murphy ($85M) and Charlie Murphy ($5M) to Chris Rock ($70M) and Tony Rock ($4M) to Shannon Sharpe and Sterling Sharpe at ($8M) each to Tiki Barber ($14M) and Ronde Barber ($12M) to those as far back as the Mowry sisters with Tamera and Tia at ($4M) each, all serving as realistic examples.

As a family unit, the Mayweathers with Floyd at ($400M), Roger at ($20M), and Floyd Sr. at ($5M); the Williams' family with Serena at ($140M), Venus at ($75M), Richard at ($20M), and Oracene Price at ($1M); the Smith's with Will ($260), Jada at ($20), Jaden at ($8M), and Willow at ($4M) are all impressive as meritocratic families. Dionne Warwick at ($10M), Cissy Houston at ($5M), the late Bobbi Kristina at ($20M), and the late great Whitney Houston at (-$20M), albeit unfortunate, still serves as a possible meritorious dynasty.

The mentioning of those who obtained non-meritorious wealth does nothing to diminish the reality of their wealth or place judgment on the manner incurred whether its through the old fashion method of inheritance, affiliation, luck, or fate, commendations to each for having arrived. Again, while nothing malicious intended, this does nothing to diminish the reality of economic polarizations within a specific culture existing from a stigmatized entertainment base.

Today, there are 400,000, 1% of the total ethnic population making this dynamic possible, The First Generation of African-American Wealth. How are they handling this wealth? Easily answered, like "New Money", "Nouveau Riche"!

> This French term means "Newly Rich" and describes people who acquired their wealth within their own generation. They usually come from middle or working class families who acquired their own wealth. They may also have acquired their wealth with help of parent's finances (who may have been above middle class). The point is, their money does not go way back in time like for the ones with "old money". "Nouveau Riche" men & women are known for splurging – sometimes exaggerating! They like to flaunt their affordability and tend to buy many status symbols to be seen as an upper class. As the naming, this means old inherited status & money. They are known for being elitists that tend to look down on the Nouveau Riche and claiming, "they lack the proper pedigree". Old money people stick together and prefer not to mix with others. They marry within "their circle" to keep as they say "the pedigree noble". They are often the "socialites" types who go to high-end events, private member's clubs and more discreet gatherings. For them fame and stardom is often not prioritized, as their circle of friends usually contain royalties, politicians and A-listers. In comparison to "Nouveau Riche", the old money folks do not flaunt their money in the same excessive way. They rather keep their head high and look above everyone they believe is not worth wasting energy on.[57]

---

[57] "Who Are the Nouveau Riche." wiseGeek. http://www.wisegeek.com/who-are-the-nouveau-riche.htm <http://jetsetbabe.com/nouveau-riche-old-money/> (accessed 2013-2016).

This is a classic example of classism within a class. Is this sub-classism? Is the "Nouveau Riche" a sub-class of "Old Money" within the wealthy class? If so, one then can conclude the inescapability of classist divisions. Therefore, not only is there a schism and extremist dichotomy between the rich and poor class of the African-American Capitalistic Culture, but there also exist polarization among the wealthy class suggesting unavoidable cultural conquest via division. If, in fact, these implied classist divisions are intentionally facilitated by conspirators, their work is both easily and automatically ingrained within humanity, as capitalism is an inherent perpetuation of the need for the existence of superiority and inferiority. How sad? Equality will never occur within the environmental dynamics of capitalism, as there always has to be those who, by their very nature, must feel better than everyone else.

Although many thereafter throughout the annals of history have either used or claimed that they were the first to voice the phrase, including Julius Caesar and Napoleon, it was Philip II, king of Macedon (382-336 BC) and father of Alexander the Great, who coined the phrase, "Divide and Conquer". The Persians used it as a routine empirical process albeit not abusively. Yet, the African and African-American have experienced and been victims of this cruel political practice more than any other people group. Nothing sabotages the democratic voting practice more than division especially related to classism. The economic taxes reliefs for the rich usually serves as an antithesis to the struggles of the poverty class.

The richest 1% of all African-American wealth does nothing to jeopardize the constructs of the American democracy. Although surprisingly criticized by the establishment, Chris Rock profoundly spoke on the differences between wealth and riches.

> For Chris Rock, being wealthy means having financial holdings so immense that they can be passed down through generations. "Shaq is rich," he said, referring to the Los Angeles Lakers' Shaquille O'Neal, "but the white man who signs his check is wealthy. Oprah is rich, but Bill Gates is wealthy. If Bill Gates suddenly woke up with Oprah's money, he'd slit his throat."[58]

Wealth has been defined and described as generational prosperity whereas riches is often times limited to first generation millionaires; "Old Money" versus "New Money". While the discussion on this difference could continue indefinitely, a much better distinction can be made. Which one is wealthier or better off, the man who has a fish or the fisherman? We have all heard the cliché', "Give a man a fish and he'll eat for a day but teach him how to fish, and he will eat for a lifetime."

Who is greater, the individual with the money to purchase and own a Rolls Royce or the individual who knows how to make a Rolls Royce? Which one is greater, the one who can make a Rolls Royce or the one who possesses the raw material whereby

---

[58] Norman, Tony. "The Big Difference Between 'Rich' and 'Wealthy'." Pittsburg Post-Gazette. http://www.post-gazette.com/opinion/tony-norman/2004/05/21/The-big-difference-between-rich-and-wealthy/stories/200405210167 (accessed May 21, 2004).

the Rolls Royce is made? Who is greater, the one who owns the raw material that's needed to make a Rolls Royce or the person who owns the land where the raw material is mined? In short, the person who owns the land that earths the raw material is greater than the manufacturer and the manufacturer is greater than the individual who possesses the money to purchase the product.

Give an African-American enough riches to purchase a Bentley, he or she will return the money in exchange for the Bentley, its comfort, and a socio-economic status where one is pit against another in an effort to reach a conclusion that one is better than the other. Therefore, there is never a danger by the host culture to give an indiscriminate amount of money to the African-American, who while being first generation millionaires and billionaires, will seek to enjoy their newly acquired riches, purchase the things for them and their families that they never experienced, in spite of liberal philanthropy by many, either genuinely or for tax shelters through their established foundations. It justifies the reality opposed to the myth that African-Americans are consumers opposed to manufacturers.

"Old Money" and the "Nouveau Riche" dichotomy is another example of internal cultural divisions. No matter how high one goes in life nor the achievement or acquisitions acquired, there still exist divisive schisms that pit and perpetuate superiority, inferiority, and a "better-than" attitude and belief system.

It hurt to watch Shaq and Kobe, two "Nouveau Riche" who won three *NBA* championships together, be at odds with one another. However, it was mighty nice to witness the reunification of their friendship.[59] It hurt even more to witness Floyd Mayweather and 50-Cent, two "Nouveau Riche" who were at one time closer than brothers, breach their brotherhood. That was divisive. However, it was sweeter to see them bury the hatchet.[60] These come with the caveat that Kobe and Floyd were not first generation celebrities and therefore may or may not be considered by some academics as "Nouveau Riche", but exceeded in wealth more than their respective fathers could ever imagine. Hopefully, one day, Nicki Minaj and Mariah Carey as well as Lil Kim, three "Nouveau Riche" will rectify their differences. Chris Brown and Drake, Drake and Diddy, Mike Epps and Kevin Hart, and Katt Williams and Kevin Hart are all further examples. With differences like these, who needs to devise a scheme or mastermind a conspiracy of "Divide and Conquer" when the most influential divide themselves from unity?

In addition, there are ingrained elements perpetually embedded on autopilot that exist among and within any plutocratic individual, group, or family. Kin cousins of the rich and famous, trust and paranoia, appear as dynamics of separatism. Those who have wealth live in a constant state of mind and being where they innately feel the need to question the motives of those who seek to

---

[59] Turner, Broderick. Eleven Years After Messy Breakup With Lakers, Kobe and Shaq Make Up On Podcast." L.A. Times. http://www.latimes.com/sports/lakers/la-sp-kobe-shaq-feud-20150830-story.html (accessed August 30, 2015).
[60] "50 Cent Buries Hatchet With Mayweather "He's My Brother." TMZ. http://www.tmz.com/2015/04/23/50-cent-buries-the-hatchet-with-mayweather/ (accessed April 23, 2015).

develop friendships or get close to them, even if they are family. Personally, the question is silently processed upon every new relationship, "Is this person with me because of my money, status, or are they holistically genuine with no ulterior motives or alternate agendas?" Publically, the celebrity exhibits anti-social behaviors, a strange irony for individuals who are unable to leave home without a mob of journalist, paparazzi, photographers, analyst, critics, pundits, and fans. Sadly, this dynamic occurs between both those who have old money wealth or new money riches. One would naturally believe that two individuals with money would not be bothered with these apparent mundane issues. Yet, as already discussed within the dynamics of "Old Money" and "New Money", belief systems, tensions, and standards of living will always clash regardless of classism. Therefore, whether public or private, it perpetuates a lonely existence. This is classism within classism!

If via conspiracy, then by default, what's the intent? If via conspiracy, the simplistic question must be asked, answered, and processed, how? Academia and scholasticism will not allow and thereby will not permit the processing thereof without due consideration as to the possibility that these dynamics and realities are intentionally intentional. What is the formula of conspiracy? In other words, how many coincidences are needed in order to make one conspiracy? The timing and affects are too coincidental. All should be able to exam certain facts and raise various questions without it neither being nor implying reverse discrimination. The facts are undeniable and real and must at some point be challenged by someone. Every significant influential threat to the establishment who sought equality and nearly accomplished it was assassinated. President Abraham Lincoln, President John Fitzgerald Kennedy, and Dr. Martin Luther King are case in point examples. Why? At the same time, certain facts can suggest a conspiracy or the co-existence of several simultaneous conspiracies with or without them being reality. In simple terms, is the African-American a victim of a conspiracy or series of conspiracies with the simplistic goal of not necessarily damaging the race, but the protection of a democratic majority, a superior class, the dynamics of superiority/inferiority, and the conservation of capitalism? All must be considered and examined for a solution to be derived.

Willie Lynch's goal was the "protection of property," Jim Crow's goal was not primarily "racism" but the "protection of superiority". One was "economic" while the other was "social" with both using politics as the vehicle of execution leading to the same conclusion, inferiority. Regardless of method, the goal has always been the same, "I'm better than you". Is 'Capitalism' well dressed as Jim Crow in 21$^{st}$ century liberalistic clothing?

After the 1865 Emancipation Proclamation, African-Americans experienced the great pioneers of ethnic thinking, Dubois, Washington, Woodson, and others. Therefore, there were some who revealed the dynamics of macro-ethnic realities. However, the masses were either still limited to the cotton fields or mere manual labor. Consequently, there was not a threat to the establishment. However, after the 1965 MLK Revolution sparked by the Rosa Parks historical incident, certain elements had to be executed in order to prevent potential threats that would ride the wave of the Vietnam, women's liberation, and anti-government protest especially after witnessing the exceptional knowledge of the aforementioned great ethnic pioneer thinkers within four decades after the Emancipation and exposure to education. Therefore, in the 1970's, America witnessed the rise of gang violence. In the 1980's, substance abuse stifled the urban ghettos of America, where the greatest population of African-Americans lived. In the 1990's, capitalism gave birth to the African-American people creating a desire for more even if it cost their freedom through criminality. Now, the rise of the wealthy class through

118

celebrity will divide and occupy the minds of the African-American for at least another decade.

First, legally and subliminally, many, long before my limited knowledge, saw and projected a conspiracy through the legal assistance of *Affirmative Action*. Blacks are inferior, so let us help them out. On the other hand, could *Affirmative Action* be so simple as an attempt to bring balance to a guilty conscience having nothing to do with the polarized elements of superiority and inferiority? In spite of Willie Lynch or Jim Crow, capitalistic assimilation, acculturation, and polarization of the African-American are the ultimate "divide and conquer" strategy. It simultaneously presents complexities and simplicities.

Second, how can one draw the conclusion that there is an intentional conspiracy or anti-African-American movement in effect when an ethnicity is being given money and therefore empowered as a result? In other words, if there is an on-going conspiracy and/or enemy, they would naturally respond, "How can one be accused of being anti-ethnic if they are giving opposed to taking?" How can one be accused of being anti-ethnic if they are the same individuals who are empowering and supply the wealth? Those receiving the wealth will automatically take the position and posture that those supplying the capital is not the enemy for they have helped me out of poverty and led to my creature comforts? They have given me opportunity I would not have otherwise achieved. Those receiving the wealth will automatically respond with the classic responses, "I'm getting paid for it"; "As long as

119

they keep lacing my pockets, they are cool with me"; "You are just hating because you ain't getting paid", etc., etc., etc. Again, the creature comforts are not the problem, nor the money, especially for those who have worked hard and/or gifted with the gateway to riches. The problem is the inability to be able to recognize possibly the greatest "divide and conquer" strategy ever devised, capitalism and classism, i.e., the great divide and polarization of the rich and poor. Its the greatest because its an *Absentee Slave Master* whereby those who are recipients of the wealth automatically become defenders of the process due to their classist status and creature comforts. The poor have been provided with imbedded incentives to hope and strive for a reality that 99% of the ethnic population will never achieve. Beyond Genius! Most of the rich will never become wealthy as they are not manufacturers but consumers, only giving the riches back to the wealthy for produced products. The rich and the poor will always remain polarized with the rich feeling a sense of betterment and the poor feeling a sense of hopelessness leading to clashing, chemical dependency, and criminality in their effort to achieve the status of the rich. If the ethnic rich ever threaten to exert their influence into political process or threaten to compromise the democracy or the establishment, true politics will then take over lending to the exposure of character defects common to all humanity. Again, beyond genius!

What's the problem? The difference between an ethnicity understanding and moving towards the "quality of life for themselves and humanity at large" versus "individualized quantity of life only for them". An irreversible reality protected by loyalist that has become the recipients of the wealth. Therefore, the supplier of the wealth never has to worry about the perpetuation of the ultimate "divide and conquer" strategy, as the loyalist will protect it as benefactors and interpret any attempt to compromise the system as a personal attack against their interest, riches, and status. Therefore, the supplier and loyalist have an impenetrable relationship. An awesome quagmire of ironic proportions exists where these theories imply a conspiracy. However, how can there be a conspiracy when the same individuals who would be accused of creating and perpetuating the conspiracy are the exact same people who are providing the money leading to an obvious wealthy class of African-Americans? In other words, its very difficult to infer that the very individual or people group that is making you rich is somehow conspiring against you. However, if it were true, it would then be one of the cleverest schemes ever devised as a conspiracy theory from one people group upon another, "give", in order to ultimately, "take"!

It is not a wonder that African-Americans are becoming sicker with mental health issues, substance abuse, and criminality based on an overwhelming desire to live within the realm of economic comforts. Heretofore, these psychological devises have historically come one at a time opposed to the genius of ethnic capitalism that permits them to occur simultaneously. Insanity, mental escape, physical incarceration, elimination from the democratic process co-existing at one time, and now capitalistic polarization have all exceeded the corruptible genius of Willie Lynch.

Third, there is no doubt that this book has racial over and under-tones. The mere fact of its title, **"CAPITALISM: The New Segregation"**, speaks directly of a certain ethnicity, historically. Capitalism and economics, population controls, classism and comparisons emanate a certain energy that appears to pit not only one socio-economic class against another but also "Black" versus "White". Based on the industries contained within *Appendix: Chart #XX*, the facts reveal no threat to the establishment as well as a comparison of *Appendix: Charts #XX and #XXI*.

However, as there appears to be no industry threats, two sports appear to be so patriotic that not only have there been limitations placed within the sport, such as "Tiger-Proofing" but also the African-American involvement within these sports are obvious.[61] They are baseball (*MLB*) and golf (*PGA*). These sports are historically heavily White dominated by both player and fan base. With the sole exception of the "Home Run" record by Hank Aaron who openly claimed to have received repeated threats when nearing Babe Ruth's record[62], an asterisk will be permanently attached to Barry Bonds' name based on a very timely performance enhancing substance scandal. Likewise, Tiger Woods

---

[61] Cox, Kevin C. "Atlanta Braves Get new Flood of Hank Aaron Hate Mail, Report Claims." CBS News. http://www.cbsnews.com/news/atlanta-braves-get-new-flood-of-hank-aaron-hate-mail-report-claims/ (accessed April 15, 2014).

[62] Christensen, Jen. "Besting Ruth, Beating Hate, How Hank Aaron Made Baseball History." CNN http://www.cnn.com/interactive/2014/04/us/hank-aaron-anniversary/ (accessed April 2014).

would have easily surpassed Jack Nicklaus in golfing majors if there was not for the well timed "Tiger-Proofing" architects within the sport of golf. Could "Tiger-Proofing" have been so intentional as to prevent and complicate the process of Tiger's ability to overtake Jack Nicklaus' 18 Majors, the long-standing golfing record? "Tiger-Proofing" is not a myth but openly recognized as reality by repetitive credible sources.[63] What I find more than strange is the timing of the process. As Tiger secured his 14th Major at the famed *2008 U.S. Open*, 4 away from tying Jack Nicklaus' 18 golfing Majors, coincidence overwhelms irony. Concurrently, questions and rumors abound as to the uniquely timed retirement of Floyd Mayweather upon tying the great Rocky Marciano at the 49-0 long held record of the exclusive undefeated legend. There is a barbershop talk belief that the American past-time sports of *MLB* and the *PGA* must remain exclusive. The 'Green Jacket' of the *Masters* that allows entrance and perks into the all-inclusive club is ethnically equivalent to the overall American classist percentage of 99-1.

Since athletics is the industry supplying the most net worth, the subliminal messages sent through sports relating to color, rules, and dynamics are relevant, significant, and overwhelmingly intriguing. Although introduced on a mass scale by Martin Lawrence in the movie, "Boomerang" using the element of comedy

---

[63] Harig, Bob. "'Tiger-proofing' Augusta Took A Toll On All." ESPN. http://espn.go.com/golf/masters11/columns/story?columnist=harig_bob&page=110329-RTTMasters (accessed April 1, 2011).

relating to the game of Pool, it doesn't diminish the reality of its content.

> It's racial... The white ball dominates everything. Knocks the shit out of the yellow ball, the red ball. Right? And the game's over when the white ball drives the black ball completely off the table. Now why is that? I don't know, but I'm sure you'll tell me, my brother...It's because of the white man's fear of the sexual potency of black balls.... It's not about jokes...Yo, man, he's getting' worse.[64]

Picking up this school of thought relating to both the subliminal impact and the subliminal messages per sport of basketball and football, the most involved by African-Americans, deals with a large brown ball. Lawrence made the balls within the game of "Pool Shooting" analogous to the male genitalia. This analogy is representative and indicative of reproduction, generational effects, and ethnic culture.

Basketball and football are both team sports requiring the sharing of the ball to secure victory. Baseball is a team sport involving nine active players using a somewhat small white ball. Golf is not a team sport requiring the use of a small white ball. However, for baseball, any single player can solely win the game without the assistance of teammates, however, not excluding the possibility of the reciprocal. In other words, one player can be at bat, one on deck, and the other seven in the dugout while the player at bat can win the game with a home run. This cannot be true in any other sport. In football, one person can return a kickoff

---

[64] "Boomerang (1992) Movie Script." Springfield.
http://www.springfieldspringfield.co.uk/movie_script.php?movie=boomerang (Accessed 1992).

for a touchdown, however, not without the assistance of blockers. In basketball, one person can score alone but not without the assistance of a teammate, at the very least, to inbound the ball. One can win, however, not alone.

Golf, on the other hand, is not a team sport. The greatest challenge of the game is the ability of the player to master the course. This is strangely consistent to how the dominant ethnicity and nationality of any country, especially America, obtains their net worth, through the mastery of the ground based on the mining and manufacturing of raw materials. The element of competition is compatible to all sports that also serve as the foundation of capitalistic thought. With golf, competition is least a factor leading to victory, success, and accomplishment than the conquest of the course.

All sports are thinking games whether it's the efficiency of the "Pick-&-Roll" or "Triangle Offensive" in basketball, the "West Coast" offense or the "Wishbone" in football, or the mastery of the course in golf. The key to the success of Floyd Mayweather in boxing is related to the precision of geometry, specifically relating to angles. Floyd's ability to always place himself at certain exact angles enabling the maximum output of both his offense and defense while simultaneously limiting these components to his opponents appears to have been the most significant contributor to his success in addition to boxing IQ, ring savvy, sheer giftedness, and extreme hard work. As stated by his former trainer and uncle,

Roger, "this is a thinking man's game." However, this is rarely, if at all, given publicity.

Therefore, in a very subtle subliminal manner, to be successful in the sports of African-American dominance, basketball and football, requires the assistance of others and the leadership of another, in the person of a coach. In football, the majority of offensive linemen are White subliminally conveying the source of protection for the most significant thinking player on the field, the quarterback. Consequently, this plants the all-important subliminal seeds of African-Americans having the need to rely on their physical athleticism perpetuating the same value and worth as slaves, the need for team support, and coaching leadership whereas Whites are capable of becoming successful by thinking independently and mastering the earth towards accomplishment.

Fourth, I admit being caught off guard when presented with a potential motive or theory behind the worst atrocity within the history of humanity, the *Holocaust*, Germany's extermination of 6 million Jews. First, some have raised the belief that Hitler was a Jew and sought the extinction of Jews so that he could be the only remaining individual labeled as the "chosen people". Most, throughout history, have discounted this to be completely absurd.

Second, many believe that America's support of Israel is related to geo-political positioning in a potentially hostile Middle East where an Islamic Empire is not a possibility but has historically occurred by overtaking the entire African Coast of the

Mediterranean and southern Europe during the Dark Ages just as America did not only possess the world's most destructive weapon, but used it to nearly extinguish the Japanese people ending World War II. The point is, once one has engaged in a certain practice, it is no longer a possibility but a potential reality. Therefore, one has to take the need for geo-military-political positioning as necessary and serious.

Third, the continued American and westernized support of the Israelis is to protect supremacy and superiority from a theorized belief that the original Jew was black consistent to the Biblical scriptures, specifically, Job 30:30, "My skin is black upon me". Because the book of Job is the oldest book of the Bible denoting the thought process of humanity's original state, this suggests that all humanity is derived from "Black people" and thus infers, 'first-ness' and thus, 'superiority'. If the present day Jew, Israeli, or Israelite were supported as an internationally recognized government, land, and people through unlimited military, political, and economic support, Blacks would never witness the opportunity to seize this position of originality and consequently, superiority. More and more African-Americans are embracing the identity of "Black Jews".

The question of Hitler's rationale behind the Holocaust has always been perplexing. His actions do not diminish the conclusion of history and the international community that the German leader was evil. Why did he do what he did? There is no rhyme or reason. Was Hitler just pure evil and there is no rhyme, reason, or rationale? Whatever his reasons, the approach taken cannot be excused. Nevertheless, the need to protect the world from a lie has to be considered based on the fundamentals of scholarship and academia. As well, while it's easy to label Hitler as evil and/or crazy, how did he manage to convince an entire country and military to commit such acts of atrocity? After examining the following alleged statement by Hitler, the protection of supremacy, but not by the Germans, has to be examined.

<u>Hitler said, even in his death, he will start World War III.</u>

**One of his soldiers asked, "How"?**

Hitler replied, "The day mankind finds out what I was trying to defend this nation, Germany, from, then that's the day World War III will start. For on that day, mankind will learn that I was trying to save my Nation from, the *Free Masons*, the *Illuminati*, and the *Jews*. For if, the Americans win the war, then, they will conquer the world and forever be a slave to the Jews and they will try to conquer God. Do you know whom America has in its possession?"

**"NO," the solider replied.**

Hitler replied, "The Americans have the jewels of God. The Americans have stolen God's precious jewels.

**"What do you mean his precious jewels?" The solider asked.**

Hitler said, "America has stolen the Jews. The Jews of God. His jewelry. The Negros. They are the true Hebrews. What a foolish move and a direct challenge to God; and they plan on moving these false white Jews into a state of Israel. America is desperate in its attempt to win this war using atom bombs on Japan. America will destroy the whole world in its attempt to conquer it. When America and its Jewish slave masters conquer the world and the world realizes I was right, then all nations will begin a third world war to dethrone America of its rule. Every nation will soon possess atom bombs of their own. It will be the end of most of the world, as we know it.

**"Why will the Jews control America?" the solider asked.**

Hitler said, "Because the white Jews know that the Negros are the real children of Israel. And to keep America's secret, the Jews will blackmail America. The Jews will extort America. Their plan for world domination won't work if the Negros knew who they were. The white citizens of America will be terrified to know that all this time they've been mistreating and discriminating and lynching the children of Israel. They will fear God who will destroy them as he destroyed Egypt for doing the same thing. So the elite, the *Illuminati* keeps this a secret at all cost. After I die, I will one day cause World War III just by this message that will be like planting a seed in people minds until it sprouts once they nurture that seed and seek more truth and learn Hitler was right. I did the world a favor by killing the false Jews before they designated a false state of Israel. But I fear I have failed. The world will fall into the hands of Satan."[65]

---

[65] "Hitler Said, Even in His Death He Will Start World War 3. One Of His Soliders Asked How? Hitler Replied....". FML. http://fmlgoneviral.com/hitler-said-even-death-will-start-world-war-3-one-soliders-asked-hitler-replied/ (accessed July 7, 2015).

Whether it is the protection of White supremacy, the prevention of Jewish or Semitic supremacy, or the promotion of Black supremacy, they all equal the sad reality of inequality.

Fifth, there are no differences in the possible motives behind the unspeakably sacred *Illuminati*. Most, who embrace the belief that African-Americans who join the *Illuminati*, are required to do so for moral reasons. They must sell their souls. However, what if the goal has always been, 'the maintenance of a superior class'. If the belief is true, those 13 families rule the world and own all of the money and power, why then would they need anything from anyone? Morality could be the ultimate deception while superiority is the ultimate accomplished goal.

Sixth, Jonathan Nolan, screenwriter of the movie, *The Dark Knight Rises* (2012), provided profound insight when he wrote and spoke through the character Bane played by Tom Hardy within the simplicity of capitalistic polarization between the elements of hope and despair relating to both, the rich and poor. These words were shared during the scene in the cave,

> Where am I...? I am home where I learned the truth about despair, as will you. There is a reason that this prison is the worst hell on earth… Hope! Every man who has rotted here over the centuries has looked up to the light and imagined climbing to freedom. So simple; so easy. And, like shipwrecked men turning to seawater from uncontrollable thirst, many have died trying. I learned that there can be no true despair without hope. So as I terrorize (the city), I will feed its people hope to poison their souls. I will let them believe they can survive so that you can watch them clamber over each other to stay in the sun…. You will

watch as I torture an entire city to cause you pain you thought you could never feel again.[66]

It is impossible for me to have described the capitalistic reality better and as a result, I will not attempt to reinvent the wheel. In order for capitalism to work, the elements of hope and despair must co-exist. Ninety-nine percent of the African-American people have to be fed hope but experience despair. They have to believe that they can make it. They must believe that wealth is at their reach. Although many have died trying, they must be so convinced that the climb to riches is ever so simple, so easy, like shipwrecked men turning to seawater to satisfy an uncontrollable thirst only to learn that although the water is there, plentiful, and accessible, it is not edible, therefore, unable to satisfy this simplistic goal of thirst. Either African-Americans seek wealth personally though attempts at celebrity status whether through music, comedy, acting, or lotto, the derivative remains the same, "hope". While most never achieve wealth as the statistics confirm, they will pretend as though they are living a life of wealth either through automobiles, homes, or celebrity interactions. How powerful then is the question posed by Langston Hughes, "What happens to a dream deferred"?[67]

---

[66] Nolan, Jonathan and Nolan, Christopher. "The Dark Knight Rises." https://alexcassun.files.wordpress.com/2012/08/tdkr.pdf,pg.90. United Kingdom: Faber and Faber LTD (accessed July 2012).

[67] Rampersad A, Roessel D., *The Collected Poems of Langston Hughes*. New York, NY: Knopf; 1994.

## DELIVER FALSE HOPE!

If 1% of the African-American population is given wealth and paraded before the remnant, it will cause the remaining 99% to believe that they too can achieve riches. *The Huffington Post* reported in the article entitled, *The Decadent Veil: Black America's Wealth Illusion*,

> The decadent veil looks at black Americans through a lens of group theory and seeks to explain an illusion that has taken form over a 30-year span of financial deregulation and newfound access to unsecured credit. This veil is trimmed with million-dollar sports contracts, *Roc Nation* tour deals and designer labels made for heads of state. As black celebrity invited us into their homes through shows like *MTV* cribs, we forgot the condition of overall African American financial affairs. Despite a large section of the 14 million black households drowning in poverty and debt the stories of a few are told as if they represent those of millions, not thousands. It is this new veil of economics that has allowed for a broad swath of America to become not just desensitized to black poverty, but also hypnotized by black celebrity. How could we not? Our channels from *ESPN* to *VH1* are filled with presentations of black Americans being paid a king's ransom to entertain. As black celebrity has been shown to millions of people, millions of times, the story of real lives has also been lost, and with it the engine that thrust forward the demand for social justice by the masses. The heartbeat of social action is to recognize your mistreatment, and demand better. With each presentation of Kobe Bryant's 25 million dollar a year contract, or Oprah's status as the sole African American billionaire a veil of false calm is created within the overall American economic psyche about the immense black wealth disparity. Young black men from ghettos across America that used to dream to make great changes in racial inequity now just dream to be a millionaire and be like Mike and dunk a ball or dance on a stage. The

decadent veil not only warps the black community's vision outward to a larger economic world, but it also distorts outside community's view of Black America's actual financial reality.... Without that veil removed, we project progress that has not yet occurred, and in doing so perpetuate an illusion that may in the end destroy us all.[68]

Seventh, the catalyst of endorsements has been used most effectively to advance the African-American Capitalistic Culture and polarization. Not only does it compensate salary disparities but pits one celebrity elite against another especially within the competitive environment of athletics where there already exists an aura of oppositionality, antagonism, and contention. Those who receive more quantitative and qualitative commercials are perceived as better than their athletic peers. Furthermore, it perpetuates a generational divide as the influential minds, especially children and adolescents who embrace the athlete of frequent and impactful endorsements as being greater than and, thus, more coveted.

> Salaries alone do not tell the entire story. Increasingly, an expanding group of African American athletes receive additional income far in excess of their salaries for endorsing products from breakfast cereals to automobiles. This was not always the case. In fact, the first Black athlete of the football Chicago Bears, Walter Payton, did not appear on the Wheaties box until 1986. Now, in 1996, Michael Jordan of basketball's Chicago Bulls and sports' highest paid athlete is expected to earn 90% of his $40 million through endorsements. While this situation does not

---

[68] Moore, Antonio. " The Decadent Veil: Black America's Wealth Illusion." Huffington Post. http://www.huffingtonpost.com/antonio-moore/the-decadent-veil-black-income-inequality_b_5646472.html (accessed August 5, 2014).

characterize the majority of Black athletes, it does include a significant number, and is in happy contrast to the 1960s and before, when the picture of an African American on a breakfast cereal box was simply unthinkable.[69]

The timing of the endorsement paradigm shift is the compelling factor. On August 8, 1991, *Gatorade* served as one of the pioneers of the capitalistic expression that partnered corporate America with professional sports supplementing iconic player's salaries with unbelievable endorsement deals. Michael Jordan was paid $1.4M per year for a decade for the, *I Wanna Be Like Mike*, commercial perpetuating classism while simultaneously planting the seeds of influence into the minds of identity searching youth.[70] Until December 8, 2015, Jordan was the highest paid endorsement athlete with a $60M lifetime deal until *Nike* renegotiated LeBron James' $30M, 10-year (2008-18), into a larger lifetime contract. March 20, 1991, *Nike* contracted with Bo Jackson's multi-sport talents for $2M a year.[71] *Nike* still remains the highest paid corporate endorsee of African-American athletes currently paying Kevin Durant $24.5M for 10 years (2014-24), Tiger Woods is presently under contract for $20M for 5 years (2013-18), and Kobe Bryant is having $15M directly deposited into his checking

[69] Walter, John C. "The Changing Status of the Black Athlete in the 20th Century United States." Liverpool John Moores University: AR Net. http://www.americansc.org.uk/Online/walters.htm (accessed 1996).

[70] Lefton, Terry. "To 'Be Like Mike,' Gatorade Had To Poach Michael Jordan From Coke." Sports Business Daily. http://www.sportsbusinessdaily.com/Journal/Issues/2014/02/17/Champions/Schmidt-Jordan.aspx (accessed February 17, 2014).

[71] Foltz, Kim. "Does Bo, Hurt, Know as Much?" NY Times. http://www.nytimes.com/1991/03/20/business/the-media-business-advertising-does-bo-hurt-know-as-much.html (accessed March 20, 1991).

account for 5 years (2013-18).[72] This makes *Nike* the leader in the capitalistic partnership of corporate America with professional sports totaling $150M exceeding *Adidas, American Express, AT&T, Beef Jerky, Buick, Campbell's Soup, Chase Bank, Dominos, Farmer's Insurance, Icy Hot, KIA, Pepsi,* and *Sprite.*

Eighth, the core of capitalism requires that the proletariat support the bourgeoisie. Because the African-American cultural *GDP* is largely based on entertainment related products and services, the great silent majority of economically disadvantaged African-Americans purchase and dance to the beat of their music, are captivated by their movies, and experience the thrill of victory and agony of defeat of their athletic competition, further contributing to the exclusivity of the oligarchic and plutocratic African-American meritocracy. Again, the poor class support, contribute, and perpetuate the wealth of the rich. Without the masses, the wealthy would not be able to sustain nor increase their riches. The process is systemic causing the rich to get richer and the poor to continue struggling while remaining hopeful, in pursuit of reserving a seat at the millionaire's table further mimicking and admiring the wealthy class. Again, the *Huffington Post* wrote in its article on *The Decadent Veil: Black America's Wealth Illusion,*

> *NBA* commissioner Adam Silver hands black teenagers, million-dollar deals and *ESPN* then projects that as a normal image of black life across the globe creating apathy for Black America's truly dire financial straits. This

---

[72] "Biggest Athlete Endorsement Deals In Sports History." Total Sportek.
http://www.totalsportek.com/money/biggest-endorsement-deals-sports-history/ (accessed January 27, 2016).

all being shown despite there being a prison rate amongst young African American males that is higher than we have seen in any modern society in history. While media projects Beyoncé signing a *Pepsi* $50 million ad campaign throughout the World Wide Web, the fact that single Black mothers across America have a median net worth of a mere $5 dollars falls in the shadow of the singularity of her financial success.[73]

Ninth, in order for there to be an achievement of wealth, those who possess the wealth must be presented and paraded in front of those who aspire providing them hope that they too can achieve wealth through the same methods of capitalism. This does not imply to any significant degree that there does not exist an economically comfortable middle-class within the African-American population made up of largely educated accomplished professionals and everyday hard working people. African-American dramatic movies maintain a consistent plot of characters made up of upwardly mobile individuals that are corporate CEO's, executives, doctors, lawyers, and entrepreneurs. This has been factually confirmed by *Ebony Magazine*, who should be commended for the decades that they have dedicated a section of their monthly publications to ordinary African-Americans who have either graduated from college, propelled themselves to success, or moved into high-level positions via exceptional resumes.

---

[73] Moore, Antonio. " The Decadent Veil: Black America's Wealth Illusion." Huffington Post. http://www.huffingtonpost.com/antonio-moore/the-decadent-veil-black-income-inequality_b_5646472.html (accessed August 5, 2014).

Tenth, as we consider whether there exist an ever-growing African-American middle class, it does not erase the fact that capitalistic ideologies have consumed this ethnicity and defines its generalized personality as a people where the wealthiest 1% owns 56% of the entire culture's wealth consistent to the majority of the overall American socio-economic ratio. While the paradigm shifted to a polarized classism within the African-American culture during the immediate post-*Cold War* years, the ever-increasing middle class was being eliminated through three significant events during the first decade of the second millennium. First, "911" (2001) initiated a war on American classism just as much as it did against global terrorism. As the military landscape changed to an unidentified mobile enemy without a host land, so also was the case relating to the war on the middle class. There is no identifiable enemy to blame although infinite theories abound relating to a secret conspirator. Second, the devastation of *Hurricane Katrina* (2005) and the New Orleans' tragedy caused a mass migration of successful upwardly mobile middle class African-Americans to the nearby cities of Oklahoma City, Houston, and Atlanta being the leading recipients of the suddenly homeless, gridlocking their housing markets and employment opportunities that rippled all throughout the south. This stifled, stagnated, and eliminated many of the general American middle class, specifically, the African-American. Finally, the *Great Recession* (2007) significantly affected all Americans, specifically eliminating a huge majority of newly experienced African-

American middle-class, like nothing else in American history. After finally making it to a point of economic comfort, it was not natural, but the possibility of intentionally egregious conspirators who robbed them of their class status, stability, opportunity, and revitalized the destructive element of hopelessness. *Inequality* reported,

> In the aftermath of the 2008 economic meltdown, wealth owned by households of color declined dramatically, as home values collapsed... present-day inequality is the poisonous result of eroding net worth among African-American and Latino households and an exploding concentration of wealth in the top 1 percent, and within that, among the richest 400 billionaires.[74]

Eleventh and hypothetically, if there was an intentional conspiracy behind the elimination of the rising African-American middle class and a polarization of cultural classism, it killed two birds with one stone as the wealthiest 5% of all American wealth possessed 95% of the entire country's net worth saw a reduction to becoming the top 1% of the entire country's wealth, owning 99% of the total American wealth. Therefore, it would not be a stretch to imagine one of these conspirators sarcastically voicing this theme, "Let's clear out all the suckers"! This concept was not limited to just the African-American people alone but also eliminated the lower 4% of the top 5% of all American wealth, truly creating an elitist class, the top wealthiest 1%.

---

[74] Collins, Chuck. "Wealth of 400 Billionaires = Wealth of All 41 Million African-Americans." Inequality. http://inequality.org/wealth-400-billionaires-wealth-41-million-africanamericans/ (accessed January 17, 2014).

Finally, if there is an intentional conspiracy, the process would be simplistic:

(1) Decrease the Population
(2) Deliver False Hope
(3) Divide by Class
(4) Divide and Conquer

## Chapter Thirteen
## CLASSISM OF AFRICAN-AMERICANS VIA CHRISTIANITY
### (1990-present)

As automatic as the sun's daily rising and setting, capitalism comes with the dynamics of "better than" or superiority. This concept is as old as Cain and Abel where Cain killed his brother over the concept of betterment. God did not tell Cain that his sacrifice was insignificant, but the implication that a sacrifice consistent with blood was "looked with favor by God' (*KJV*), had "regard" (*Holman*), or "accepted" (*NLT*) than the edible plants that emanated from the ground.[75] The analogy was based on the ultimate misunderstood symbolism of Christology in that salvation could not be acquired by works opposed to the life of an innocent lamb. However, Cain could not fathom the feeling or perception of inferiority after knowing that he worked harder than his brother toiling with the thorns and thistles of the ground where the fruit that he produced was not better than the sheep that his brother, Abel, tended.

Do titles, ethnicity, education, family origin, "old money" versus "new money", and net worth make one better than another? African-American Churches are filled with clicks, the sin of covetousness, and divisions by socio-economic class. This over-shadows the goal of Christianity, to be Christ-like and conform to the image of Christ Jesus who thought it not robbery to be equal with both God and man as He was God incarnate in flesh. If a

---

[75] Gen. 4:4.

component of capitalism is the division of people groups, as is the case with clashing internally, no external assistance nor devilishly evil scheme needs to be devised to accomplish this goal within Christianity as *Protestantism* has successfully achieved this by developing over 33,000 denominations. Because there cannot be a unified consensus among the professionals of the field, i.e., theologians, professors, pastors, bishops, seminaries, Bible colleges, and denominational leaders as to what they believe, it is of limited shock that the plethora of denominational followers are so fragmented.

> My personal view is that Christians divide and give themselves denominational- type names too easily. Jesus said his followers should be "one", and many of these separate organizations are the result of serious divisions. It would be better if we emphasized what we have in common more, and worried less about these divisions.[76]

The African-American Church, regardless of denomination, has experienced seven major paradigm shifts in worship, modality, and ministry approach. First, there was the "Age and Era of Oppression" that gave us *Liberation Theology* from the leading authority and pioneer legend, James Cone, in his book, *A Black Theology of Liberation: 1970*, initiating the traditional Church modality where the sermons and songs were geared around freedom and the relief from a slave or oppressed reality.[77] Second,

---

[76] "How Many Christian Denominations Worldwide?" Following Jesus in the 21st Century. https://theway21stcentury.wordpress.com/2012/11/23/how-many-christian-denominations-worldwide/ (accessed November 23, 2012).
[77] Cone, James. *A Black Theology of Liberation.* Maryknoll, NY: Orbis Books, 1970.

we witnessed the rise of the "Charismatic Movement" (1960-present) where the cognitive evolved into the emotional with remnants of the traditional serving as the base. The "Charismatic Movement" emphasized 'spiritual gifts', the 'laying on of hands', 'speaking in tongues', and the need to feel something to suffice the worshipper. Third, we experienced the "Age of the Mega-Church" (1970-present) where African-Americans flocked in groves to certain pastoral personalities. This era still exists. The movement also hung on the coattails of "seeker-sensitivity" where the approach, the Church environment, and both in-reach and outreach ministries were created and perpetuated in such a way that does not offend or make the invitee feel uncomfortable, thus, lending to the mass growth. Fourth, the African-American Church embraced the renowned ministry approach of Rick Warren's *Purpose Driven Church Model* (1980/1995*-present) where worship alone did not suffice the spiritual needs of people but asked the all-important question, "What can the Church do for me?"[78] Until one discovers their God-given purpose in life, they will never experience true peace, serenity, and the idealism of living within the will of God.

Fifth, the African-American Church has now entered the 'Age of the Cell Church" (1990/2002*-present) also known as 'Small Groups'.[79] [80] This is an approach that offers a support system for those struggling with spiritual issues to receive

---

[78] Warren, Rick. *The Purpose Driven Church*. Grand Rapids, MI: Zondervan, 1995.

[79] Neighbor, Ralph & Jenkins, Lorna. *Where Do We Go from Here: A Guidebook for the Cell Group Church, 1st Ed.* Condell Park, Australia: Torch Publications Inc., 1990.

[80] The variation in date origins denote the lapse between the origin of the modality and the time the African-American culture embraced the concept.

immediate attention or outreach ministry. While there remains a main campus, the 'Cell Church' offers small cells (also called "small groups") over geographic clusters. Therefore, if one needs transportation to worship, employment, instant emergency assistance, or basic ministry, these needs are met through their local 'Cell/Small Group'. The 'Cell/Small Group' also offers frequent, even daily prayer meetings and Bible studies while also receiving ministry services corporately at a main campus in weekly increments. Sixth, although the traditional Church will probably always serve as the base, the African-American Church now practices either one of these modalities, a combination of two, more, or all of the above.

Seventh, in spite of there being pros and cons to each Church modality, none has caused more damage to the African-American soul like the "Prosperity Movement".

> Critics have charged that the focus on individual financial gain has turned black churches away from addressing the broader issues of racism and economic inequality. Personal scandals involving figures such as Eddie Long, accused of sexual misconduct with young men in one of his church organizations, and Gaston Everett Smith, pastor of *Friendship Missionary Baptist Church* in Liberty City, Florida, who was convicted of stealing public grants made to his church to aid the poor, have also raised questions about a number of celebrity ministers who contravene the sexual and financial standards they preach in their ministries.[81]

---

[81] Weisenfeld, Judith. "Religion in African American History." Oxford University Press: http://americanhistory.oxfordre.com/view/10.1093/acrefore/9780199329175.001.0001/acrefore-9780199329175-e-24 (accessed March 2015).

Critics of the 'Traditional' approach claim it to be reverse discrimination suggesting that the need for freedom within *Liberation Theology* automatically implies the existence of an oppressor, who is assumed to be White, based on historical racism. In addition to being racist, pundits believe the concept is exclusive and against a Church made up of the "whosoever wills". Critics of the 'Charismatic Movement' argue that the executions of the spiritual gifts, specifically, are inconsistent to sound Biblical doctrine. Critics of the 'Mega-Church Movement' believe it to perpetuate casual and inactive believers, as there is no accountability towards ministry involvement. Critics of the *Purpose Driven Church* model take more of an issue with the "seeker-sensitivity approach" which served as the foundation of its massive growth opposed to the Purpose-Driven format, in that seeker-sensitivity in its intent to not offend the potential candidate of baptism is counter to basic Biblical fundamentals, which by intent, are designed to offend any and all carnality. As a result, "Seeker-Sensitivity" is oxymoronic, a conflict of interest, and counter to the basic fundamentals of the Biblical problem, i.e., sin. Therefore, sound fundamental Biblical preaching and teaching offends, for it ought to always attack sin. Critics of the 'Cell/Small Church Movement' fear the ever-potential disunity of the Church, whereby, instead of having one unified Church, there is always the possibility of mini Churches within the macro-Church lending to already existing Church clicks and fragmentation. Therefore, while all methods have imperfections, as is the case with all Churches, none has corrupted the Church more than the "Prosperity Movement".

It is the Prosperity Movement's preaching, teaching, and ideologies that has inundated the masses with false hopes of material wealth.

> The prosperity gospel goes by many names: "Word of Faith", "Health and Wealth", "Name It and Claim It". This "different gospel" teaches that God provides rewards, including personal happiness, financial wealth and physical health, for believers who have sufficient faith. Prosperity theology developed in America in the last century and has been called a "baptized form of capitalism."[82]

There are two distinct components of capitalism that has infiltrated and defiled Christianity and the African-American Christian Church regardless of denomination. First, the ideology of the "Prosperity Gospel" has planted the false seeds and perception that prosperity is equivalent to the blessings of God while poverty and tragedy are evidence of the curse of God as well as being outside of the will of God. Second, the Pastors, Bishops, and so-called "Apostles" who parade around as celebrities fuel the insanity of the "Prosperity Gospel" providing pseudo-visualizations of prosperity that influence the fragile mind.

As a thirty year ordained Baptist minister of the gospel, a seminary graduate, and an eye witness to Churches of all faiths and

---

[82] Mitchell, Corrie. "Ten Bible Verses Prosperity Gospel Preachers Need To Stop MisUsing." On Faith. http://www.faithstreet.com/onfaith/2014/05/09/ten-verses-prosperity-gospel-preachers-need-stop-misuising/32019 (accessed May 9, 2014).

denominations across America over the last half-century, especially the African-American Christian Church, I am saddened by the fact that capitalism and capitalistic ideologies have infiltrated, dominated, and overtaken the prime objective of Biblical Christianity, i.e., 'salvation and life everlasting through the death, burial, and resurrection of Jesus Christ'. Pastors who place guilt trips onto their congregations for not possessing the latest helicopter are quintessential examples of capitalistic invasion and domination.

As per a *TIME* cover story on the September 15, 2006 edition: *Does God Want You to Be Rich*, denoting,

> Prosperity soft-pedals the consequences of Adam's fall — sin, pain and death — and their New Testament antidote: Jesus' atoning sacrifice and the importance of repentance.[83]

Instead, preachers have accentuated the economic principals of the Bible to extreme excesses and consequently either built up the hopes of believers, instilled guilt towards those in poverty, or burnt out the ears of doubters. "The message of many churches has been co-opted by American capitalism," said the Rev. Frederick Haynes III of the Friendship-West Baptist Church in South Dallas."[84] Haynes shared this as he hosted a summit on the subject of "Mega-Church Impact within the African-American Culture" with such great names as Joseph Lowery, Al Sharpton, Jesse Jackson, Cornel

---

[83] Van Biema, David & Chu, Jeff. "Does God Want You to Be Rich?" Time Magazine. http://content.time.com/time/magazine/article/0,9171,1533448,00.html (accessed September 10, 2006).

[84] Glick, Julia. "Black Leaders Blast Megachurches, Say They Ignore Social Justice." Religion News Blog. http://www.religionnewsblog.com/15084/black-leaders-blast-megachurches-say-they-ignore-social-justice (accessed June 29, 2006).

West, and T.D. Jakes. Creflo Dollar declined attendance. Sharpton took the position that mega-Church pastors are using their influence to 'fight morality opposed to social injustice' which is completely ludicrous as its the antithesis of the Church's core purpose towards morality and holiness opposed to politics. Lawrence Mamiya, professor of religion and Africana studies at Vassar College, said,

> Black Word of Faith mega-churches attract mostly middle-class blacks, who respond to their self-affirming message rather than more traditional churches' messages of guilt or obligation. It is really a question of whether the black middle class will continue to support the black poor. If they don't, I would see in that a big influence from Word of Faith or prosperity gospel.[85]

The plan towards capitalistic idealism leading to the goal of an elitist class within African-American Christianity is to target the upwardly mobile middle class. The African-American middle class is largely made up of educated hard working self-acclaimed professionals who deem themselves one step away from bourgeoisie. Therefore, a message of hope and its possibility is so potentially attainable that it is ripe for this audience. Through either a few good investments, a single economic breakthrough, or via routine opportunities, a seat at the millionaire's table appears to be a decision away. Consequently, a message of hope captivates the thought process of the African-American middle class.

---

[85] Ibid.

On the other hand, the African-American middle class benefits the ministry of the African-American mega-Church because their tithe and offering is optimal among the ethnic classes. They offer the most income and appear to pay for a product opposed to the giving of the tithe or an offering as they purchase seminar information from a motivational speaker towards riches and a life of comfort. The mega-Church pastor has assumed the role of a motivational speaker providing the service, details, process, and product towards the next economic class. On the one hand, the African-American middle class serves as the best ethnic economic people group ripe and hungry for higher monetary aspirations while simultaneously fueling the most cumulative revenue to the mega-Church ministry. As a result, the African-American middle class is magnetized to the mega-Church because of the sermonic content of hope, emotional experiences complements of performance-based entertainment whether through celebrity gospel singing, praise dancing, or the like, the affiliation with the local mega-Church in the geographic area of their residency, and the charismatic dynamics of a celebrity pastoral personality.

Is God a capitalist? Certainly not! God does not embrace capitalistic ideologies, whether economic or classist. Economically, God is the polar opposite of basic capitalistic principles in that the currency that satisfies the penalty of sin and provides salvation cannot be paid with money; only the shedding of the pure blood of Jesus Christ is able to pay the price of salvation.

Is God classist? Certainly not! As a matter of fact, God is the polar opposite of basic capitalistic principles of classism as salvation is offered to the "whosoever will". Everybody is the same in the eyes of God as all are sinners. Both Apostles Peter and Paul Biblically concurred that God does not show partiality or favoritism. Luke wrote in Acts, "Then Peter opened his mouth, and said, of a truth I perceive that God is no respecter of persons"[86]; Paul wrote, "For there is no respect of persons with God."[87] Scholarship requires me to reason the scriptures relating to the issue of equality. Although all are the same based on class as, "All have sinned and come short of the glory of God"[88], another scripture renders, "To whom much is given, of him much is required".[89] This certainly implies that while all are simultaneously in the same spiritual class, as all are sinners, there appears to be a differentiation of possessions, as not all are given the same, whether by spiritual or material gifts.

True scholasticism requires one to consider and argue each side of a debate. On one side of the academic argument relating to the "Prosperity Gospel" are the initial requirements of discipleship, "If any man will come after me, let him deny himself, take up his cross, and follow me."[90] Paul states, "Though he was rich, yet for

---

[86] Acts 10:34 (KJV)
[87] Romans 2:11 (KJV)
[88] Romans 3:23 (KJV)
[89] Luke 12:48 (KJV)
[90] Matthew 16:24 (KJV).

your sake he became poor, so that you through his poverty might become rich."[91] The academic argument continues within the story of the "Rich Young Ruler". He was three things that most modern-day capitalist desire. He was RICH. He was a ROOKIE ("young"). He was a RULER.[92] The occasion of Peter and John, who were used as instruments by God to endow the Holy Spirit unto a new believer through the laying on of hands, was met by a New Testament capitalist who saw their gifts as an economic opportunity towards wealth.[93] Many modern-day African-American pastors possess this same spirit whereby any innovative dynamic that appears to provide economic opportunities are quickly embraced, attempted, and implemented. This was no different from their first evangelical experience with the lame man who was lying at the gate entering Jerusalem facilitating the response, "Silver and gold have I none, but such as I have, I give unto thee. In the name of Jesus of Nazareth, rise up and walk."[94] Jesus offers His response to the element of money versus the concept of true values in three consecutive parables: the woman with the alabaster box, Jesus' expression that the impoverished are the world's permanent companions, and Judas' distorted belief of the importance of money.[95] None of these passages remotely compare to the fact that Jesus never owned nor sought to place

---

[91] 2 Corinthians 8:9 (KJV).
[92] Mark 10:16-24 (KJV).
[93] Acts 8:14-20 (KJV).
[94] Acts 3:1-10 (KJV).
[95] Matthew 26:6-16 (KJV)

value onto any materialistic possession as He moved His disciples from the realm and mentality of the carnal to that of the spiritual.

Many advocates of the 'Prosperity Movement' will require a response to the meaning of the following passages, "Ask and it shall be given;"[96] "You may ask me for anything in my name, and I will do it;"[97] "You do not have because you do not ask God;"[98] "He will do exceeding abundantly more than ye could ask or think."[99] First, if I properly exegete each passage, it will be a chapter within itself if not a book. Second, it will deflect from the primary theme of infiltrated capitalism within the African-American Church as the content of each passage, although appears economic, has absolutely no economic nor materialistic context. God wants us to be spiritually rich and each passage leads to that conclusion.

The African-American Church has become a business opposed to a salvation and spiritual growth center. The sad reality is that African-American pastors have deemed their congregations to be rebellious or problematic when the offering doesn't meet a certain pre-determined amount while simultaneously failing to understand that these same congregants have grown weary of hearing and seeing these same pastors live lavish lifestyles while they are left, as lowly congregants, to go home to bills that they cannot pay and hopes of prosperity complements of their most

---

[96] Mt. 7:7 (KJV).
[97] John 14:14 (KJV).
[98] James 4:2 (KJV).
[99] Eph. 3:20 (KJV).

recent sermon. As a result, the African-American Church has moved from a 'help center' to a 'hedge center' for those who desire material insurance opposed to spiritual assurance.

When the Old Testament writer spoke of prosperity, the context had absolutely no relationship to monetary blessings as the existence of money did not historically arrive until the period of *Roman Empire* as confirmed by Jesus' famous quote when He commented on the inscription of a Roman coin, "Give unto Caesar that which is Caesar's and unto God that which is God's." The Jewish system or equivalence of money was defined by the exchange of goods and services, especially among the *Twelve Tribes of Israel* who were brothers and generational relatives. Consequently, the barter of exchange was not money but the proceeds of the ground, true wealth, as described in the next chapter, whether agricultural, livestock, or precious metals.

While these facts are sufficient to connect the infiltration of capitalism within Christianity, it does not remotely compare to the celebrity personalities within the African-American Church. It was processed within my seminary experience that the *Catholic Church* has viewed *Protestants* as wayward children since the *Reformation* who would and will one day come back home and reaffirm the true meaning of the word "Catholic" as the "Church Universal". Therefore, it is believed that for five hundred years, the Catholic Church has constructed and maintained think tanks that are committed night and day to merging Protestants back with Catholics re-assembling the "Universal Church". One believed option out of these think tanks is to create mega-Churches all over the United States. Consequently, African-American Churches instantly embraced this think tank outcome in pursuit of greed, popularity, celebrity, large memberships, and money. The short-term goal is to follow the simplistic logic of celebrities who are the trendsetters of the African-American culture. As adults and children alike seek to be like and follow the personalities, philosophies, and lifestyles of the rich and famous, the same would hold true with the African-American Church related to celebrity pastoral personalities. The theorized long-term goal of the Catholic think tanks is as average pastors and parishioners look towards celebrity pastors who are default leaders because of their celebrity, likewise, the celebrity pastor, on auto pilot, will look towards the best in their field, industry, and profession. The celebrity Pastor will continue to look until they reach the height of their profession, as is the case with all professions. The largest figure in the Christian Church is the pope, the papacy, and the *Office of the Vatican*. Consequently, celebrity pastors will continue to conform to the mannerisms and methods of the Pope until full assimilation has been accomplished.

There are two popular responses from mega-Church millionaire pastors. First, they embrace and readily publicize a belief that God wants His children to have the best and use scriptural prosperity sermonic approaches to support this belief. Second, the essence, spirit, and pros and cons of capitalism are best expressed within the highest paid professions in the United States today, i.e., plastic surgery, where the basics of economics, "supply and demand", meet the bases of a meritocracy as an extremely gifted surgeon of high demand would naturally have a problem embracing a reality where he or she received compensation commensurate to an average *Internal Medicine* doctor. If people are willing to pay more for a skill that one possesses and wants it so badly that no amount is too much, why shouldn't the former, embrace the spirit of capitalism? Here, the two most prestigious professions, medicine and law, meet and prevent universal health care. People will always pay unlimited and infinite amounts of money to feel well, pain free, and without discomfort. Because of a lawsuit culture, malpractice continues to drive the cost of health care to unaffordable limits. The lawyer takes the same approach as the doctor claiming, why should I receive the same compensation for the required services of a public defender? In other words, if an attorney has the skill to protect a doctor's license who cannot work nor practice medicine without their license and therefore is willing to pay more for these services no matter the cost based on critical importance and professional necessity, he or she should consequently receive more. Likewise, the prosperity Pastor assumes the same ideology. I have the ability to reach MORE people from a gifted meritocratic perspective. Therefore, I should receive MORE as my gift is worth MORE. In addition, my sheepfold requires MORE workload as there are obviously MORE members within a mega-Church. Furthermore, my innovative abilities relating to ancillary gifts, book sales, celebrity, and preaching engagements equally produce a greater compensation. Thus, why shouldn't I benefit from the capitalistic spirit? It is a good question with significant merit.

The list goes on all serving as examples of an obvious prosperity movement. This is not an absolute, for not all pastors possess financial motives towards ministry nor does it imply that all celebrity pastors engage the ministry for the purpose of money. Personally, I have followed most of the pastors listed in *Appendix: Chart XVII* for over thirty years and through effective ministry, approached systems have been instruments of God towards mega-ministries. Therefore, this is not an attack, an indictment, condemnation, or anti-compensation campaign for those, who through gift, wisdom, and the guidance of the Holy Spirit, are reaping the benefits of their hard labor. Nevertheless, it doesn't erase the reality that a capitalistic culture has been created within the African-American Church that will be canned, followed, and coveted by the masses of struggling pastors. Likewise, it doesn't erase the reality that the African-American Church has become trendy, following the latest fad. In conclusion, the African-American Church has, just as much acculturated into capitalism, motivated by celebrity, wealth, and upper socio-economic classism, as the African-American has assimilated into the American Capitalism.

## Chapter Fourteen

## CLASSISM OF AFRICAN-AMERICANS VIA CORRUPTION

### (1990-present)

Most, which make it to celebrity, come to realize a sad reality. One of the basic fundamentals of capitalism, as well as democracy, is removal from the political process through the exposure of character defects and scandals. Although the newly found status of the wealthy will inherently embrace the mentality that they are better than the struggling majority by virtue of their riches, the consistent publicity of African-American imperfections inevitably leads to their elimination from the political process. As wealth is automatically assumed to provide power and influence, disqualification from the political process is as immediate through perceived or engaged immorality.

In 1991, Andre Young (a.k.a., "Dr. Dre) was convicted for assault.[100] In 1992, Michael Jordan, who is the greatest basketball player to have ever taken the hard wood and arguably the greatest athlete of all times, admitted to gambling under oath.[101] In June 1999, Curtis Jackson (best known as "50-Cent") was sentenced to a three-to-nine year prison sentence for possession of crack cocaine, heroin, and firearms. In 2003, Jackson was arrested for weapons possession. In 2005, he was charged with assault. Finally, in August 2013, Jackson was charged with domestic violence and

---

[100] Noel, Peter. "Revenge of the Mad Rappers". The Village Voice. http://www.villagevoice.com/news/revenge-of-the-mad-rappers-6423066 (accessed December 1, 1998).

[101] Wojciechowski, Gene. "Jordan Hit On Gambling : Golf Bets: San Diego Man Says The Bulls' Star Played Him For Four Years, Once Owed Him $1.252 Million." L.A. Times. (accessed June 3, 1993).

vandalism.[102] Kobe Bryant, five-time world champion and third all-time *NBA* leading scorer, was charged for sexual assault although later exonerated.[103] In 2005, Sean Combs (better known as, "Diddy") was accused of sexual assault by one of his employees and in 2013; he was questioned by the FBI on alleged charges of child molestation and rape. In 2005, Michael Jackson, the undisputed 'King of Pop" was aquitted of child molestation allegations before the revelation of his addiction to the habit-forming anesthetic, *Propofol*, which ultimately led to his untimely and unfortunate death in 2009.[104][105] In December 2009, Tiger Woods provided a personal confession of repetitive marital indiscretions over the entire period of the marriage that led Woods into a residential sexual addiction treatment center.[106] It is no secret that Floyd Mayweather, the biggest boxing icon and largest athletic cash cow served two-thirds of a 90-day sentence after accepting a plea on domestic violence charges in August 2012.[107] In December 2013, Magic Johnson had a transparent session with Oprah Winfrey as to the mystery of his HIV disease transmitter

[102] Duke, Alan. "50 Cent pleads not guilty in domestic violence case". CNN. (accessed August 5, 2013).
[103] "Kobe Bryant Charged With Sexual Assault." CNN.
http://www.cnn.com/2003/LAW/07/18/kobe.bryant/ (accessed December 16, 2003).
[104] Broder, John M. and Madigan, Nick. "Michael Jackson Cleared After 14-Week Child Molesting Trial." NY Times. http://www.nytimes.com/2005/06/14/us/michael-jackson-cleared-after-14week-child-molesting-trial.html?_r=0 (accessed June 14, 2005).
[105] Alexander, Brian. "Jackson's Death: How Dangerous Is Propofol?" Time Magazine.
http://content.time.com/time/arts/article/0,8599,1918363,00.html (accessed August 25, 2009).
[106] "Tiger Woods' Affair: Has Golfer's Image Finally Recovered From Infidelity Scandal?" Huffington Post. http://www.huffingtonpost.com/2013/06/10/tiger-woods-reputation_n_3417137.html (accessed June 10, 2013).
[107] "Floyd Mayweather Released From Jail." ESPN and The Associated Press.
http://espn.go.com/boxing/story/_/id/8228834/floyd-mayweather-jr-released-vegas-jail-serving-2-months (accessed August 3, 2012).

reporting that he repeatedly had unprotected sex with multiple partners simultaneously.[108] On May 14, 2014, Shawn Carter (widely acclaimed as "Jay-Z") was alleged to have had a physical altercation with his sister-in-law. Sheila Johnson, the wife of the first African-American billionaire, Robert Johnson, reported to a publishing author that their marriage was terminated due to chronic extra-marital affairs by her ex-husband.[109] Bill Cosby, 'Mr. Squeaky Clean' and one of the greatest influential figures within the African-American culture, especially as it relates to educational encouragements and pursuits, was accused in a barrage of sexual assault claims by multiple victims in November 2014, whereby, the initial complaint was reported in 2002.[110] Lastly, Jesse Jackson, the defacto spokesman of the African American people and 'Shadow-Senator of the *District of Columbia*', admitted to an extra-marital affair resulting in a child out of wedlock and has since been flying under the radar from the socio-political process.[111]

The blatant indisputable fact is that the democratic process must be protected at all cost. If any single individual, ethnicity, people group, or culture seeks to threaten the democracy, they

[108] "Magic Johnson Opens Up About His Promiscuous Past - Oprah's Next Chapter - Oprah Winfrey Network." You Tube. http://www.youtube.com/watch?v=S9pZd3Em6ag (accessed December 2, 2013).
[109] Leiby, Richard. "The Ex-Spouse Who Roared: Shelia Johnson's Revelations." The Washington Post. http://www.washingtonpost.com/wp-dyn/articles/A1887-2004May30.html (accessed May 30, 2004).
[110] Giles, Matt and Jones, Nate. "A Timeline of the Abuse Charges Against Bill Cosby [Updated]." Vulture. http://www.vulture.com/2014/09/timeline-of-the-abuse-charges-against-cosby.html (accessed December 30, 2015).
[111] "Jesse Jackson Admits Affair, Illegitimate Child." ABC News. http://abcnews.go.com/Politics/story?id=122032 (accessed January 18, 2016).

must be silenced. Politics is the 'art of silence' as perfected by the late great J. Edgar Hoover and the 'art of compromise' according to the late great President Richard Nixon. This is either achieved by silence, secrets, or compromise. No matter the extent of wealth or the sphere of influence, the shovel of politics requires that each individual's dirt is uncovered if perceived to be a threat to the capitalistic establishment. As a result, this work will be scrutinized, dismissed by benefactors of capitalistic wealth, embraced by those who identify with its contents, or attacked by those who would seek to eclipse the cited facts by my own personal indiscretions. However, none of these things will erase the facts contained within this book and chapter that most of the wealthiest African-Americans have been dismissed from the democratic and political process through politics relating to character defects, public indiscretions, and scandals.

## Chapter Fifteen

## CLASSISM OF AFRICAN-AMERICANS VIA CAPITALISM
### (1990-present)

As democracy is said to be the worst form of government except for all others, likewise, capitalism is absolutely the worst form of economics with the exception of all existing alternatives. As communism has corruption as the enemy to its success, capitalism has greed as its inevitable downfall. While providing limitless possibilities, capitalism also perpetuates unhealthy competition, greed, and debt.

Twenty years after the fall of the *Berlin Wall*, the end of a fifty-year *Cold War*, and the believed victory of capitalism over communism, the question lingers on *Wall Street* and *Main Street* alike, "Did Capitalism really win"? The credit downgrade of America, the debt ceiling crisis, the maxing out of the American credit limit via *Gross Domestic Product* (*GDP*) excess, and the bankruptcy of Greece has highlighted the argument of capitalism versus communism. Upon the "fall of the *Berlin Wall*" on November 9, 1989, the world believed that capitalism triumphed over communism and socialism. However, on August 5, 2011 when America's credit was downgraded after exceeding its credit limit with a *GDP* of $15 trillion, the question arose, "Is (present tense) communism currently victorious over capitalism and a better form of government"? If as a country, America has spent $19+ trillion in the last thirty years since the Reagan administration with his motif of "*Peace through Strength*", the question must be reiterated, "Did capitalism truly triumph over communism? The late great President Ronald Reagan was truly one of the best presidents in United States' history. He ended the *Cold War*, committed America to *Star Wars* that increased communication as well as warfare whereby war is fought today via satellite with America having a significant advantage, and ultimately revitalized the American economy. However, President Reagan began a trend that has since addictively escalated, i.e., borrowing. One historian wrote,

> The U.S. government each year spends roughly 30 percent more money than it takes in. It took 39 Presidents and 200 years to accumulate a debt of $1 trillion dollars. But it has taken only the past 12 years for that debt to triple to more than $5.9 trillion. Interest payments on the deficit alone add up to more than what our government pays for unemployment compensation, veteran's benefits, postal operations, housing, education, and highways combined.[112]

Borrow your way through! If America is at its debt ceiling, i.e., 104% of the American credit card in comparison to China who is only at 41%, ask yourself, Is capitalism a better form of government than communism?

> Under the first *Bretton Woods*, America had all the world's money, so the periphery countries needed to sign up in order to borrow. Under BW2, the center country is still America, but it is now the world's biggest borrower and has a weak currency, while it is the periphery countries that have all the money.[113]

---

[112] Bilbray, James, "Quote from James Bilbray." Liberty Tree. http://quotes.liberty-tree.ca/quote/james_bilbray_quote_6fe2 (accessed 2016).
[113] Morris, Charles. *The Two Million Dollar MeltDown*. New York, NY: Pubic Affairs; 2008; 92-93.

The facts reveal that the major Westernized countries, consumed by greed, have severely troubled economies. USA's borrowing is 104% of its *GDP* at $19 trillion. The European Union is at 93%. The United Kingdom is at 90%. France is at 90%. Canada is at 86%. Germany is at 82%. Italy is at 127% and Japan is over 200%. Greece filed bankruptcy at 158% of their *GDP*. On the other hand, communist China, the 3$^{rd}$ largest economy at $10 trillion, has only borrowed 41% of their *GDP*. This is seen and evident in *Appendix: Chart #XX* that is a compilation of the data derived from the *CIA World Fact Book*, *The World Bank*, and principally *The International Monetary Fund (IMF)*.

African-Americans embraced debt as a vehicle to wealth just as quickly as any other people group. *The American Prospect* reports, "The median net worth for black households is $4,955, or about 4.5 percent of whites' median household wealth, which was $110,729 in 2010, according to Census data."[114] Based on the data of the average household size provided in *Appendix: Chart VI* as being 2.36 makes the average single individual's net worth for each African-American at $2100.

There are several classifications of African-Americans to consider. First, there are those who are not homeowners, own their own vehicle, have no education, no debt, and no savings, however, is employed. It is these who are considered to be of the poverty class because they have absolutely no net worth. I will offer further

---

[114] Breunig, Matt. "The Racial Wealth Gap." The American Prospect. http://prospect.org/article/racial-wealth-gap (accessed November 6, 2013).

commentary on these individuals shortly. Second, there are those who are not homeowners, has a car payment, no education, and savings via employment that is less than the outstanding debt of their vehicle who are the beginning of those with limited negative net worth. Third, there are those who are not homeowners, have car payments, educated, and savings via employment that is less than the outstanding debt of the vehicle but with school loans who are those with moderate negative net worth. Fourth, there are those who are homeowners with limited equity, have car payments, highly educated, and savings via employment that is far less than the outstanding debt of their home, vehicle, school loans, and random debt that have significant negative net worth. There are obvious variations of persons two, three, and four. Fifth, there are those who own their own home, own their vehicles, are highly educated due to wise supportive parents and/or scholarships, and have savings through prestigious careers. It is these that live comfortable lives, yet, make up a very small percentage of the African-American population. If 56% make up the top 1%, and 35% have little, no, or negative net worth which adds up to 91% of this culture's wealth, this leaves only a remaining 9% that we believe to be person number five who is named above.

> Yet, the wealth difference between the American black household in the top 1 percent and the average black household is several times worse. As reported by *MSNBC* the median net worth of the few black households in the top 1 percent was $1.2 million dollars, while according to the Census median net worth for all black households was about $6,000 in total.... According to the Pew Research Study, 35 percent of Black households have Negative or No Net Worth. Another 15 percent have less than

$6,000 in total household worth, that's nearly 7 million of the total 14 million black households that have little or no security.[115]

Finally, there is the wealthy class who acquired their riches through a variety of means ranging from inheritance, celebrity, meritocratic gifts and talents, wise decisions and investments, or just good old fashion hard work. This is the top 1%.

In the final analysis, what is sad is the belief that the first individual identified is not the better off especially if they live happy lives. Material possessions and wealth is not what gratifies all. The unfortunate reality for those who seek higher learning, yet, are not gifted with athleticism or college scholarships, incur immense debt due to the skyrocketing cost of education and they dare not consider the attempt to own a reliable car. This base existence immediately leads one into the realm of negative net worth especially if they are not the benefactors of parental support. Debt is automatically accelerating when the inevitable unplanned and inconvenient emergencies of life occur.

If this is true, how many persons with a $2100 average net worth does it take to make the $19B of the top 39 wealthiest African-Americans as indicated in *Appendix: Chart #XX*? The answer is 4,000,000 African-Americans, exactly 10% of the entire ethnic population within the *USA*. The net worth of the top 39

---

[115] Moore, Antonio. "The Decadent Veil." Huffington Post. http://www.huffingtonpost.com/antonio-moore/the-decadent-veil-black-income-inequality_b_5646472.html (accessed August 5, 2014).

wealthiest African-Americans owns the equivalent wealth of 4,000,000 others or 10% of the entire ethnic culture. Wow!!!

Worst of all is that wealth is attempted through the slave component of debt. Competition, debt, and both, the lack and disinterest in true raw material wealth serve as the African-American's new and improved slave master. It is unquestionable that capitalism, greed, image, and not being satisfied with what one has that has consumed the African-American culture and serves as its new segregationist. These elements promote the same concepts as clashing and a migration back into a tribal mentality. Charles Morris, one of the leading authorities in the field of economics and author of the book, *The Two Million Dollar Meltdown*, wrote,

> The prosperity of 2000 was fake, based on massive borrowing on bubble-priced assets. Now consumers are deeply in debt, and the price of the favored assets are falling, while both employment and incomes are falling along with them.[116]

All forms of government have pros and cons. Communism battles corruption and liberties specifically relating to the freedom of speech. Dictatorships and Kingdoms wrestle with the issues of integrity from a single leader that provides any given country with its global reputation. However, Capitalism struggles with greed and carnality. Theology has long argued that the cause, premise, and the root of all sin is greed as displayed by Adam and Eve based on the quintessential interpretation of "not being satisfied with what they had".

---

[116] Morris, Charles. The Two Million Dollar MeltDown. New York, NY: Pubic Affairs; 2008; 111.

Is this also true with capitalism? Is the greed of capitalism greater than the corruption of communism? Is there a form of government that offers a perfect balance between capitalism and communism? If unchecked, will the fate of Greece become the fate of America? In the on-going debt ceiling debate, does America increase taxes and thus, increase revenue or cut expenses and thus, reduce the national budget? It's evident from the major westernized countries that satisfaction is not capitalism's strong suit, especially America, which requires them to slow their spending. While America and Europe offers the greatest comforts of life, are they living beyond their means?

If $19t hasn't solved America's problems, what will? America has more homelessness, helplessness, and hopelessness, drug and alcohol addiction, insanity, and crime than ever before. A $19t+ debt is equivalent to one million billionaires loaning the government $5B each. This would appear to satisfy the *National Debt*. However, because of unfunded liabilities, specifically in the areas of *Interest* on the *National Debt, Social Security*, and *Medicare* deficits which is not included in the total *National Debt* due to the inability for placement onto the *National Balance Sheet*, this would not solve the debt problem.

Three problems continue to contribute to America's economic woes. First, the absence of a nationalized health care system based on two principle reasons, pharmaceutical companies or the increasing cost of medication and legal cost based on the frequency of malpractice cases in a lawsuit-ridden culture is unacceptable, and intolerable. Both, pharmaceuticals and legalities are fueled by the capitalistic spirit. Lobbyist for pharmaceutical companies, lawyers, malpractice insurance companies, and classism within the community of medical doctors continues to be elements that prevent a national health care system. In spite of the critics and kinks within the *Affordable Care Act*, commendation must be given to President Obama for not only tackling this massive issue, but also in the progress that he has been able to make in establishing the foundation of a nationalized health care system. Having traveled through Europe, I have witnessed the presence of nationalized health care resulting in a belief that America is archaic relating to this issue and knowledge of its possibilities. Having worked for *Haight Ashbury Free Clinics* in San Francisco for ten years, founded in 1967 upon the Mission Statement that, "Health Care is right, not a privilege", I agree to health care being as fundamental to humanity's basic needs as is the entity of water. Therefore, health care should be just as much a right of citizenship as military protection.

Second, the abuse of the *Social Security* system, fueled by greed and caused by mismanagement that disallowed the government from treating these funds as sacrosanct, led to its continuous use as supplemental compensation for annual deficits. Simultaneously, the routine practice of using *Social Security* funds, as available and budgetary revenue, prevents an on-going surplus and ever increasing assets. The Congressman/Congresswomen and Senators who consider and bring to the floor of Congress, the possibility of cutting or eliminating the *Social Security* system is intolerable at the very least and inhumane at worst.

Third, the absence of a balanced budget that continues to allow the government to withdraw these funds directly from the common laborer's paycheck but fails to park these funds in a dedicated account that would incur perpetual interest is inexcusable. The refusal to adopt a *Balance Budget Amendment* only fuels the economic problems. Although there are legitimate pros and cons to both sides of the *Balanced Budget Amendment* debate, the government's continuance to demand of its citizens what it is unwilling to do as a government, is illogical, unfair, and contagious preventing the ability to teach its citizens to live within their means. Easy answer, budget for it! Its called "savings" officially and a "rainy day fund" informally. President Clinton not only became the third President to push a *Balance Budget Amendment* through Congress unsuccessfully, but went a step further and said, in essence, I'll not only ask you but show you how its done. As a result, all have come to know that an unplanned tragedy is not the compelling factor preventing a *Balance Budget Amendment* but "greed".

President Bill Clinton, as is the case with all Presidents, inherited the twin dilemmas of debt and deficit. After being the first President in U.S. history since LBJ to balance the national budget, if President Clinton's economic trends would have continued, America would have soon thereafter experienced annual surpluses that could have been used to pay on the debt until resolved. In other words, the attack of the deficit first and the debt second would have led to stability and surplus. However, because of America's capitalistic greed, they went from $5.7t to $19t+ in debt and $1.3B in daily deficit. Let the record speak for itself as the obvious Clinton years led not only to a decreased overall debt but also to obvious annual deficit reduction in sequential years leading to an ever-creasing equally annual surplus.

# United States Deficit: 1969 – 2014:

1. *President Lyndon B. Johnson*: **Total** = $42 billion (1969)
   FY 1969 - $3 billion **surplus**;

2. *President Jimmy Carter*: **Total** = $253 billion (1981)

3. *President Ronald Reagan*: **Total** = $1.412 trillion; (1989)

4. *President George H.W. Bush*: **Total** = $1.03 trillion; (1993)
   FY 1993 - $255 billion;

5. *President Bill Clinton*: **Total** = $63 billion surplus; (1994-2001)
   FY 1994 - $203 billion;
   FY 1995 - $164 billion;
   FY 1996 - $107 billion;
   FY 1997 - $22 billion;
   FY 1998 - $69 billion **surplus**;
   FY 1999 - $126 billion **surplus**;
   FY 2000 - $236 billion **surplus**;
   FY 2001 - $128 billion **surplus**;

6. *President George W. Bush*: **Total** = $3.294 trillion; (2002-2010)
   FY 2002 - $158 billion;

7. *President Barack Obama*: **Total** = $6.619 trillion; (2010-2014);
   FY 2010 - $1.547 trillion;
   FY 2011 - $1.300 trillion;
   FY 2012 - $1.087 trillion;
   FY 2013 - $680 billion;
   FY 2014 - $485 billion;[117]
   FY 2015 – pending;

---

[117] "Deficit by President." About News. http://useconomy.about.com/od/people/fl/Deficit-by-President.htm (accessed March 1, 2016).

Although President Obama has the very obvious overall total debt increase, there is an equally obvious and significant documented decrease in annual deficits throughout his leadership. If these trends continue, without a *Balanced Budget Amendment* or the usual enemies of budget management, i.e., war or natural disaster, history, America, and the Obama legacy will be more greatly appreciated in years to come based on his economic management. This absolutely has no reflection onto the presidency of George W. Bush who had to deal with possibly the worst crisis in American history, *911*. Consequently, one would expect some debt and deficit increase. Likewise, the record setting debt increase of the Obama presidency cannot be attributed to the common partisan stigmas of "tax and spend" since he inherited the second worst economic crisis in American history, *The Great Recession* and the unprecedented crash of the housing market. Joseph Joyce, author of the book, *The IMF and Global Economic Crisis*, wrote,

> Among the many surprising features of the global financial crisis of 2008-9 was the emergence of the *International Monetary Fund (IMF)* as a leading player in the response to what has become known as the *"Great Recession.*[118]

As of the submission of this manuscript to the publisher, the *National Debt* was $19.2t. The daily deficit was $1.3B. The *Unfunded Liabilities* of *Social Security* was $14.9t and *Medicare* at $27.6t totaling $42.5t.[119] If the $19.2t *National Debt* is added,

---

[118] Joyce, Joseph P. The IMF and Global Financial Crisis. New York: Cambridge University Press, 2013; 1.

[119] "U.S. Debt Clock." United States Debt Clock. http://www.usdebtclock.org (accessed 2016).

$61.7t would appear to be the true 'Total National Debt'. The *United States Treasury* defines the *US National Debt* as:

> The National Public Debt Outstanding represents the face amount or principal amount of marketable and non-marketable securities currently outstanding.[120]

The *United States Federal Reserve* defines the *US Total Debt* as:

> US Total Debt includes Household, Business, State and Local Governments, Financial Institutions, and the Federal Government.[121]

Because the *United States Treasury* defines the *US **National** Debt* differently from the *United States Federal Reserve's* definition of the *US **Total** Debt*, there is a huge disparity. In the most simplistic explanation possible, the difference between the *US National Debt* of the *US Treasury* and the *US Total Debt* of the *US Federal Reserve* is $19.3t vs. $64.8t, respectively. Finally, *US Unfunded Liabilities* has been defined as:

> Total US Unfunded Liability includes Social Security, (Medicare Parts A, B, and D), Federal Debt held by the Public, plus Federal Employee and Veteran Benefits.[122]

The *US Treasury* reports the *US Unfunded Liabilities* as $102t.[123] This is what is needed in order to correct the broken budgetary practices and for America to reach a point of economic homeostasis.

---

[120] Ibid.
[121] Ibid.
[122] Ibid.
[123] Ibid.

While the complexities of governmental economics are severely problematic for the *Treasury Department* and *Federal Reserve*, the simplicity is as equally easy as the requirements of the basic household. Balance the budget, inclusive of line items for emergencies, such as war and natural disasters, maintain the sanctity of *Social Security* revenues, eliminating any jeopardy attached from its intended use, and ensure health care for every American citizen, serves as the most simplistic solution.

There is some strange irony attached to the fact that it only took thirty years, 1980-2010, for America to borrow itself into the *Great Recession* leading to a global economic crisis whereby in the same period African-American's experienced its greatest economic growth. If a generation is determined to be two decades, then it only took a little over one generation for America to borrow its way into trouble. Will this exact same dynamic repeat itself for any who follows these capitalistic practices of borrowing after perceived victory? The health and quantity of the African-American middle class is just as much of a myth as the American middle class. If 99% of the American wealth is owned by 1% of the American population, where then is the American middle class? The same holds true with the African-American, where, in two decades, the African-American culture mirrors the polarizations of the general American population, rich and poor. Millions of Americans are working longer hours for lower wages, and yet almost all of the new income and wealth being created is going to the top one percent. Senator Bernie Sanders said during the first *2015 Democratic Debate* (10/13/2015):

> What democratic socialism is about is saying that it is immoral and wrong that the top one-tenth of 1 percent in this country own almost 90 percent – almost own almost as much wealth as the bottom 90 percent. That it is wrong, today, in a rigged economy, that 57 percent of all new income is going to the top 1 percent. That when you look around the world, you see every other major country providing health care to all people as a right, except the *United States*..... Those are some of the principles that I believe in, and I think we should look to countries like Denmark, like Sweden and Norway, and learn from what they have accomplished for their working people....A Gallup poll says half the country would not put a socialist in the *White House*....Do I consider myself part of the casino capitalist process by which so few have so much and so many have so little by which Wall Street's greed and recklessness wrecked this economy? No, I don't. I believe in a society where all people do well. Not just a handful of billionaire.... This is a great country, but we have many, many serious problems. We should not be the country that has the highest rate of childhood poverty of any major country and more wealth and income inequality than any other country.[124]

Secretary Clinton responded to Senator's Sanders comments by saying,

> When I think about capitalism, I think about all the small businesses that were started because we have the opportunity and the freedom in our country for people to do that and to make a good living for themselves and their families.... And I don't think we should confuse what we

[124] Parnass, Sarah. " The CNN Democratic Debate Transcript, Annotated." The Washington Post. https://www.washingtonpost.com/news/the-fix/wp/2015/10/13/the-oct-13-democratic-debate-who-said-what-and-what-it-means/ (accessed October 13, 2015).

have to do every so often in America, which is save capitalism from itself. And I think what Senator Sanders is saying certainly makes sense in the terms of the inequality that we have…. But we are not Denmark. I love Denmark. We are the *United States of America*. And it's our job to rein in the excesses of capitalism so that it doesn't run amok and doesn't cause the kind of inequities we're seeing in our economic system. [125]

What did Secretary Clinton mean when she said, "I don't think we should confuse what we have to do every so often in America, which is to save capitalism from itself?" When capitalism's greed becomes excessive, it is the responsibility of the Federal Reserve to adjust interest rates by either increasing or decreasing spending until the general economy has been stabilized.

> William McChesney Martin, who served as *Chairman of the Federal Reserve* for eighteen years, spanning presidential administrations from Truman through Nixon said, "The function of the *Federal Reserve* is to take away the punch bowl just as the party is getting good." [126]

Alan Greenspan, possibly, the most popular and powerful *Federal Reserve Chairman in USA* history who served from Bush I to Bush II was labeled as "an enemy of fun" especially based upon the ideologies and policies of his leadership as identified in his book, *The Age of Turbulence*. [127] On the other hand, the capitalist continue to resound loudly, let the greed continue. While Secretary Clinton readily comes to the defense of capitalism, the self-termed

---

[125] Ibid.

[126] Morris, Charles. *The Two Million Dollar MeltDown*. New York, NY: Pubic Affairs, 2008; 62.

[127] Greenspan, Alan. *The Age of Turbulence*. London, U.K.: Penguin Group, 2007.

"Democratic Capitalist", Senator Bernie Sanders cites Denmark as an example of a better way of life. There is a minimum of five (5) weeks' paid holiday for all wage earners, $20/hour minimum wage, 33-hour workweek, free university, free childcare, and free national healthcare for all citizens. As a result, Denmark deems the quality of life more valuable than quantity of materialism.

> Quality of life and a good work-life balance characterize Danish welfare society. Work-life balance literally means prioritizing between work (career and ambition) on one hand and life (health, pleasure, leisure, spirituality, and family) on the other. Danes enjoy a high degree of flexibility at work – often being able to choose when they start their working day and having the flexibility of working from home. The lunch break is often at a designated time each day, enabling colleagues to interact and eat together, thus getting away from their desks.[128]

Kobe, in response to the constant comparison between he and Jordan, commented with a profound statement, "I don't want to be the next Michael Jordan; I only want to be the best Kobe Bryant I can be."[129] Likewise, America is not the Danes but can be a better nation, as African-Americans can be a better ethnicity. The only way for this to occur is when the quality of life becomes far more valuable than quantity in life. The ability to prioritize spirituality, family, childcare, elderly-care, healthcare, education, career, recreation, and the overall quality of life far outweighs any standard of living. If all things are to be done in moderation and

---

[128] Steed, Richard. Denmark. "Work/Life Balance - The Danish Way." The Official Website of Denmark. http://denmark.dk/en/meet-the-danes/work-life-balance-the-danish-way/ (accessed 2016).
[129] "Kobe Bryant." BrainyQuote.com, Xplore Inc, 2016.
http://www.brainyquote.com/quotes/quotes/k/kobebryant167158.html, accessed April 9, 2016.

thus, the achievement of an optimal balance, inequality can never be a consideration. No one ever has to be homeless, uneducated, unemployed, without health care, or permit money be the ultimate determinate of superiority between one person and another. My godfather, Dr. E.E. Stafford, use to say, "There is no perfect organization, however, if you manage to find one, don't join it; as the day you become a part of it, it will no longer be perfect." Consequently, the goal is not to mirror the Danes but to re-examine American priorities.

# DIVIDE BY CLASS!

It is the lack of qualitative 'standard of living' focus that has led to the rise of the celebrity class that has promoted this New Segregation and the extremism of Capitalism, the rich and the poor. The same holds true for the African-American culture where there appears to be only rich and poor. Exactly two decades after the *Fall of the Berlin Wall* and the victory celebrations of Capitalism over Communism, the Communistic countries are currently posing the question, "Did Capitalism really win since it has only taken twenty years for the greed of Capitalistic ideologies to cause America to borrow itself into the excess of its *GDP* and total net worth?" Greece has already filed bankruptcy, America's credit has been downgraded by *Standard and Poor's*, the *United States Congress* has defaulted and continues to threaten default as partisan political leverage causes the other credit rating agencies who monitor each country's credit, *Fitch*, *Moody*, and *Standard & Poor's* to further consider downgrading USA's credit, moving their status from "stable" to "negative" while most of the other westernized countries have exceeded 80% of their borrowing power. As a result, the question is valid, "Did Capitalism really win?" There are three agencies that determine each country's credit ratings, *Standard and Poor's* (S&P), *Moody's*, and the *Fitch Group* monitor and rate each country's credit as *Equifax*, *Experian*, and *Transunion* monitor individual USA consumer credit scores and reports.

On August 5, 2011, S&P downgraded the U.S. credit rating for the first time in history. The move, lowering U.S. debt to AA+, came after weeks of congressional wrangling over the deficit and debt ceiling. The eventual deal to avert a default did not, in the opinion of S&P, implement adequate measures to reduce the U.S. deficit over the next ten years.[130]

Within three decades, the African-American experienced extraordinary wealth through celebrity. African-Americans gained riches through athletics, music, acting, and comedy. Of course, other opportunities availed themselves through education, CEO's of *Fortune 500* companies, politics, and business. However, the largest and most significant percentage of the overall African-American population who has been able to successfully gain riches is tantamount to the overall American percentage of wealth distribution, whereby, approximately 1% of the African-American population owns 56% of the total African-American wealth. In an effort for the remaining 99% of the African-American population to gain the wealth of the richest 1%, debt appears to be the preferred route.

*Inequality* provides the total net worth for the entire African-American people as a culture to be $2 trillion. As well, *Inequality* and the *Huffington Post* reports that 35% of the African-American population has zero or negative net value. The *Huffington Post* wrote in its article on *The Decadent Veil: Black America's Wealth Illusion*,

---

[130] "CFR Backgrounders" Council on Foreign Relations. http://www.cfr.org/financial-crises/credit-rating-controversy/p22328 (accessed 2016).

Yet, the wealth difference between the American black household in the top 1 percent and the average black household is several times worse. As reported by *MSNBC* the median net worth of the few black households in the top 1 percent was $1.2 million dollars, while according to the Census median net worth for all black households were about $6,000 in total.... According to the *Pew Research Study*, 35 percent of Black households have Negative or No Net Worth. Another 15 percent have less than $6,000 in total household worth, that's nearly 7 million of the total 14 million black households that have little or no security.[131]

This is proof positive evidence of true cultural capitalistic assimilation and acculturation of the African-American people. If the top wealthiest 1% owns more than $1.12t or nearly 60% of the total cumulative African-American net worth, by default, $88B of total remaining cultural wealth is divided among the remaining 40% of this ethnicity. This is internal segregation and capitalism in its finest!

At these alarming rates of ethnic wealth, polarization lies at the realities of an inevitable time when the African-American will reach a point of complete assimilation into the capitalistic dynamic of extreme classism and neo-segregation. If it has taken exactly two decades or 20 years from 1989 to 2009, from the end of the *Cold War*, to the one of worst periods in USA history, *The Great Recession*, for the wealthiest 1% to acquire 56% of the total cultural wealth, the case for a New Segregation, subtle, yet, real, is

---

[131] Moore, Antonio. "The Decadent Veil." Huffington Post. http://www.huffingtonpost.com/antonio-moore/the-decadent-veil-black-income-inequality_b_5646472.html (accessed August 5, 2014).

evident and proven. This would provide us with the formula that exactly 28% of the ethnic population is assimilating each decade. Therefore, at 30 years, in 2021, it will be 84% and at 35 years, 2026, complete capitalistic acculturation will be achieved as the wealthiest 1% will own 98%. In just 10 more years, one additional decade, the polarization of the African-American socio-economic classes will mirror American classist statistics, cultural divisions, and segregationism.

The African-American's hatred, disdain, and promise to never return to the cotton fields had pros and cons. While it freed the African-American from the oppression of slavery, it permanently removed the African-American from manufacturing and made them sole consumers. The manufacturing field places one in the realm of true wealth derived from raw material that comes directly from the ground. The person who owns a luxurious car is impressive. However, the individual who is more impressive than the owner is the maker. Nonetheless, the one who holds the greatest degree of impressiveness is the supplier of the raw material or the individual(s) who owns the land wherein the material was mined. This is certainly true as it relates to wood from a forest that is used to build homes, steel and iron ore that is used to build buildings, and diamonds, gold, silver, and precious stones used to make jewelry. The African-American is enslaved and dependent on manufacturers and landowners to sustain its culture. This is extremely true as it relates to the tools of each trade contributing to the height of African-American industrial wealth. If music or film-based entertainment is the major contributor to African-American wealth, studios, studio equipment, film cameras, and film props are created, manufactured, distributed, supplied, and sold largely by Japanese and Caucasian American producers. It is not a wonder as to why African-Americans are given millions of dollars in all phases of the entertainment industry whether athletes, actors/actresses, singers, comedians, or producers; for they will return their fortunes to those who make, distribute, and extract these products by using studios, purchasing state-of-the-art studio equipment, homes, expensive cars, private *Learjet's*, televisions, play stations, clothing, and other popular products.

Every African-American historian since Booker T. Washington, Carter G. Woodson, W.E.B. Dubois, and Marcus Garvey, from the early 1900's, provided an assessment and overview of the African-American "state of the union" addressing the very issue of inequality. Martin Luther King Jr., and Malcolm X were also bold enough to provide an outcry of the African-American plight and place it within the larger American cultural society during the 1960's. While Martin Luther King Jr. fought for the cause of equality, no one can tell me that this is what he had in mind; equal in economic opportunity but separation by economic class.[132] Bob Lord, of the *Institute for Policy Studies*, calls this

---

[132] "Black America: Waking Life." The Economist.
http://www.economist.com/news/briefing/21584003-his-i-have-dream-speech-martin-luther-king-threw-out-challenge-america-how-has-it (accessed August 24, 2013).

"Dr. King's Nightmare."[133] The Westernized countries dedicated trillions of dollars and the lives of thousands of covert operatives within the 50 years of the *Cold War* in order to maintain this way of life that perpetuates betterment under the guise of a free market economy. However ironic, the same dynamics of inequality came during the same decade synonymous to the previous century when legal enforcements against the monopolistic practices of the industrial pioneers, such as the John D. Rockefeller and Andrew Carnegie in manufacturing, Cornelius Vanderbilt in railroading, J. P. Morgan in banking, and many others. Therefore, the concept is not new as it continued throughout the period of the *Industrial Revolution* (1875-1914).

> The was a period of relative peace in which liberal consciousness, with its faith in the natural progress of reason, rationality and the rule of law, combined with an assumption of racial superiority to justify European economic and political domination of large parts of the non-industrialized world.[134]

There always has to be a winner and loser in a competitive free-market system. Corporately, Pepsi or Coke; in sports, a Super Bowl winner and a conference finalist; There are so many pros and cons to the competition of capitalism.

> *Bretton Woods* also represents the aggressive desire of the capitalist market to expand globally beyond the boundaries of the developed industrial world. Owing

[133] Collins, Chuck. "Wealth of 400 Billionaires = Wealth of All 41 Million African-Americans." Inequality. http://inequality.org/wealth-400-billionaires-wealth-41-million-africanamericans/ (accessed January 17, 2014).
[134] Peet, Richard. *Unholy Trinity: The IMF, World Bank, and WTO*, 2nd Ed. London: Zed Books, 2008; 37.

to the influence of Keynes, however, such an expansion had to regulated and controlled - the market should not be left to its whims, and all nations should participate in regulating its forces.[135]

Two of the greatest under-estimated strengths within capitalism are unity and patriotism. Some of us would never know as a commonality, the cities of Cleveland, Green Bay, or Fresno if it was not for the professional basketball *Cavaliers*, professional football *Packers*, or college football *Bulldogs* within sports. Before every sporting event, regardless of the sport, the *Star Spangled Banner* is sung facilitating the continuity of patriotic unity. On the other hand, possibly the greatest divisive factor to the world's largest continent, i.e., Africa is tribalism. If Africa could unite their states as the *USA*, imagine the greatness. Ironically, the same unity that simulates the ultimate patriotic connectedness also promotes the most severe extremism, winners and losers, the best and the rest. In capitalism, there always has to be a "best" and the "rest", a "winner" and a "loser", and unfortunately, a "rich" and a "poor".

The African-American would be best served by examining the dynamics of the Korean people. While no one condones the actions of Kim Jong-un, (unlike his grandfather, Kim Il Sung, who worked towards peace through diplomacy with Fidel Castro of Cuba, Mao Zedong of China, President Richard Nixon, and each Westernized leader), with his nuclear ambitions in defiance of the international community, one should be able be objectively

---

[135] Peet, 42.

understand the root of his emotional reactions. The Korean peninsula is made up of one people, Koreans, sisters and brothers. However, they approach life and live in different political and economic climates, as well as lifestyles. North Korea, one of the three remaining Communistic governments alongside China and Cuba, has come to a point of hatred and bitterness towards westernized cultures. Again, while not condoning the actions of the North Korean people as it relates to their nuclear ambitions and defiance of the international community, they certainly appear angry for several valid reasons. First, the geographic separation from their people, the South Koreans in 1953 at the *38th Parallel* is certainly cause. Second, because they have chosen a form of government termed Communism that facilitates "equality among all" in spite of its many imperfections, they have been separated from their southern brothers and sisters because of the latter's choice to embrace westernization and capitalism. Third, because capitalism is a westernized form of government, they are supported by those powerful allies to the west making their way of life and economic reality so far more comfortable than their northern family lending to the hatred, bitterness, despair, and covetousness of the latter. Finally, the reality of living a life of struggle and poverty in the north, while your very same family to the south are supported by those who ally and ensure a better livelihood, with the harsh directive that it cannot be shared with your northern brothers and sisters due to political reasons, fuels obvious hatred. While the term "KIA" actually means, "Rising out of Asia" and others embrace the shadow definition of "Korean Automotive International", cynics critically and sarcastically render KIA's backdrop interpretation as, "Korea in America", which has become one of the leading automotive leaders by both sales and ownership in America. No example expresses this reality more than the *GDP* of South Korea at $1.4t compared to North Korea's $15B, as indicated in *Appendix: Chart XXII*. If this is not an indication of segregated polarization, rich and poor, there is no such thing. The ultimate result can only be division. This is in no wise a new concept, as the *38th Parallel* is older than the *Berlin Wall*. This does not advocate communism as it has its share of problems, principally corruption, the lack of checks and balances, and the absence of any abusive corrective processes through freedom of speech and the presence and protections of a public media. At the same time, capitalism has its own share of problems in that it is fueled by greed. Once the cucumber has become a pickle, it can never return to being a cucumber again.

This has been one of the theorized basics of Arab contempt for centuries specifically relating to its women. Once the taste of greed and the liberties of capitalism have been experienced, the cucumber has become pickled and will never return to the traditional cultural roots or gender-based oppression. Once the veils have been replaced by skirts and heels, women experience the freedom from male domination, and Arab women's refusal to participate in the traditional male harem of multiple wives, there is no turning back. The result is Arab hatred of western civilization principally by the Arab male, and the continuance of Arab radicalism by Islamic militants. The Arab woman has become pickled by capitalism and this newly found liberation would make Arab traditionalism an extinct cucumber.

The African-American is the Korean people with the exception of not having their own land and laws. The South Koreans have been pickled with money being the quintessential element. The African-American does not care about the division of its people once they have become the benefactors of capitalistic pseudo-wealth and greed. It then becomes competitive as to who has the most and thereby a default division of a new, subtle, and sophisticated segregation within the ethnicity. While it is evident in Korea because of the land, it is so far less obvious within African-Americans because it exists solely within a culture. However, the outcome is the same; division and poverty upon most while support to another; most importantly, hope to some while despair to others.

*Inequality*, in its article, *Wealth of (Top) 400 Billionaires = Wealth of All 41 Million African-Americans*, posted on January 17, 2014 by Chuck Collins, provides the total net worth for the entire African-American people to be $2 trillion reporting, "Both groups, (the top 400 billionaires and African-Americans as a culture) possess some $2 trillion, about three percent of the national net worth of $77 trillion." Please note that there is a significant difference between "National Net Worth" and "Gross Domestic Product". The "National Net Worth" is the total asset value of each individual citizen whereas the "Gross Domestic Product" is the total value of any given country based on the total goods and services produced. "The National Net Worth" is simplistically cumulative individual worth compared to the nation's cumulative corporate worth per "Gross Domestic Product." The top African-American wealthiest 1% currently owns more than $1.12t, 56% of the total cumulative African-American net worth. The projections show that in 2021, it will be 84%, and in 2026, complete capitalistic acculturation will be achieved, as the wealthiest African-American 1% will own 98% of all African-American net worth. In just 10 more years, one additional decade, the polarization of the African-American socio-economic classes will mirror American classist statistics and cultural divisions. This is not a stretch to believe or conceive with Jordan being forecasted to move from his current $1.2B of personal net worth to $4.5B by

2020. Consequently, the reality still remains that there is a huge schism between the "haves" and "have not's" that will only progressively grow wider into a new and improved segregation.

There is an intentional missing chapter from this book. No work should be complete without solutions. After identifying the problems and issues affecting an entire ethnicity and culture, what are the recommended corrective actions? How are these processes reversed?

First, Communism, Socialism, and Fascism have all been proven to be failed forms of economics as well as political governments, as capitalism will soon join.

Second, we know that *Keynesian Economics* is not the solution although the preferred approach by President Nixon according to his popular statement, "We are all Keynesians now."[136] Not only is it not a stretch to prove that Keynesianism is a direct contributor to each country's debt, especially those which are excessive, but the belief that a capitalistic economy that is guided by the private sector needing supplemental assistance from the government for both stabilization and perpetuation has been well proven to be ineffective as the greed of the corporate world will always lead to excess.[137] Since the Keynesianism of the *Great Depression* and *The New Deal*, markets have and always will rise and fall through war, natural disasters, politics, and market collapse. From *The Great Depression* to *The Great Recession*,

---

[136] Gilpin, Robert. *Global Political Economy*. Princeton, N.J: Princeton University Press, 2001; 70.

[137] Sullivan, Arthur; Steven M. Sheffrin. *Economics: Principles in Action*. Upper Saddle River: Pearson Prentice Hall, 2003.

Keynesianism has been a failure. Furthermore, the belief that Keynesianism ask of troubled capitalistic government assistance during troubled times with the belief that the private sector will repay the loans and assistance during periods of revitalization, prosperity, and surplus is textbook insanity. Because greed will always disallow this reality, all who continue to embrace this form of economics is tantamount to serious denial.

Third, Reagan's "Trickled-Down Economics", popularized as *Reaganomics*, based on my proposed theory that the borrowing of the Reagan Administration is the primary contributor to the excessive historical borrowing and current debt of America, westernized countries, and the global economy. Using Keynesian principles, a shot in the arm of economic stimulus from the government during periods of crisis that are provided directly to the capitalist, i.e., corporations, for the purpose of trickling down to the masses, has failed to drip, let alone trickle. Equally, the belief that borrowing during economic hardships will not only be replaced but provide a surplus upon re-stabilization never occurs. As is the case with *Social Security*, anywhere the government can access funds at any time, good or bad, it will occur.

Fourth, it has already been established that if there were an alliance between "*Main Street*" and "*Wall Street*", would it end the capitalistic experiment and thus, no longer be deemed as capitalism. If a country ceased to be a "democracy" but a hybrid government, somewhere in between, where decisions are not made exclusively by the people nor the government, but an intermediate, which then is the intermediate? Capitalist? If this is ever a reality, there must be an assurance of non-monopolistic practices and power vacuums. Richard Peet's, within the book, *Unholy Trinity: The IMF, World Bank, and WTO, 2nd Ed.*, wrote, "The present time, however, finds an advanced process of de-establishment of the hegemonic ideas of Washington-Wall Street alliance within an overall crisis of global financial crisis.[138] Peet went on to say,

> We suggest that a historical economics grounded more in empirical generalizations, with more attention to contexts and cases would do no more to end inequality and poverty than unrealistic mathematical elegance. Further, we think that the political an economic interest controlling global governance institutions and their policies, especially banking and the multinational corporations, should be further revealed to show that policies that damage the poor result from considerations limited to the rich.[139]

If there are simultaneous economic and political actions taken by both, the government and corporate America, it is no longer a "democracy" but as close to "socialism" as one can possibly get.

Peet suggests that three organizations, the *World Bank*, the *International Monetary Fund* (*IMF*), and the *World Trade Organization* (*WTO*), operate the global economy. While the *World Bank* loans the money to governments as a local bank would to an ordinary consumer for personal, car, and housing loans, the *World Bank* provides funds for governments to operate their daily affairs with borrowing power based on the country's *Gross*

---

[138] Peet, 258.
[139] Peet, 258-259.

*Domestic Product* (*GDP*). If the country defaults on the loan, the *IMF* enforce steps in with corrective action plans, operates the country's revenues, especially if bankrupt, and works closely with the *World Trade Organization* (*WTO*) to regulate the given government's revenues and diplomacy. As a point in case example, Iraq's greatest revenue asset is oil. If the *IMF, United Nations,* or other globally influential organizations place sanctions or trade limits on the respective country, the *WTO* serve as either the authority or enforcement of the *IMF* who mandates, even to the point of threatening, placing sanctions, or trade limits on any country who would defy these international regulations. Peet's conclusion is that these three organizations, the *IMF, World Bank,* and *WTO* currently rule the world, have inter-related members lending to an oligarchy and are responsible for global economic crisis as well as worldwide "Bear" and "Bull" markets.

Fifth, Joseph Joyce concurs advocating for more influence of the IMF as a permanent solution to global economic crisis stating,

> The recent global crisis shows the need to address the volatility of the financial linkages of the global economy and demonstrates that an empowered *IMF* can provide valuable services to its members."[140]

Sixth, Peet, comprehensively and compassionately argued to the conclusion that three global organizations, The *World Bank,*

---

[140] Joyce, 195.

the *IMF*, and the *WTO* rule of the world, is inter-related, and served as the primary cause leading to the global economic crisis.

> Practically, we think that the *IMF* should revert to its original role as a place to deposit surpluses that can be withdrawn on demand, in hard currency, as emergency loans. Failing this, the *IMF* should be disbanded. The *WTO* is a nasty organization run by directors and a secretariat that propagate the rightest elitism in the guise of consumer populism. The *WTO* has either to be transformed into a fair trade organization, or it should be allowed to collapse in confusion, as it shows every sign of doing – either way, it has to go. And finally, some hope for the *World Bank,* were it to listen seriously to its many critics and were it to undergo the changes that even its own conscience and many of its own staff suggest.... Globalization has to be directed into becoming something finer by a democratic alliance of social movements that opposes the alliance of the rich, the famous, and the gratuitously philanthropic.[141]

Seventh, it is impossible to entertain the discussion of "capitalism" without including Richard Wolff's concept of "Workers' Self-Directed Enterprise" (*WSDE*), which would only occur through an employee revolution. Wolff proposes,

> This cure involves, first, replacing the current capitalistic organization of production inside offices, factories, stores, and other-places in modern societies. In short, exploitation – the production of a surplus appropriated and distributed by those other than its producers – would stop. Much as earlier forms of class structure (lords exploiting serfs in feudalism and masters exploiting slaves in slavery) have been abolished, the capitalist class structure (employers exploiting wage laborers) would have to be abolished, as well. In corporations, the dominant form of modern capitalist enterprises, no longer would small boards of

---

[141] Peet, 259-260.

194

directors selected by a typical tiny number of major shareholders appropriate and distribute the surplus produced by employees. Instead the surplus-producing workers themselves would make the basic decisions about production and distribution.[142]

Of these seven approaches that might cure the ills of classist inequality caused by capitalism and its ugly twin of greed, the Wolff Doctrine of *WSDE* appears to be the most effective. One problem still outstanding to its execution is a united front from the worker class.

Eighth, it is my conclusion and belief that there is no solution to avoid the capitalistic assimilation of the African-American people. Of course, the African-American can terminate self-genocide and discontinue the killing and clashing. African-Americans can remain crime free. The African-American can remain drug-free. However, the African-American is unable to release themselves from the hope and actions that lead to wealth. Like Arab women who tasted the liberties of westernization that has enraged the Arab male, African-Americans are addicted to money. There is and never will be any alternative lifestyle that seeks higher standards of living than materialism once wealth and capitalism has been tasted. The chase for the old mighty dollar has already begun and the sad reality is, just like chasing a cheetah, 99% of those running in the race of capitalism, will never catch him.

---

[142] Wolff, 11-12.

# DIVIDE and CONQUER

The divide between rich and poor, i.e., segregation, will continue as hope is dangled in front of those climbing the ladder towards wealth. This divide between rich and poor cannot be prevented but will only widen. It is as inevitable as the social divide of the entire capitalistic world. Once the cucumber has become a pickle, it can never become a cucumber again. As the watchmaker who finely crafts a watch and it continues to maintain the precision of time independent of its creator regardless of possession or ownership, capitalistic dynamics within the African-American culture are on autopilot and will continue without the aid, assistance, or conspiracy of external factors. This is the reality of the African-American people relating to the comforts and greed of wealth. They are irreversible.

Unfortunately, African-Americans have reached a point of no return. The pendulum has swung and the paradigm has shifted. However, the African-American is unable to release themselves from the hope and actions that lead to wealth and to the most popular methods that has historically led to cultural ethnic wealth.

> Superstar players of the '80s and '90s saw their salaries jump to levels never before thought possible. And yet, when you look back now, these deals still seem somewhat stunted. It's hard to believe that Michael Jordan, the greatest basketball player of all time, earned just $2-3 million a season for most of his career. This only changed as he neared the end of his career, signing a $30 million contract with the Bulls for the '96-'97 season. No NBA player since has ever come close to topping Jordan's

pay, not even LeBron, whose current salary is $19.3 million.[143]

As stated in Chapter 9, classist divisions appear as automatically ingrained within humanity, as capitalism is an inherent perpetuation of the need for the existence of superiority and inferiority, segregated classism. Adam and Eve were guilty of a basic principal, "not being satisfied with what they had". Cain could not accept that his brother, Abel's offering, was more respected than his as defined by God. Equality will never occur within the environmental dynamics of capitalism, as there always has to be those who, by their very nature, must feel better than everyone else.

The sad dynamic of the "Old Money" and the "Nouveau Riche" dichotomy is another example of segregation of internal cultural division. Billionaires fighting millionaires, as we witness with every professional sport "Lockout", when billionaire owners feud with millionaire players while poverty flourishes, is a prime example. No matter how high one goes in life nor the achievement or acquisitions acquired, there will still exist divisive schisms that pit and perpetuate superiority, inferiority, a "better-than" attitude, and belief system.

African-Americans embrace the compulsion and need to flaunt their riches. This exploitation of material prosperity is an attempt to propel one's self above another. This is not just limited

---

[143] Stephenson, Debbie. "When Did Athletes Start Getting Rich." The Deal Room. http://www.firmex.com/thedealroom/when-did-athletes-start-getting-rich/ (accessed June 24, 2014).

to the size of one's house, the neighborhood of their home, and the luxury of one's car, but the standard of university degree acquired, the esteem of one's professional career; whether a man is wearing a custom suit versus a rack suit; whether a woman is carrying a *Luis Vuitton* bag versus a *Coach* bag; the quality of a woman's weave; gel nails versus traditional polish; *I-Phones* versus *Galaxy's*; are all examples of ethnic segregation or capitalistic betterment comparisons that pits one African-American against another. Unfortunately, the compulsion for better than is not limited to material prosperity but also is evident in social media post where one African-American feels the need to post a statement of deeper wisdom than another on *Facebook*. Capitalism perpetuates popular clichés that has, is, and continues to stagnant the African-American people, "Keep Up with the Jones", "One Must Out-Do Another, "He Who Dies with The Most Toys Wins", not understanding that raw materials and the manufacturing field places one in the realm of true wealth that is derived directly from the ground especially when more than 60% of African-Americans are living from paycheck to paycheck.

The common cliché that "Only Nixon Could Go to China," is applicable, as someone from the millionaire club would have to provide the formula, precedent, and antidote for capitalistic separatism. The "Haymon Approach" indicative of Al Haymon, boxing manager and promoter, provides a prime example for all. Haymon, who is by far, the most successful personality in the sport of boxing, has presented components to achievement that has displaced, disgraced, and made many disgruntle. Haymon's long-standing competitors, Don King, Bob Arum, and Oscar De La Hoya have net worth's ten times that of Haymon. Al has had every opportunity to exceed their net worth in one night from a single fight card. Many are economic recipients of fight nights inclusive of State Boxing Commissions, the networks, pay-per-view, sponsors, the venue or host, the promoters, and the boxers. However, Haymon intentionally chooses to allow the fighters to retain more of the general purse than he does his own profit. At the end of the day, Haymon does not appear to be consumed by greed. He has no interest in popularity or fame as he refuses interviews, and makes intentional contractual arrangements to NOT be seen on camera. What then is his motive? We can easily assess it to his Harvard education, the possibility of being satisfied with what he has and who he is, or a genuine need to right the ship. The "Haymon Approach" is an excellent example of one's quest to achieve the best without the barometer of success being measured by money?

Haymon is not the only African-American with this mindset. As Al Haymon has unlimited potential towards wealth from the sport of boxing, Dr. Cornel West has unlimited potential towards wealth based solely on knowledge. From his own website, Dr. West states,

> I've never spent a weekend in Princeton. I would like to be at home, but my calling beckons me. I've got places to go, from schools to community centers to prisons to churches to mosques to universities to trade unions. There's

academic lectures, political lectures, religious lectures. It's just my regular weekly travel…I stay in hotels. They provide for me. None of this is out of my pocket; I'm as broke as I can be.[144]

Capitalism has now been unarguably proven to be a failed system and experiment evident by the element of greed revealed by the increasing debt of the largest westernized civilizations. With the borrowing of certain key countries such as the USA at 106%, the European Union is at 93%, the United Kingdom at 90%, France at 90%, Canada at 86%, and Germany at 81%, is evidence in itself. Even the hybrid economy of communist China has increased its borrowing to 41% raising questions as to its stability. The ultimate end of capitalism is debt, division, decadence, and demoralization. These FACTS are enough for any assimilating culture within capitalism to take caution against acculturation of this way of life. Why would the outcome and fate of African-Americans be any different?

If uncorrected, what is the worst outcome? The continued sub-priming of the African-American culture is one way to put it. **Debt has become the ultimate sophisticated *Absentee Slave Master* while Capitalism has become the ultimate sophisticated Neo-Segregationist.** What has enslaved the present-day African-American more than anything else is debt? Debt does not require an active slave master. First, it pits one African-American against

---

[144] Buckley, Cara. "Dr. Cornel West: Reviews, Heeding The Call, The Places He Goes." Dr. Cornel West. http://www.cornelwest.com/reviews.html#.Vxb2o6tX_zI (Accessed January 22, 2010).

another through competition, desire, and greed. Second, it perpetuates and enslaves without the need for external assistance. How is this known? It has already been well documented and proven through every westernized country that unmanageable debt is both the ultimate conclusion and demise evident by the final *Appendix: Chart XXII* of this book. Is the true goal of capitalism to fuel betterment, opposed to a free-market economy? What the facts reveal is that the African-American has been divided by class using capitalism as the vehicle and instrument of division into a rich and poor class, a competition of one against another, a sense of betterment, entitlement, a culture of superiority versus inferiority, and a highly sophisticated Neo-Segregation. The enemy is no longer racism, its classism!

I cannot help but to entertain, consider, and give due process to the possibility that the ultimate and inevitable resolve for America's severely problematic debt will lie in what will be historically termed as the *Greatest Loan Forgiveness Act* the world will ever witness. Because the United States provided the United Kingdom with the *Anglo-American Loan Agreement* during the post-World War II periods of economic hardships, thereby offering collateral relief to the U.K. and many other affected countries, it gives the global aura that the world owes America an indefinite favor that the United States can call in whenever needed. In 1946, negotiated by John Maynard Keynes, the U.S. loaned the U.K. nearly $4B (the modern day equivalent of $57B) that was paid off by the Brits in 2006. The former led to the *London Debt*

*Agreement* of 1953 that allowed the U.K. to reduce Germany's World War I reparations by 50% and *The Marshall Plan* whereby the U.S. cancelled certain debts to Germany. Therefore, instead of America having to file bankruptcy if they default or exhaust all other options risking the inevitability of default as the national debt increases further and further over the 100% marker of their *GDP*, they will be very likely to call in that global favor and remind the world of their historical act of debt relief generosity. If America is granted loan forgiveness or the *New World Order* provides global relief for every debt-ridden country, a new economic start has the potential of continuing American empirical dominance, maintaining the elitist class, generally and ethnically, and cause the world to ignore the failure of capitalism.

If corrected, what is the best outcome? First, the African-American will have come to the knowledge that money has not, is not, and never will be the primary objective. **The quality of life will always outweigh the quantity in life.** Second, each African-American person must find satisfaction in being the best and doing the best with the best that God has given them individually! Best is not measured in dollars and cents but in democracy and sense. I must disagree with the ultimate cliché of African-American capitalistic verbiage, "If it doesn't make dollars, it doesn't make sense." I have come to know through life's experiences, "If it doesn't bring serenity, it doesn't make sense!" Some will respond to my antithesis with the embrace that it is money that brings them serenity. To this, I have no argument as to each their own.

However, I will recommend that they read my "Prologue". Abraham Lincoln rendered these words, "Whatever you are, be a good one." Third, the African-American should set the goals identified by Dr. Martin Luther King Jr., stated in his *I Have a Dream Speech*, quoting the *U.S. Constitution*,

> I have a dream that one day this nation will rise up and live out the true meaning of its creed: We hold these truths to be self-evident: that all men are created equal.[145]

Fourth, the African-American people should come to the realization of the words of President John Fitzgerald Kennedy who said in the commencement speech at *American University* on June 10, 1963,

> For, in the final analysis, our most basic common link is that we all inhabit this small planet. We all breathe the same air. We all cherish our children's future. And we are all mortal.[146]

Finally, the African-American culture will have to embrace the words of President Barack Obama who said at the *NAACP Centennial Celebration* on July 16, 2009,

> No one has written your destiny for you. Your destiny is in your hands. That's what we have to teach all our children. No excuses. This notion, that through striving anyone, can achieve and create his or her own destiny is central to American ideology. This ideology asserts that the *United States* is a meritocracy and that its

[145] King Jr., Martin Luther. "I Have a Dream Speech." National Archives and Records Administration: United States Government. https://www.archives.gov/press/exhibits/dream-speech.pdf. (accessed August 28, 1963).

[146] Clymer, Adam. "When Presidential Words Led to Swift Actions." The New York Times. http://www.nytimes.com/2013/06/09/us/remembering-two-seminal-kennedy-speeches.html?pagewanted=all&_r=0 (accessed June 8, 2013).

citizens regardless of the social stratum from which they start should aspire to, and in fact can attain, the height of social and economic success described as the American Dream. American meritocracy, the claim goes, has liberated its citizens from old-world confines of class and heritage. President Obama personifies the promise of American meritocracy, an African American man in a country with a long history of racism, rising from very modest means.[147]

---

[147] Kwate, PhD., Naa Oyo A. and Meyer, PhD., Ilan H. "The Myth of Meritocracy and African American Health." National Center for Biotechnology Information: United States National Library of Medicine: National Institutes of Health. http://www.ncbi.nlm.nih.gov/pmc/articles/PMC2936997/ (accessed October 2010).

Money can buy a house, but not a home.

Money can buy a bed, but not sleep.

Money can buy a clock, but not time.

Money can buy pleasure, but not love.

Money can buy food, but not an appetite.

Money can buy medicine, but not health.

Money can buy psychiatry, but not sanity.

Money can buy cosmetics, but not beauty.

Money can buy plastic surgery, but not eternal youth.

Money can buy positions, but not personality.

Money can buy you friends, but not friendship.

Money can buy status, but not respect.

Money can buy insurance, but not assurance.

Money can buy knowledge, but not wisdom.

Money can buy entertainment, but not happiness.

Money can buy sex, but not life.

Money can buy solitude, but not serenity.

Money can buy an expensive knitted sweater, but not unity.

Money can buy religion, but not salvation.

# APPENDIX

# CHARTS

| CHART I | United States Historical Populations | |
|---|---|---|
| **Census** | **Population** | **% +/-** |
| 1790 | 3,929,214 | — |
| 1800 | 5,236,631 | 33.30% |
| 1810 | 7,239,881 | 38.30% |
| 1820 | 9,638,453 | 33.10% |
| 1830 | 12,866,020 | 33.50% |
| 1840 | 17,069,453 | 32.70% |
| 1850 | 23,191,876 | 35.90% |
| 1860 | 31,443,321 | 35.60% |
| 1870 | 38,558,371 | 22.60% |
| 1880 | 49,371,340 | 28.00% |
| 1890 | 62,979,766 | 27.60% |
| 1900 | 76,212,168 | 21.00% |
| 1910 | 92,228,531 | 21.00% |
| 1920 | 106,021,568 | 15.00% |
| 1930 | 123,202,660 | 16.20% |
| 1940 | 132,165,129 | 7.30% |
| 1950 | 151,325,798 | 14.50% |
| 1960 | 179,323,175 | 18.50% |
| 1970 | 203,211,926 | 13.30% |
| 1980 | 226,545,805 | 11.50% |
| 1990 | 248,709,873 | 9.80% |
| 2000 | 281,421,906 | 13.20% |
| 2010 | 308,745,531 | 9.70% |
| Est. 2013 | 316,364,000 | 2.50% |

[148]

---

[148] Sources: Data derived from *United States Census Bureau* for Charts I – IV, supporting data contained within the "Introduction" chapter of this book. These charts are not direct copies, thus, does not require the need for citations but is intentionally organized to support the book's material and to make population, demographic, and ethnic comparisons.

United States 2010 Population by Ethnicity

| CHART II | United States 2010 Population by Ethnicity | |
|---|---|---|
| Race / Ethnicity | Number | % US Population |
| Total Population | 308,745,538.00 | 100% |
| White | 163,635,135.14 | 53.00% |
| Hispanic | 50,325,522.69 | 16.30% |
| African-American | 38,901,937.79 | 12.60% |
| Asian Americans | 14,819,785.82 | 4.80% |
| American Indian/Alaskan Native | 2,778,709.84 | 0.90% |
| Native Hawaiian/Pacific Islander | 617,491.08 | 0.20% |
| Other | 28,095,843.96 | 9.10% |

# US POPULATION COMPARING WHITES, BLACKS, & HISPANICS (1610-2010)

| CHART III | US POPULATION COMPARING WHITES, BLACKS, & HISPANICS (1610-2010) | | | | | |
|---|---|---|---|---|---|---|
| YEAR | POPULATION | WHITES | WHITES % | BLACKS | BLACKS % | HISPANIC % |
| 1630 | 4,586 | 4,586 | 98.7% | 60 | 1.3% | -- |
| 1640 | 26,037 | 26,037 | 97.8% | 597 | 2.2% | -- |
| 1650 | 48,768 | 48,768 | 96.8% | 1,600 | 3.2% | -- |
| 1660 | 72,138 | 72,138 | 96.1% | 2,920 | 3.9% | -- |
| 1670 | 107,400 | 107,400 | 95.9% | 4,535 | 4.1% | -- |
| 1680 | 144,536 | 144,536 | 95.4% | 6,971 | 4.6% | -- |
| 1690 | 193,643 | 193,643 | 92.0% | 16,729 | 8.0% | -- |
| 1700 | 223,071 | 223,071 | 88.9% | 27,817 | 11.1% | -- |
| 1710 | 286,845 | 286,845 | 86.5% | 44,866 | 13.5% | -- |
| 1720 | 397,346 | 397,346 | 85.2% | 68,839 | 14.8% | -- |
| 1730 | 538,424 | 538,424 | 85.5% | 91,021 | 14.5% | -- |
| 1740 | 755,539 | 755,539 | 83.4% | 150,024 | 16.6% | -- |
| 1750 | 934,340 | 934,340 | 79.8% | 236,420 | 20.2% | -- |
| 1760 | 1,267,819 | 1,267,819 | 79.6% | 325,806 | 20.7% | -- |
| 1770 | 1,688,254 | 1,688,254 | 78.6% | 459,822 | 20.0% | -- |
| 1780 | 2,780,369 | 2,204,949 | 79.3% | 575,420 | 20.0% | -- |
| 1790 | 3,929,214 | 3,172,006 | 80.7% | 757,208 | 19.3% | -- |
| 1800 | 5,308,483 | 4,306,446 | 81.1% | 1,002,037 | 18.90% | -- |
| 1810 | 7,239,881 | 5,862,073 | 81.0% | 1,377,808 | 19.00% | -- |
| 1820 | 9,638,453 | 7,866,797 | 81.6% | 1,771,656 | 18.40% | -- |
| 1830 | 12,860,702 | 10,532,060 | 81.9% | 2,328,642 | 18.10% | -- |
| 1840 | 17,063,353 | 14,189,705 | 83.2% | 2,873,648 | 16.80% | -- |
| 1850 | 23,191,876 | 19,553,068 | 84.3% | 3,638,808 | 15.70% | -- |
| 1860 | 31,443,321 | 26,922,537 | 85.6% | 4,441,830 | 14.10% | -- |
| 1870 | 38,558,371 | 33,589,377 | 87.1% | 4,880,009 | 12.70% | -- |
| 1880 | 50,155,783 | 43,402,970 | 86.5% | 6,580,793 | 13.10% | -- |
| 1890 | 62,947,714 | 55,101,258 | 87.5% | 7,488,676 | 11.90% | -- |
| 1900 | 75,994,575 | 66,809,196 | 87.9% | 8,833,994 | 11.60% | -- |
| 1910 | 91,972,266 | 81,731,957 | 88.9% | 9,827,763 | 10.70% | 0.9% |
| 1920 | 105,710,620 | 94,820,915 | 89.7% | 10,463,131 | 9.90% | 1.2% |
| 1930 | 122,775,046 | 110,286,740 | 89.8% | 11,891,143 | 9.70% | 1.3% |
| 1940 | 131,669,275 | 118,214,870 | 89.8% | 12,865,518 | 9.80% | 1.5% |
| 1950 | 150,697,361 | 134,942,028 | 89.5% | 15,042,286 | 10.00% | 2.1% |
| 1960 | 179,323,175 | 158,831,732 | 88.6% | 18,871,831 | 10.50% | 3.2% |
| 1970 | 203,210,158 | 178,119,221 | 87.7% | 22,539,362 | 11.10% | 4.4% |
| 1980 | 226,545,805 | 188,371,622 | 83.1% | 26,495,025 | 11.70% | 6.4% |
| 1990 | 248,709,873 | 199,686,070 | 80.3% | 29,986,060 | 12.10% | 9.0% |
| 2000 | 281,421,906 | 211,460,626 | 75.1% | 34,658,190 | 12.30% | 12.5% |
| 2010 | 308,745,538 | 223,553,265 | 72.4% | 38,929,319 | 12.60% | 16.3% |

# UNITED STATES FERTILITY AND MORTALITY DEMOGRAPHICS (1990-2010)

| CHART IV | UNITED STATES FERTILITY AND MORTALITY DEMOGRAPHICS (1990-2010) | | | | | | | | |
|---|---|---|---|---|---|---|---|---|---|
| -- | WHITES | | | BLACKS | | | HISPANICS | | |
| YEAR | Live Births[1] | Deaths | *NFM | Live Births2 | Deaths | *NFM | Live Births[3] | Deaths | *NFM |
| 1990 | -- | 595,073 | -- | 2,626,500 | -- | -- | 661,701 | -- | -- |
| 1991 | -- | 623,085 | -- | 2,589,878 | -- | -- | 666,758 | -- | -- |
| 1992 | -- | 643,271 | -- | 2,527,207 | -- | -- | 657,450 | -- | -- |
| 1993 | -- | 654,418 | -- | 2,472,031 | -- | -- | 641,273 | -- | -- |
| 1994 | -- | 665,026 | -- | 2,438,855 | -- | -- | 619,198 | -- | -- |
| 1995 | -- | 679,768 | -- | 2,382,638 | -- | -- | 587,781 | -- | -- |
| 1996 | -- | 701,339 | -- | 2,358,989 | -- | -- | 578,099 | -- | -- |
| 1997 | -- | 709,767 | -- | 2,333,363 | 1,895,461 | 437,902 | 581,431 | 273,381 | 308,050 |
| 1998 | -- | 734,661 | -- | 2,361,462 | 1,912,802 | 448,660 | 593,127 | 275,264 | 317,863 |
| 1999 | 35,662 | 764,339 | -728,677 | 2,346,450 | 1,953,197 | 393,253 | 588,981 | 281,979 | 307,002 |
| 2000 | 37,144 | 815,868 | -778,724 | 2,362,968 | 1,959,919 | 403,049 | 604,346 | 282,676 | 321,670 |
| 2001 | 38,618 | 851,851 | -813,233 | 2,326,578 | 1,962,810 | 363,768 | 589,917 | 284,343 | 305,574 |
| 2002 | 40,049 | 876,642 | -836,593 | 2,298,156 | 1,981,973 | 316,183 | 578,335 | 286,573 | 291,762 |
| 2003 | 41,501 | 912,329 | -870,828 | 2,321,904 | 1,979,465 | 342,439 | 576,033 | 287,968 | 288,065 |
| 2004 | 43,024 | 946,349 | -903,325 | 2,296,683 | 1,933,382 | 363,301 | 578,772 | 283,859 | 294,913 |
| 2005 | 44,606 | 985,505 | -940,899 | 2,279,768 | 1,967,142 | 312,626 | 583,759 | 289,163 | 294,596 |
| 2006 | 46,197 | 1,039,077 | -992,880 | 2,308,640 | 1,944,617 | 364,023 | 617,247 | 286,581 | 330,666 |
| 2007 | 47,794 | 1,062,779 | -1,014,985 | 2,310,333 | 1,939,606 | 370,727 | 627,191 | 286,366 | 340,825 |
| 2008 | 49,327 | 1,041,239 | -991,912 | 2,267,817 | 1,981,198 | 286,619 | 623,029 | 285,959 | 337,070 |
| 2009 | 50,790 | 999,548 | -948,758 | 2,212,552 | 1,944,606 | 267,946 | 609,584 | 282,982 | 326,602 |
| 2010 | 52,045 | 945,180 | -893,135 | 2,162,406 | 1,967,619 | 194,787 | 589,808 | 282,750 | 307,058 |
| 2011 | -- | 918,129 | -918,129 | 2,146,566 | 2,005,481 | 141,085 | 582,345 | 287,482 | 294,853 |
| 2012 | -- | 907,405 | -907,405 | 2,133,115 | -- | 2,133,115 | 583,080 | -- | 583,080 |
| TOTAL | -- | -- | -12,539,483 | -- | -- | 7,139,483 | -- | -- | 5,249,659 |

* "NFM" = NET FERTILITY VS. MORTALITY

**PROJECTIONS THROUGH 2060**

| CHART V | POPULATION PROJECTION THROUGH 2060 | | | | |
|---|---|---|---|---|---|
| **Race/Ethnic Group** | **2020** | **2030** | **2040** | **2050** | **2060** |
| **Total Population** | 333,896,000 | 358,471,000 | 380,016,000 | 399,803,000 | 420,268,000 |
| White | 255,346,000 | 267,604,000 | 276,438,000 | 282,959,000 | 289,587,000 |
| Hispanic (any race) | 63,784,000 | 78,655,000 | 94,876,000 | 111,732,000 | 128,780,000 |
| Black | 44,810,000 | 49,246,000 | 53,412,000 | 57,553,000 | 61,822,000 |
| American Indian, Eskimo, & Aleut | 4,328,000 | 4,889,000 | 5,407,000 | 5,881,000 | 6,308,000 |
| Asian and Pacific Islander | 19,708,000 | 23,802,000 | 27,945,000 | 31,967,000 | 35,815,000 |
| Two or more races | 9,704,000 | 12,929,000 | 16,814,000 | 21,443,000 | 26,737,000 |
| Non-Hispanic White | 199,313,000 | 198,817,000 | 193,887,000 | 186,334,000 | 178,951,000 |

Racial and Ethnic Demographics of the United States **(Percentages)** Between 2020 and 2060 (Projected)

| Race/Ethnic Group | 2020 | 2030 | 2040 | 2050 | 2060 |
|---|---|---|---|---|---|
| White | 76.50% | 74.70% | 72.70% | 70.80% | 68.90% |
| Hispanic (of any race) | 19.10% | 21.90% | 25.00% | 27.90% | 30.60% |
| Black | 13.40% | 13.70% | 14.10% | 14.40% | 14.70% |
| American Indian, Eskimo, & Aleut | 1.30% | 1.40% | 1.40% | 1.50% | 1.50% |
| Asian and Pacific Islander | 5.90% | 6.60% | 7.40% | 8.00% | 8.50% |
| Two or more races | 2.90% | 3.60% | 4.40% | 5.40% | 6.40% |

149

[149] Colby, Sandra L. and Ortman, Jennifer M. "The Baby Boom Cohort in the United States: 2012 to 2060: Population Estimates and Projections, Table 1." U.S. Census Bureau. (accessed May 2014) 11.

*World Historical Total Fertility Rate (1950–2015)*

| CHART VI | World Historical Total Fertility Rate (1950–2015) UN, medium variant, 2010 |
|---|---|
| Years | Total Fertility Rate |
| 1950–1955 | 4.95 |
| 1955–1960 | 4.89 |
| 1960–1965 | 4.91 |
| 1965–1970 | 4.85 |
| 1970–1975 | 4.45 |
| 1975–1980 | 3.84 |
| 1980–1985 | 3.59 |
| 1985–1990 | 3.39 |
| 1990–1995 | 3.04 |
| 1995–2000 | 2.79 |
| 2000–2005 | 2.62 |
| 2005–2010 | 2.52 |
| 2010–2015 | 2.36 |

150

---

[150] UN data: Total fertility rate (children per woman). esa.un.org. Retrieved 2012-09-17.[dead link]

Chart VII

# Forms of Government
## ARCHON: "Ruled by"

**(1) Aristocracy:** rule based on inherited hereditary right by a few;

**(2) Autocracy:** rule by a single self-appointed ruler;

**(3) Corporatocracy:** ruled by a corporation or group of corporations;

**(4) Demarchy:** a political system executed by random selection;

**(5) Democracy:** ruled by the people

**(6) Epistemocracy:** a utopian type of society and government ruled by people of rank and status;

**(7) Ethnocracy:** ruled by a dominant ethnicity;

**(8) Exilarchy:** a theocratic or monarchic form of gov't that rules an ethnic or religious Diaspora;

**(9) Futarchy:** rule based on the idea of a certain voted outcome & then figure out how to achieve it;

**(10) Geniocracy:** rule, which advocates problem-solving and creative intelligence;

**(11) Gerontocracy:** ruled by the old;

**(12) Kakistocracy:** ruled or government by the worst;

**(13) Kleptocracy;** ruled by thieves wherein the government officials live on the citizens;

**(14) Kratocracy:** ruled by those who are strong enough to seize power through force;

**(15) Kritocracy or Krytocracy:** ruled by judges.

**(16) Logocracy:** ruled by words.

**(17) Meritocracy:** ruled by those appointed based on demonstrated talent and ability.

**(18) Minarchy:** rule whereby the government's only function is the protection of individuals;

**(19) Mobocracy or Ochlocracy:** ruled by mob or the intimidation;

**(20) Monarchy:** ruled by one with supreme power for life or until abdication;

**(21) Noocracy:**, a social and political system that is based on the priority of human mind;

**(22) Oligarchy,** ruled by a few;

**(23) Panarchracy:** a person's right to choose any form of gov't without being forced to move;

**(24) Plutocracy:** ruled by the wealthy or power provided by wealth;

**(25) Sociocracy:** ruled by structuring and governing organizations;

**(26) Stratocracy:** ruled equally between the military and civil power:

**(27) Technocracy:** ruled by engineers, scientists, and other technical experts;

**(28) Theocracy:** ruled by God, faith, or doctrine or representative thereof; .

**(29) Theodemocracy:** a simultaneous rule of faith and the republic; .

**(30) Timocracy:** ruled by property owners only or where rulers are predicated on peer honor.

## AFRICAN-AMERICAN WEALTHIEST ATHLETES I

| Chart VIIIA | | | | African-American Wealthiest Athletes I | | |
|---|---|---|---|---|---|---|
| # | NAME | $M | | # | NAME | $M |
| 1 | Michael Jordan | 1200 | | 36 | Kevin Durant | 80 |
| 2 | Tiger Woods | 700 | | 37 | Chris Paul | 75 |
| 3 | Magic Johnson | 500 | | 38 | Jason Kidd | 75 |
| 4 | Floyd Mayweather | 400 | | 39 | Karl Malone | 75 |
| 5 | Ulysses Bridgeman Jr. | 400 | | 40 | Rasheed Wallace | 75 |
| 6 | Shaquille O'Neal | 350 | | 41 | Tony Parker | 75 |
| 7 | Kobe Bryant | 320 | | 42 | Tracey McGrady | 75 |
| 8 | Alex Rodriguez | 300 | | 43 | Venus Williams | 75 |
| 9 | LeBron James | 300 | | 44 | Vernon Wells | 75 |
| 10 | George Foreman | 250 | | 45 | Alonzo Mourning | 70 |
| 11 | Kevin Garnett | 190 | | 46 | Amare Stoudemire | 70 |
| 12 | Derek Jeter | 185 | | 47 | Antawn Jamison | 70 |
| 13 | Grant Hill | 180 | | 48 | David Robinson | 70 |
| 14 | Don King | 150 | | 49 | Elton Brand | 70 |
| 15 | Serena Williams | 140 | | 50 | Jermaine O'Neal | 70 |
| 16 | Gary Payton | 130 | | 51 | Paul Pierce | 70 |
| 17 | Tim Duncan | 130 | | 52 | Michael Finley | 65 |
| 18 | CC Sabathia | 125 | | 53 | Zach Randolph | 65 |
| 19 | Dwayne Johnson | 125 | | 54 | Antonio McDyess | 60 |
| 20 | Julius Peppers | 125 | | 55 | Baron Davis | 60 |
| 21 | Terrell Suggs | 125 | | 56 | Bernie Williams | 60 |
| 22 | Sugar Ray Leonard | 120 | | 57 | Frank Thomas | 60 |
| 23 | Dwight Howard | 100 | | 58 | Jalen Rose | 60 |
| 24 | Ray Allen | 100 | | 59 | Jayson Williams | 60 |
| 25 | Dwayne Wade | 95 | | 60 | Jerry Stackhouse | 60 |
| 26 | Michael Redd | 91 | | 61 | Joe Johnson | 60 |
| 27 | Carmelo Anthony | 90 | | 62 | Kenyon Martin | 60 |
| 28 | Gary Sheffield | 90 | | 63 | Mike Bibby | 60 |
| 29 | Reggie Miller | 90 | | 64 | Mo Vaughn | 60 |
| 30 | Derrick Rose | 85 | | 65 | Rashad Lewis | 60 |
| 31 | Ken Griffey | 85 | | 66 | Shawn Marion | 60 |
| 32 | Patrick Ewing | 85 | | 67 | Torrii Hunter | 60 |
| 33 | Barry Bonds | 80 | | 68 | Vince Carter | 60 |
| 34 | Chris Webber | 80 | | 69 | Alan Houston | 55 |
| 35 | Juwan Howard | 80 | | 70 | Deron Williams | 55 |
| *Figures should not be held to be completely accurate. *RIP! | | | | | TOTAL | See XIV |

151

---

[151] See "Copyright Page" for all sources and permissions for Charts VIII – XIX.

# AFRICAN-AMERICAN WEALTHIEST ATHLETES II

| Chart VIIIB | | | | African-American Wealthiest Athletes II | | |
|---|---|---|---|---|---|---|
| # | NAME | $M | | # | NAME | $M |
| 71 | Jerry Rice | 55 | | 106 | Michael Strahan | 45 |
| 72 | Tyson Chandler | 55 | | 107 | Ray Lewis | 45 |
| 73 | Brian Grant | 52 | | 108 | Sharef Abdur-Rahim | 45 |
| 74 | Charles Oakley | 52 | | 109 | Stephon Marbury | 45 |
| 75 | Aeneas Williams | 50 | | 110 | Theo Ratliff | 45 |
| 76 | Ben Wallace | 50 | | 111 | Corey Maggette | 44 |
| 77 | Chris Bosh | 50 | | 112 | A.L. Harrington | 40 |
| 78 | Doug Christie | 50 | | 113 | Andre Miller | 40 |
| 79 | Gale Sayers* | 50 | | 114 | Ben Gordon | 40 |
| 80 | Gilbert Arenas | 50 | | 115 | Bernard Hopkins | 40 |
| 81 | James Harden | 50 | | 116 | Brandon Phillips | 40 |
| 82 | Jim Brown | 50 | | 117 | Bryant Young | 40 |
| 83 | Larry Fitzgerald | 50 | | 118 | Charles Barkley | 40 |
| 84 | Marcus Camby | 50 | | 119 | Deion Sanders | 40 |
| 85 | Muhammad Ali | 50 | | 120 | Derek Fisher | 40 |
| 86 | Penny Hardaway | 50 | | 121 | Edgerrin James | 40 |
| 87 | Richard Hamilton | 50 | | 122 | Garrett Anderson | 40 |
| 88 | Richard Jefferson | 50 | | 123 | Jason Terry | 40 |
| 89 | Scottie Pippen | 50 | | 124 | LaMarcus Aldridge | 40 |
| 90 | Vincent Jackson | 50 | | 125 | Ndamukong Suh | 40 |
| 91 | Antrel Rolle | 48 | | 126 | Ne-Ne | 40 |
| 92 | Damon Stoudamire | 46 | | 127 | Nick Van Excel | 40 |
| 93 | Adam Jones | 45 | | 128 | Steve Francis | 40 |
| 94 | Albert Belle | 45 | | 129 | Tim Thomas | 38 |
| 95 | Albert Haynesworth | 45 | | 130 | Dale Davis | 35 |
| 96 | Andrew Bynum | 45 | | 131 | DeMarcus Ware | 35 |
| 97 | Carl Crawford | 45 | | 132 | Donovan McNabb | 35 |
| 98 | Carlos Boozer | 45 | | 133 | Glenn Rice | 35 |
| 99 | Chauncey Billups | 45 | | 134 | Horace Grant | 35 |
| 100 | Derrick Coleman | 45 | | 135 | Jamal Crawford | 35 |
| 101 | Jamal Mashburn | 45 | | 136 | Lamar Odom | 35 |
| 102 | Jason Richardson | 45 | | 137 | Rajon Rondo | 35 |
| 103 | Larry Hughes | 45 | | 138 | Ron Artest | 35 |
| 104 | Lavar Arrington | 45 | | 139 | Roy Jones | 35 |
| 105 | Marvin Hagler | 45 | | 140 | Russell Westbrook | 35 |
| *Figures should not be held to be completely accurate. *RIP! | | | | | TOTAL | See XIV |

216

# AFRICAN-AMERICAN WEALTHIEST ATHLETES III

| Chart VIIIC | | | | African American Wealthiest Athletes III | | |
|---|---|---|---|---|---|---|
| # | NAME | $M | | # | NAME | $M |
| 141 | Shane Mosley | 35 | | 177 | P.J. Brown | 26 |
| 142 | LaDainian Tomlinson | 32 | | 178 | Steve McNair | 26 |
| 143 | Adrian Petersen | 30 | | 179 | Leonard Davis | 25.5 |
| 144 | Andrew McCutchen | 30 | | 180 | Bernard Berrian | 25 |
| 145 | Billy Blanks | 30 | | 181 | Bobbie Banilla | 25 |
| 146 | Blake Griffin | 30 | | 182 | Bobby Bonds | 25 |
| 147 | Calvin Johnson | 30 | | 183 | Brendon Hayward | 25 |
| 148 | Champ Bailey | 30 | | 184 | Cam Newton | 25 |
| 149 | Darius Miles | 30 | | 185 | Chone Figgins | 25 |
| 150 | Darnell Dockett | 30 | | 186 | Clyde Drexler | 25 |
| 151 | Darrelle Revis | 30 | | 187 | Dwayne Bowe | 25 |
| 152 | Derrick Brooks | 30 | | 188 | Earl Campbell | 25 |
| 153 | Emeka Okafor | 30 | | 189 | Giancarlo Stanton | 25 |
| 154 | Erick Dampier | 30 | | 190 | Hank Aaron | 25 |
| 155 | Fred McGriff | 30 | | 191 | Joe Smith | 25 |
| 156 | Jamaal Charles | 30 | | 192 | John Starks | 25 |
| 157 | Justin Houston | 30 | | 193 | Kenny Lofton | 25 |
| 158 | Kwame Brown | 30 | | 194 | Kyle Arlington | 25 |
| 159 | Mario Williams | 30 | | 195 | Michael Bourn | 25 |
| 160 | Ray Durham | 30 | | 196 | Nazr Mohammed | 25 |
| 161 | Speedy Claxton | 29.5 | | 197 | Randy Moss | 25 |
| 162 | Ty Law | 28.4 | | 198 | Shane Battier | 25 |
| 163 | Andre Iguodala | 28 | | 199 | Sidney Rice | 25 |
| 164 | Barry Sanders | 28 | | 200 | Stephen Jackson | 25 |
| 165 | Donnell Marshall | 28 | | 201 | Tayshan Prince | 25 |
| 166 | Gerald Wallace | 28 | | 202 | Cuttino Mobley | 24 |
| 167 | Jahri Evans | 28 | | 203 | Darren Oliver | 24 |
| 168 | Jimmy Graham | 28 | | 204 | Darren Sproles | 24 |
| 169 | Rickey Henderson | 28 | | 205 | Derek Anderson | 24 |
| 170 | Tim Hardaway | 28 | | 206 | Kevin Martin | 24 |
| 171 | Juliann Peterson | 27 | | 207 | Terrell Brandon | 24 |
| 172 | Marvin Harrison | 26.8 | | 208 | Aaron McKie | 23 |
| 173 | Caron Butler | 26 | | 209 | Alan Henderson | 23 |
| 174 | Elden Campbell | 26 | | 210 | Bobby Simmons | 23 |
| 175 | Greg Jennings | 26 | | 211 | Brandon Roy | 23 |
| *Figures should not be held to be completely accurate. *RIP! | | | | | TOTAL | See XIV |

# AFRICAN-AMERICAN WEALTHIEST ATHLETES IV

| Chart VIIID | | | African American Wealthiest Athletes IV | | |
|---|---|---|---|---|---|
| # | NAME | $M | # | NAME | $M |
| 212 | Josh Smith | 23 | 247 | Randy Winn | 20 |
| 213 | Malik Rose | 23 | 248 | Ray Lankford | 20 |
| 214 | Milton Bradley | 23 | 249 | Reggie Jackson | 20 |
| 215 | Pat Williams | 23 | 250 | Richard Williams | 20 |
| 216 | Darius Johnson- | 22.5 | 251 | Robert Horry | 20 |
| 217 | Jonathan Ogden | 22.4 | 252 | Roger Mayweather | 20 |
| 218 | Larry Allen | 22 | 253 | Rohan Marley | 20 |
| 219 | Patrick Surtain | 20.5 | 254 | Tony Gwynn | 20 |
| 220 | Darren McFadden | 20 | 255 | Trevor Ariza | 20 |
| 221 | DeAngelo Hall | 20 | 256 | Walter Jones | 20 |
| 222 | Devin Harris | 20 | 257 | Dre Bly | 19.2 |
| 223 | Dimitri Young | 20 | 258 | Paris Lenon | 19 |
| 224 | Dontrelle Willis | 20 | 259 | Trevor Pryce | 19 |
| 225 | Dusty Baker | 20 | 260 | Vince Wilfork | 19 |
| 226 | Eric Snow | 20 | 261 | Chris Samuels | 18.6 |
| 227 | Gerald McCoy | 20 | 262 | Tyson Jackson | 18.2 |
| 228 | Glenn Robinson | 20 | 263 | Willie Anderson | 18.2 |
| 229 | J.R. Smith | 20 | 264 | A.J. Green | 18 |
| 230 | Jameer Nelson | 20 | 265 | Brandon Marshall | 18 |
| 231 | Jason Williams | 20 | 266 | Brian Dawkins | 18 |
| 232 | Joakim Noah | 20 | 267 | Clinton McDonald | 18 |
| 233 | John Salmons | 20 | 268 | Desagana Diop | 18 |
| 234 | Justin Upton | 20 | 269 | Dwyane Wade | 18 |
| 235 | Kareem Adul-Jabbar | 20 | 270 | Emmitt Smith | 18 |
| 236 | Kelvin Cato | 20 | 271 | James Stewart Jr. | 18 |
| 237 | Kerry Kittles | 20 | 272 | John Henson | 18 |
| 238 | Kevin Carter | 20 | 273 | Justin Smith | 18 |
| 239 | Keyshawn Johnson | 20 | 274 | Kendrick Perkins | 18 |
| 240 | Larry Johnson (NBA) | 20 | 275 | Larry Holmes | 18 |
| 241 | Larry Johnson (NFL) | 20 | 276 | Marvin Williams | 18 |
| 242 | Maurice Taylor | 20 | 277 | Michael Duncan | 18 |
| 243 | Mitch Richmond | 20 | 278 | T.J. Ford | 18 |
| 244 | Mo Williams | 20 | 279 | Wesley Person | 18 |
| 245 | Nnamidi Asomougha | 20 | 280 | Antoine Winfield | 17.2 |
| 246 | Paul George | 20 | 281 | Anthony Mason | 17 |
| *Figures should not be held to be completely accurate. *RIP! | | | | TOTAL | See XIV |

218

# AFRICAN-AMERICAN WEALTHIEST ATHLETES V

| Chart VIIIE | | | | African American Wealthiest Athletes V | | |
|---|---|---|---|---|---|---|
| # | NAME | $M | | # | NAME | $M |
| 282 | Michael Bennett | 17 | | 317 | Vernon Davis | 16 |
| 283 | Michael Waddell | 17 | | 318 | Michael Huff | 15.2 |
| 284 | Red Bryant | 17 | | 319 | A.C. Green | 15 |
| 285 | Rudy Gay | 17 | | 320 | Al Haymon | 15 |
| 286 | Tory Holt | 16.7 | | 321 | Andre Dawson | 15 |
| 287 | Sylvester Williams | 16.2 | | 322 | Buster Douglas | 15 |
| 288 | Andre Carter | 16 | | 323 | Charles Woodson | 15 |
| 289 | Antrel Rolle | 16 | | 324 | Charlie Strong | 15 |
| 290 | Bo Jackson | 16 | | 325 | Chike Okeafor | 15 |
| 291 | Brandon MeBane | 16 | | 326 | Deion Branch | 15 |
| 292 | Brian Westbrook | 16 | | 327 | Emanuel Steward* | 15 |
| 293 | Clint Dempsey | 16 | | 328 | Gene Upshaw | 15 |
| 294 | Colin Kaepernick | 16 | | 329 | Greg Oden | 15 |
| 295 | Corey Webster | 16 | | 330 | Jim Jackson | 15 |
| 296 | DeAngelo Williams | 16 | | 331 | Joe Giraardi | 15 |
| 297 | Doc Rivers | 16 | | 332 | Joe Horn | 15 |
| 298 | Donald Driver | 16 | | 333 | Kabeer Gbaja- | 15 |
| 299 | Earl Watson | 16 | | 334 | Kyrie Irving | 15 |
| 300 | Etan Thomas | 16 | | 335 | Maverick Carter | 15 |
| 301 | Greg Gumbel | 16 | | 336 | Michael Irvin | 15 |
| 302 | Hines Ward | 16 | | 337 | Mike Adams | 15 |
| 303 | Isaac Bruce | 16 | | 338 | Mugsy Bouges | 15 |
| 304 | Jason Collins | 16 | | 339 | Nate Clemens | 15 |
| 305 | Jerome James | 16 | | 340 | Priest Holmes | 15 |
| 306 | John Salley | 16 | | 341 | Randall Thomas | 15 |
| 307 | Julius Erving | 16 | | 342 | Randy Thomas | 15 |
| 308 | Kordell Stewart | 16 | | 343 | Raymond Felton | 15 |
| 309 | Laron Landry | 16 | | 344 | Rod Smith | 15 |
| 310 | Lynn Swan | 16 | | 345 | Shaun Alexander | 15 |
| 311 | Michael Crabtree | 16 | | 346 | Stuart Scott* | 15 |
| 312 | Michael Vick | 16 | | 347 | Terrance Newman | 15 |
| 313 | Mike Tomlin | 16 | | 348 | Trindon Holliday | 15 |
| 314 | NaVorro Bowman | 16 | | 349 | Udonis Haslem | 15 |
| 315 | Pierre Garion | 16 | | 350 | O'Brien Schofield | 14.9 |
| 316 | Quentin Jammer | 16 | | 351 | Adewale Ogunleye | 14 |
| *Figures should not be held to be completely accurate. *RIP! | | | | | TOTAL | See XIV |

219

# AFRICAN-AMERICAN WEALTHIEST ATHLETES VI

| Chart VIIIF | | | | African American Wealthiest Athletes VI | | | |
|---|---|---|---|---|---|---|---|
| # | NAME | $M | | | # | NAME | $M |
| 352 | Bob Sanders | 14 | | | 387 | Wes Matthews | 14 |
| 353 | Byron Scott | 14 | | | 388 | Will Beatty | 14 |
| 354 | Calvin Pace | 14 | | | 389 | Will Shields | 14 |
| 355 | Caylin Hauptman | 14 | | | 390 | Heath Farwell | 13.8 |
| 356 | Desean Jackson | 14 | | | 391 | Maurkice Pounce | 13.8 |
| 357 | Desmond Howard | 14 | | | 392 | Bernard Pollard | 13.5 |
| 358 | Desmond Walker | 14 | | | 393 | Julius Thomas | 13.2 |
| 359 | Dominique Wilkins | 14 | | | 394 | Al Harris | 13 |
| 360 | Eric Jordan | 14 | | | 395 | Anthony Davis | 13 |
| 361 | Fred Miller | 14 | | | 396 | Brandon Lloyd | 13 |
| 362 | JaVale McGheee | 14 | | | 397 | Brian Shaw | 13 |
| 363 | Jerome Bettis | 14 | | | 398 | Brian Walters | 13 |
| 364 | Joey Porter | 14 | | | 399 | DeAndre Jordan | 13 |
| 365 | John Henderson | 14 | | | 400 | DeMarco Murray | 13 |
| 366 | Kris Jenkins | 14 | | | 401 | Derrick Mason | 13 |
| 367 | Lee Evans | 14 | | | 402 | Eddie Murray | 13 |
| 368 | LeSean McCoy | 14 | | | 403 | Eric Moulds | 13 |
| 369 | Mario Chalmers | 14 | | | 404 | Kareem McKenzie | 13 |
| 370 | Marshawn Lynch | 14 | | | 405 | Kevin Sumlin | 13 |
| 371 | Marvin Lewis | 14 | | | 406 | LeMuel Jean-Pierre | 13 |
| 372 | Michael Bowie | 14 | | | 407 | Levi Jones | 13 |
| 373 | Michael Oher | 14 | | | 408 | Marty Booker | 13 |
| 374 | Michael Robinson | 14 | | | 409 | Matt Forte | 13 |
| 375 | Ray Rice | 14 | | | 410 | Nate Robinson | 13 |
| 376 | Reggie Bush | 14 | | | 411 | Orlando Pace | 13 |
| 377 | Ron Brown | 14 | | | 412 | Orpheus Roye | 13 |
| 378 | Roy Hibbert | 14 | | | 413 | Robert Griffin III | 13 |
| 379 | Roy Williams | 14 | | | 414 | Royce Clayton | 13 |
| 380 | Russell Okung | 14 | | | 415 | Shaun Ellis | 13 |
| 381 | Russell Wilson | 14 | | | 416 | Shawn Merriman | 13 |
| 382 | Sam Madison | 14 | | | 417 | Tarik Glenn | 13 |
| 383 | Stephen Curry | 14 | | | 418 | Tubby Smith | 13 |
| 384 | Tiki Barber | 14 | | | 419 | Ty Lawson | 13 |
| 385 | Tommie Harris | 14 | | | 420 | Wayne Gandy | 13 |
| 386 | Virgil Green | 14 | | | 421 | Will Smith (NFL) | 13 |
| *Figures should not be held to be completely accurate. *RIP! | | | | | | TOTAL | See XIV |

220

# AFRICAN-AMERICAN WEALTHIEST ATHLETES VII

| Chart VIIIG | | | | African American Wealthiest Athletes VII | | |
|---|---|---|---|---|---|---|
| # | NAME | $M | | # | NAME | $M |
| 422 | Keith Bullock | 12.75 | | 457 | Ken Lucas | 12 |
| 423 | Martellus Bennett | 12.6 | | 458 | Kevin Ollie | 12 |
| 424 | Ricardo Lockett | 12.6 | | 459 | Lance Briggs | 12 |
| 425 | Bryant McKinney | 12.5 | | 460 | LaRoi Glover | 12 |
| 426 | Aaron Brooks | 12 | | 461 | Larry Sanders | 12 |
| 427 | Adrian Wilson | 12 | | 462 | London Fletcher | 12 |
| 428 | Anthony Henry | 12 | | 463 | Marshall Faulk | 12 |
| 429 | Assante Samuel | 12 | | 464 | Michael Wilborn | 12 |
| 430 | Betrand Berry | 12 | | 465 | Mike McKenzie | 12 |
| 431 | Brad Hopkins | 12 | | 466 | Mike Peterson | 12 |
| 432 | Braylon Edwards | 12 | | 467 | Peter Boulluare | 12 |
| 433 | Brian Orakpo | 12 | | 468 | Quinton Rampage | 12 |
| 434 | Bruce Bowen | 12 | | 469 | Ron Harper | 12 |
| 435 | Bruce Smith | 12 | | 470 | Ronde Barber | 12 |
| 436 | Chad Brown | 12 | | 471 | Sam Hurd | 12 |
| 437 | Damien Woody | 12 | | 472 | Takeo Spikes | 12 |
| 438 | Darren Howard | 12 | | 473 | Tarvaris Jackson | 12 |
| 439 | Dave Winfield | 12 | | 474 | Thomas Jones | 12 |
| 440 | David Bruton | 12 | | 475 | Thurman Thomas | 12 |
| 441 | Delonte West | 12 | | 476 | Tim Raines | 12 |
| 442 | DeWayne | 12 | | 477 | Tra Thomas | 12 |
| 443 | Ed Reed | 12 | | 478 | Tyson Gay | 12 |
| 444 | Fred Smoot | 12 | | 479 | Vince Coleman | 12 |
| 445 | Fred Taylor | 12 | | 480 | Vontez Burfiet | 12 |
| 446 | Freddy Adu | 12 | | 481 | Will Witherspoon | 12 |
| 447 | Glenn Davis | 12 | | 482 | Willie McGhee | 12 |
| 448 | Greg Willis | 12 | | 483 | Willie McGinest | 12 |
| 449 | Herschel Walker | 12 | | 484 | Rodney Harrison | 11.5 |
| 450 | Jamal Williams | 12 | | 485 | Ahman Green | 11 |
| 451 | James Harrison | 12 | | 486 | Amani Toomer | 11 |
| 452 | Jason Ferguson | 12 | | 487 | Anquan Boldin | 11 |
| 453 | Javon Walker | 12 | | 488 | Chris Chambers | 11 |
| 454 | Jim Caldwell | 12 | | 489 | Corey Dillon | 11 |
| 455 | Josh Childress | 12 | | 490 | Gary Walker | 11 |
| 456 | Kellen Winslow | 12 | | 491 | Jonathan Vilma | 11 |
| *Figures should not be held to be completely accurate. *RIP! | | | | | TOTAL | See XIV |

221

# AFRICAN-AMERICAN WEALTHIEST ATHLETES VIII

| Chart VIIIH | | | | African American Wealthiest Athletes VIII | | |
|---|---|---|---|---|---|---|
| # | NAME | $M | | # | NAME | $M |
| 492 | Marcus Shroud | 11 | | 527 | Javaris Crittenton | 10 |
| 493 | Marvel Smith | 11 | | 528 | Joe Dumars | 10 |
| 494 | T.J. Ward | 11 | | 529 | Joey Galloway | 10 |
| 495 | Ted Washington | 11 | | 530 | Jon Bones | 10 |
| 496 | Tony Carter | 11 | | 531 | Justin Tuck | 10 |
| 497 | Warrick Dunn | 11 | | 532 | Kam Chancellor | 10 |
| 498 | Samuri Rolle | 10.8 | | 533 | Kenny Smith | 10 |
| 499 | Alvin Bailey | 10.4 | | 534 | Kevin Johnson | 10 |
| 500 | Bobby Wagner | 10.4 | | 535 | Kevin Williams | 10 |
| 501 | Anthony Mosley | 10 | | 536 | Laila Ali | 10 |
| 502 | Bill Russell | 10 | | 537 | Larry Johnson (NBA) | 10 |
| 503 | Bobby McCray | 10 | | 538 | Leonard Little | 10 |
| 504 | Brandon LaFell | 10 | | 539 | Lovie Smith | 10 |
| 505 | Charles Tellman | 10 | | 540 | Matt Barnes | 10 |
| 506 | Chris Duhon | 10 | | 541 | Maurice Jones-Drew | 10 |
| 507 | Cliff Avril | 10 | | 542 | Michael Singletary | 10 |
| 508 | D. Brickashaw- | 10 | | 543 | Mookie Blaylock | 10 |
| 509 | Damian Lillard | 10 | | 544 | Norm Nixon | 10 |
| 510 | Damon Jones | 10 | | 545 | Ozzie Newsome | 10 |
| 511 | Darren Woodson | 10 | | 546 | Patrick Peterson | 10 |
| 512 | Dave Stewart | 10 | | 547 | Randall Cunningham | 10 |
| 513 | David Otunga | 10 | | 548 | Reggie Wayne | 10 |
| 514 | DeShawn Stevenson | 10 | | 549 | Rich Paul | 10 |
| 515 | Doug Williams | 10 | | 550 | Richard Sherman | 10 |
| 516 | Dwight Freeney | 10 | | 551 | Robert Parish | 10 |
| 517 | Eric Dickerson | 10 | | 552 | Shannon Briggs | 10 |
| 518 | Frank Gore | 10 | | 553 | Shaun Livingston | 10 |
| 519 | Gerrard Warren | 10 | | 554 | Spudd Webb | 10 |
| 520 | Greg Anthony | 10 | | 555 | Steven A. Smith | 10 |
| 521 | Harry Carson | 10 | | 556 | Terrell Davis | 10 |
| 522 | Hugh Douglas | 10 | | 557 | Tom Jackson | 10 |
| 523 | Isaiah Rider | 10 | | 558 | Tony Allen | 10 |
| 524 | Jacque Vaugh | 10 | | 559 | Von Miller | 10 |
| 525 | James Brown | 10 | | 560 | Warren Moon | 10 |
| 526 | James Worthy | 10 | | 561 | Wilt Chamberlain* | 10 |
| *Figures should not be held to be completely accurate. *RIP! | | | | | TOTAL | See XIV |

# AFRICAN-AMERICAN WEALTHIEST ATHLETES IX

| Chart VIIII | | | | African American Wealthiest Athletes IX | | |
|---|---|---|---|---|---|---|
| # | NAME | $M | | # | NAME | $M |
| 562 | Shawn Springs | 9.75 | | 597 | Ken Norton Jr. | 8 |
| 563 | James Carpenter | 9.6 | | 598 | Kevin Mitchell | 8 |
| 564 | Jordan Hill | 9.6 | | 599 | Mark Blount | 8 |
| 565 | Demaryius Thomas | 9.5 | | 600 | Muhsin Mohammad | 8 |
| 566 | Lou Williams | 9.5 | | 601 | Nate Irving | 8 |
| 567 | Golden Tate | 9.4 | | 602 | Nick Young | 8 |
| 568 | Casey Hamilton | 9 | | 603 | Odell Beckman | 8 |
| 569 | Chris Carter | 9 | | 604 | Santana Moss | 8 |
| 570 | Daniel Gibson | 9 | | 605 | Sebastian Telfain | 8 |
| 571 | Earl Thomas | 9 | | 606 | Shannon Brown | 8 |
| 572 | Eddy Lacy | 9 | | 607 | Shannon Sharpe | 8 |
| 573 | Jason Paul | 9 | | 608 | Sterling Sharpe | 8 |
| 574 | Monty Williams | 9 | | 609 | Tim Brown | 8 |
| 575 | Victor Cruz | 9 | | 610 | Tristan Thomas | 8 |
| 576 | Rashad Evans | 8.5 | | 611 | Wayman Tisdale | 8 |
| 577 | Ahmad Rashad | 8 | | 612 | Winkey Wright | 8 |
| 578 | Anthony Dixon | 8 | | 613 | Tony McDaniels | 7.6 |
| 579 | Cadillac Williams | 8 | | 614 | LaVeranues Coles | 7.5 |
| 580 | Carl Nicks | 8 | | 615 | Andre Caldwell | 7 |
| 581 | Chris Ivory | 8 | | 616 | Antonio Gates | 7 |
| 582 | Darren Sharper | 8 | | 617 | Charles Jones | 7 |
| 583 | Dee Brown | 8 | | 618 | Chris Clemons | 7 |
| 584 | Dell Curry | 8 | | 619 | DeMarcus Cousins | 7 |
| 585 | DeMar Rozan | 8 | | 620 | Donte Stallworth | 7 |
| 586 | Devin McCarty | 8 | | 621 | Harold Reynolds | 7 |
| 587 | Eugene Parker | 8 | | 622 | James Jones | 7 |
| 588 | Flozell Adams* | 8 | | 623 | Jayson Heyward | 7 |
| 589 | Harvey Grant | 8 | | 624 | John Stallworth | 7 |
| 590 | Herman Edwards | 8 | | 625 | LaGarrette Blount | 7 |
| 591 | James Blake | 8 | | 626 | Michael Johnson | 7 |
| 592 | Jeremy Mincey | 8 | | 627 | Osi Umenylora | 7 |
| 593 | John Mobley | 8 | | 628 | Timothy Bradley | 7 |
| 594 | Julio Jones | 8 | | 629 | Winston Justice | 7 |
| 595 | K.J. Wright | 8 | | 630 | Ben Jarvus-Green-Ellis | 6 |
| 596 | Kellen Davis | 8 | | 631 | Benson Mayowa | 6 |
| *Figures should not be held to be completely accurate. *RIP! | | | | | TOTAL | See XIV |

223

# AFRICAN-AMERICAN WEALTHIEST ATHLETES X

| Chart VIIIJ | | | | African American Wealthiest Athletes X | | |
|---|---|---|---|---|---|---|
| # | NAME | $M | | # | NAME | $M |
| 632 | Chris Howard | 6 | | 667 | Clinton Portis | 5 |
| 633 | Chris Johnson | 6 | | 668 | Cory Spinks | 5 |
| 634 | Curtis Martin | 6 | | 669 | DaMarcus Beasley | 5 |
| 635 | David Wilson | 6 | | 670 | Danny Green | 5 |
| 636 | Dominique | 6 | | 671 | Darryl Dawkins | 5 |
| 637 | Dwayne Casey | 6 | | 672 | Dave Bing | 5 |
| 638 | Earl Boykins | 6 | | 673 | Ed Hartwell | 5 |
| 639 | Ezekiel Ansah | 6 | | 674 | Ed Jordan | 5 |
| 640 | Fletcher Smith | 6 | | 675 | Floyd Mayweather Sr. | 5 |
| 641 | Hakeem Nicks | 6 | | 676 | Isaiah Mustafa | 5 |
| 642 | Jerod Mayo | 6 | | 677 | JaMarcus Russell | 5 |
| 643 | Joel Dreessen | 6 | | 678 | Jamie Dukes | 5 |
| 644 | Juan Dixon | 6 | | 679 | Jerome Kersey | 5 |
| 645 | Klay Thompson | 6 | | 680 | Joe Morgan | 5 |
| 646 | Mark Jackson | 6 | | 681 | Kawhi Leonard | 5 |
| 647 | Marques Colston | 6 | | 682 | Ken Norton Sr. | 5 |
| 648 | Mike Tirico | 6 | | 683 | Lisa Leslie | 5 |
| 649 | Nyjah Huston | 6 | | 684 | Marcellus Wiley | 5 |
| 650 | Patrick Willis | 6 | | 685 | Michael Spinks | 5 |
| 651 | Plaxico Burress | 6 | | 686 | Moses Malone | 5 |
| 652 | Ralph Sampson | 6 | | 687 | Pernell Whitaker | 5 |
| 653 | Randy Starks | 6 | | 688 | Ron Washington | 5 |
| 654 | Robert Ayers | 6 | | 689 | Ronnie Lott | 5 |
| 655 | Terrell Fletcher | 6 | | 690 | Rosey Grier | 5 |
| 656 | Wyjah Huston | 6 | | 691 | Shaun Gayle | 5 |
| 657 | Glenn Pakulak | 5.5 | | 692 | Shawn Kemp | 5 |
| 658 | James Lofton | 5.4 | | 693 | Tony Delk | 5 |
| 659 | Akeem Ayers | 5 | | 694 | Tony Dorsett | 5 |
| 660 | Althea Gibson | 5 | | 695 | Tony Dungy | 5 |
| 661 | Artis Reed | 5 | | 696 | Willis Reed | 5 |
| 662 | Bart Scott | 5 | | 697 | Zab Judah | 5 |
| 663 | Ben Tankard | 5 | | 698 | Jannero Pargo | 4.5 |
| 664 | Chad Johnson | 5 | | 699 | Mark Henry Jr. | 4.5 |
| 665 | Cheryl Miller | 5 | | 700 | Walt Frazier | 4.5 |
| 666 | Chris Brossard | 5 | | 701 | Aaron Ross | 4 |
| *Figures should not be held to be completely accurate. *RIP! | | | | | TOTAL | See XIV |

224

# AFRICAN-AMERICAN WEALTHIEST ATHLETES XI

| Chart VIIIK | | | | African American Wealthiest Athletes XI | | |
|---|---|---|---|---|---|---|
| # | NAME | $M | | # | NAME | $M |
| 702 | Arthur Ashe* | 4 | | 737 | Andrew Wiggins | 3 |
| 703 | Brandon Jacobs | 4 | | 738 | Antonio Smith | 3 |
| 704 | Brandon Jennings | 4 | | 739 | Archie Griffin | 3 |
| 705 | David Tyree | 4 | | 740 | Austin Carr | 3 |
| 706 | Dez Bryant | 4 | | 741 | Bo Kimble | 3 |
| 707 | Dhani Jonas | 4 | | 742 | Bob Sapp | 3 |
| 708 | Greg Hardy | 4 | | 743 | Brittney Griner | 3 |
| 709 | Harrison Barnes | 4 | | 744 | Calvin Murphy | 3 |
| 710 | Iman Shuperd | 4 | | 745 | Candace Parker | 3 |
| 711 | Jay Williams | 4 | | 746 | Charles Haley | 3 |
| 712 | Jerome Williams | 4 | | 747 | Cobi Jones | 3 |
| 713 | Jimmy Smith | 4 | | 748 | Curt Menafee | 3 |
| 714 | Knowshon Moreno | 4 | | 749 | Devin Hester | 3 |
| 715 | Logan Ryan | 4 | | 750 | Devon Still | 3 |
| 716 | Marcus Allen | 4 | | 751 | Donta' Hightower | 3 |
| 717 | Mateen Cleaves | 4 | | 752 | Eddy Curry | 3 |
| 718 | Matt Parker | 4 | | 753 | Franco Harris | 3 |
| 719 | Miles Austin | 4 | | 754 | Frank Robinson | 3 |
| 720 | Nick Foles | 4 | | 755 | Gabby Douglas | 3 |
| 721 | Oscar Robertson | 4 | | 756 | Jamie Collins | 3 |
| 722 | Patrick Chung | 4 | | 757 | Jason Campbell | 3 |
| 723 | Percy Harvin | 4 | | 758 | Jason Pierre-Paul | 3 |
| 724 | Randall Cobb | 4 | | 759 | John Thompson | 3 |
| 725 | Rashad McClants | 4 | | 760 | Jonas Gray | 3 |
| 726 | Rick Mahon | 4 | | 761 | Kedrick Brown | 3 |
| 727 | Ron Dayne | 4 | | 762 | KiJana Carter | 3 |
| 728 | Ron Prince | 4 | | 763 | Kirby Puckett | 3 |
| 729 | Ryan Clady | 4 | | 764 | Kofi Kingston | 3 |
| 730 | Steven Ridley | 4 | | 765 | Len Dale White | 3 |
| 731 | Vernon Maxwell | 4 | | 766 | Lionel Hollins | 3 |
| 732 | Willie Randolph | 4 | | 767 | Mark Aquirre | 3 |
| 733 | Willis McGahee | 4 | | 768 | Mark May | 3 |
| 734 | Bob Whitfield | 3.5 | | 769 | Matthew Slater | 3 |
| 735 | Dennis Green | 3.5 | | 770 | Rashard Mendenhall | 3 |
| 736 | Adrien Bronner | 3 | | 771 | Ray Buchanan | 3 |
| *Figures should not be held to be completely accurate. *RIP! | | | | | TOTAL | See XIV |

| Chart VIIIL | | | | African American Wealthiest Athletes XII | | | |
|---|---|---|---|---|---|---|---|
| # | NAME | $M | | # | NAME | $M | |
| 772 | Ricky Williams | 3 | | 807 | Desmond Clark | 2 | |
| 773 | Rob Konrad | 3 | | 808 | Dion Waiters | 2 | |
| 774 | Ron Simmons | 3 | | 809 | Donald Young | 2 | |
| 775 | Sam Perkins | 3 | | 810 | Draymond Green | 2 | |
| 776 | Sean May | 3 | | 811 | Duke Ihenacho | 2 | |
| 777 | Theodore Long | 3 | | 812 | Geno Smith | 2 | |
| 778 | Tim Hardaway Jr. | 3 | | 813 | Glover Quinn | 2 | |
| 779 | Walter Payton | 3 | | 814 | Jahil Okafur | 2 | |
| 780 | Wesley Woodyard | 3 | | 815 | James Edwards | 2 | |
| 781 | Willie Mays | 3 | | 816 | James Toney | 2 | |
| 782 | Chad Dawson | 2.8 | | 817 | Jimmy Butler | 2 | |
| 783 | Torrey Smith | 2.7 | | 818 | Jonathan Martin | 2 | |
| 784 | Antonio Brown | 2.6 | | 819 | Justin Gatlin | 2 | |
| 785 | T.Y. Hilton | 2.6 | | 820 | Kaelin Burnett | 2 | |
| 786 | Dominique Dawes | 2.5 | | 821 | LaMichael James | 2 | |
| 787 | Doug Edwards | 2.5 | | 822 | Lance Stephenson | 2 | |
| 788 | Jeremy Stephens | 2.5 | | 823 | LoMas Brown | 2 | |
| 789 | Le'Veon Bell | 2.5 | | 824 | Malcolm Smith | 2 | |
| 790 | Phil Heath | 2.5 | | 825 | Mark Breland | 2 | |
| 791 | Adrian Dantley | 2 | | 826 | Matthew Hatchette | 2 | |
| 792 | Alfred Morris | 2 | | 827 | Meadow Lark-Lemon | 2 | |
| 793 | Andre Ward | 2 | | 828 | Mean Joe Green | 2 | |
| 794 | Antonio Cromartie | 2 | | 829 | Michael Smith | 2 | |
| 795 | Benson Henderson | 2 | | 830 | Montee Ball | 2 | |
| 796 | Bernard King | 2 | | 831 | Nelson Frazier Jr. | 2 | |
| 797 | Brandon Bolden | 2 | | 832 | Nick Gordon | 2 | |
| 798 | Brett Rodgers | 2 | | 833 | Philip Buchanon | 2 | |
| 799 | Cari Champion | 2 | | 834 | Quinn Buckner | 2 | |
| 800 | Charles Davis | 2 | | 835 | Robert Turbin | 2 | |
| 801 | Charlie Batch | 2 | | 836 | Roy Tarpley | 2 | |
| 802 | Christian Okoye | 2 | | 837 | Sage Steele | 2 | |
| 803 | Chuck Smith | 2 | | 838 | Shani Davis | 2 | |
| 804 | Clark Kellogg | 2 | | 839 | Terry Porter | 2 | |
| 805 | David Nelson | 2 | | 840 | Tim Wright | 2 | |
| 806 | Dawn Harper | 2 | | 841 | Todd Blackledge | 2 | |
| *Figures should not be held to be completely accurate. *RIP! | | | | | TOTAL | See XIV | |

# AFRICAN-AMERICAN WEALTHIEST ATHLETES XIII

| Chart VIIIM | | | | African American Wealthiest Athletes XIII | | |
|---|---|---|---|---|---|---|
| # | NAME | $M | | # | NAME | $M |
| 842 | Tony Thompson | 2 | | 877 | Cynthia Cooper | 1 |
| 843 | Tyron Woodley | 2 | | 878 | Dawn Staley | 1 |
| 844 | William Perry | 2 | | 879 | Eddie George | 1 |
| 845 | Zina Garrison | 2 | | 880 | Eddie Jackson | 1 |
| 846 | Doug Baldwin | 1.8 | | 881 | Jamal Wilkes | 1 |
| 847 | Tyrod Taylor | 1.6 | | 882 | Jamelle Hill | 1 |
| 848 | Akile Smith | 1.5 | | 883 | Josh Gordon | 1 |
| 849 | Andre Ware | 1.5 | | 884 | Josh Owens | 1 |
| 850 | Bernard Pierre | 1.5 | | 885 | Justin Tucker | 1 |
| 851 | Byron Maxwell | 1.5 | | 886 | Kai Greene | 1 |
| 852 | C.J. Anderson | 1.5 | | 887 | Kara Lawson | 1 |
| 853 | Christine Michael | 1.5 | | 888 | Katrina Adams | 1 |
| 854 | Herb Dean | 1.5 | | 889 | LaMont Peterson | 1 |
| 855 | Ivy Calvin | 1.5 | | 890 | Marcus Vick | 1 |
| 856 | Kayvon Webster | 1.5 | | 891 | Marion Jones | 1 |
| 857 | Marion Barber III | 1.5 | | 892 | Mike Tyson | 1 |
| 858 | Mike Rozier | 1.5 | | 893 | Mynique Smith | 1 |
| 859 | Pat White | 1.5 | | 894 | O.J. Simpson | 1 |
| 860 | Ronnie Hillman | 1.5 | | 895 | Pam Oliver | 1 |
| 861 | Sage Steele | 1.5 | | 896 | Rudy Gobert | 1 |
| 862 | San Derrick Marks | 1.5 | | 897 | Shawn Porter | 1 |
| 863 | Sandra Richards- | 1.5 | | 898 | Sheryl Swoopes | 1 |
| 864 | Seneca Wallace | 1.5 | | 899 | Syklar Diggins | 1 |
| 865 | Shane Vereen | 1.5 | | 900 | Terrelle Pryor | 1 |
| 866 | Sloane Stephens | 1.5 | | 901 | Tigresa Caliente | 1 |
| 867 | Terrance Kinsey | 1.5 | | 902 | Vin Baker | 1 |
| 868 | Troy Smith | 1.5 | | 903 | Wes Unseld | 1 |
| 869 | Vince Young | 1.5 | | 904 | William Moore | 1 |
| 870 | Vinnie Johnson | 1.5 | | 905 | William Spearmon | 1 |
| 871 | Walter Thurmond | 1.5 | | 906 | Antonio Freeman | 0 |
| 872 | Antonio Tarver | 1 | | 907 | Art Monk | 0 |
| 873 | Booker Huffman | 1 | | 908 | Bubba Franks | 0 |
| 874 | Charles Johnson | 1 | | 909 | Cliff Branch | 0 |
| 875 | Charlie Bell | 1 | | 910 | Dana Stubblefield | 0 |
| 876 | Curtis Ennis | 1 | | 911 | Dante Hall | 0 |
| *Figures should not be held to be completely accurate. *RIP! | | | | | TOTAL | See XIV |

# AFRICAN-AMERICAN WEALTHIEST ATHLETES XIV

| Chart VIIIN | | | | African American Wealthiest Athletes XIV | | | |
|---|---|---|---|---|---|---|---|
| # | NAME | $M | | # | NAME | $M | |
| 912 | David Garrard | 0 | | 947 | Warren Sapp | -1 | |
| 913 | Deacon Jones | 0 | | | | | |
| 914 | Derrick Thomas | 0 | | | | | |
| 915 | Dexter Manley | 0 | | | | | |
| 916 | Donnie Shell | 0 | | | | | |
| 917 | Drew Hill | 0 | | | | | |
| 918 | Drew Pearson | 0 | | | | | |
| 919 | Duante Culpepper | 0 | | | | | |
| 920 | Ed "Too Tall" Jones | 0 | | | | | |
| 921 | Eric Allen | 0 | | | | | |
| 922 | Eric Martin | 0 | | | | | |
| 923 | Everson Walls | 0 | | | | | |
| 924 | Freeman McNeil | 0 | | | | | |
| 925 | Henry Ellard | 0 | | | | | |
| 926 | Jack Tatum | 0 | | | | | |
| 927 | Jeremiah Trotter | 0 | | | | | |
| 928 | Jevon Kearse | 0 | | | | | |
| 929 | Joseph Addai | 0 | | | | | |
| 930 | Keenan McCardell | 0 | | | | | |
| 931 | Kenny Anderson | 0 | | | | | |
| 932 | Leon Lett | 0 | | | | | |
| 933 | Mel Blount | 0 | | | | | |
| 934 | Mike Wallace | 0 | | | | | |
| 935 | Reggie White | 0 | | | | | |
| 936 | Rod Woodson | 0 | | | | | |
| 937 | Terry Metcalf | 0 | | | | | |
| 938 | Tim McDonald | 0 | | | | | |
| 939 | Wes Chandler | 0 | | | | | |
| 940 | Allen Iverson | -1 | | | | | |
| 941 | Andre Rison | -1 | | | | | |
| 942 | Dennis Rodman | -1 | | | | | |
| 943 | Jamal Lewis | -1 | | | | | |
| 944 | Jevon Kearse | -1 | | | | | |
| 945 | Lawrence Taylor* | -1 | | | | | |
| 946 | Terrell Owens | -1 | | | | | |
| *Figures should not be held to be completely accurate. *RIP! | | | | | TOTAL | $21B | |

## AFRICAN-AMERICAN WEALTHIEST MUSICIANS I

| Chart IXA | | | | African American Wealthiest Musicians I | | |
|---|---|---|---|---|---|---|
| # | NAME | $M | | # | NAME | $M |
| 1 | Michael Jackson* | 600 | | 36 | Little Richard | 40 |
| 2 | Mariah Carey | 520 | | 37 | Macy Gray | 40 |
| 3 | Beyoncé Knowles | 450 | | 38 | R. Kelly | 40 |
| 4 | Quincy Jones | 350 | | 39 | Rick James* | 35 |
| 5 | Berry Gordy | 345 | | 40 | Chaka Khan | 30 |
| 6 | Russell Simmons | 340 | | 41 | Kelly Rowland | 30 |
| 7 | Prince* | 300 | | 42 | Luther Vandross* | 30 |
| 8 | Diana Ross | 250 | | 43 | Monica Scott Young | 30 |
| 9 | Percy Miller | 250 | | 44 | Rodney Jenkins | 30 |
| 10 | Tina Turner | 250 | | 45 | Troy Carter | 30 |
| 11 | Lionel Richie | 200 | | 46 | Diahann Carroll | 28 |
| 12 | Usher Raymond IV | 180 | | 47 | Eric Benet | 28 |
| 13 | Janet Jackson | 175 | | 48 | Gladys Knight | 28 |
| 14 | Jimie Hendrix* | 175 | | 49 | Vanessa Williams | 28 |
| 15 | Rihanna | 160 | | 50 | Bill Withers | 25 |
| 16 | Billy Paul | 145 | | 51 | Pebbles | 25 |
| 17 | Babyface | 120 | | 52 | Chris Brown | 22 |
| 18 | Steve Wonder | 110 | | 53 | Barry White* | 20 |
| 19 | James Brown* | 100 | | 54 | Bobbi Kristina* | 20 |
| 20 | Smokey Robinson | 100 | | 55 | Bobby Womack* | 20 |
| 21 | Anita Baker | 80 | | 56 | Evan Ross | 20 |
| 22 | Donna Summers | 75 | | 57 | Gloria Gaynor | 20 |
| 23 | Nile Rodgers | 70 | | 58 | James Ingram | 20 |
| 24 | Cortez Bryant | 66 | | 59 | Jennifer Hudson | 20 |
| 25 | Byron Michael Cot | 65 | | 60 | John Legend | 20 |
| 26 | Aretha Franklin | 60 | | 61 | Kierra Sheard | 20 |
| 27 | Nathan Morris | 60 | | 62 | Roberta Flack | 20 |
| 28 | Sade | 60 | | 63 | Benny Medina | 20 |
| 29 | Jimmy Jam | 50 | | 64 | Eddie Levert | 18 |
| 30 | Patti LaBelle | 50 | | 65 | Ciara | 17 |
| 31 | Toni Braxton | 50 | | 66 | Etta James* | 16 |
| 32 | Alicia Keys | 45 | | 67 | Ne-Yo | 16 |
| 33 | Shawn Stockman | 45 | | 68 | Shirley Caesar | 16 |
| 34 | Ashanti | 40 | | 69 | Brian McKnight | 15 |
| 35 | Lenny Kravitz | 40 | | 70 | Charlie Wilson | 15 |
| *Figures should not be held to be completely accurate. *RIP! | | | | | TOTAL | See IV |

229

## AFRICAN-AMERICAN WEALTHIEST MUSICIANS II

| Chart IXB | | | | African American Wealthiest Musicians II | | |
|---|---|---|---|---|---|---|
| # | NAME | $M | | # | NAME | $M |
| 71 | LaShawn Daniels | 15 | | 106 | Peabo Bryson | 10 |
| 72 | Rickey Bell | 15 | | 107 | Percy Sledge | 10 |
| 73 | Johnny Wright | 15 | | 108 | Siedah Garrett | 10 |
| 74 | Warryn Campbell | 15 | | 109 | Stan Lathan | 10 |
| 75 | Yandy Smith | 15 | | 110 | Tamia Hill | 10 |
| 76 | Al Jarreau | 14 | | 111 | Trey Songz | 10 |
| 77 | Tatyana Ali | 13 | | 112 | Versine Walker | 10 |
| 78 | Brandy Norwood | 12 | | 113 | Harvey Mason Jr. | 10 |
| 79 | Erykah Badu | 12 | | 114 | Memphitz Wright | 10 |
| 80 | Herbie Hancock | 12 | | 115 | Vincent Herbert | 10 |
| 81 | Isaac Hayes* | 12 | | 116 | Kirk Franklin | 8.5 |
| 82 | Jill Scott | 12 | | 117 | Anthony Hamilton | 8 |
| 83 | Shelia E | 12 | | 118 | Corrie Bailey Rae | 8 |
| 84 | Tariq Trotter | 12 | | 119 | Hezekiah Walker | 8 |
| 85 | Cory Rooney | 12 | | 120 | Mary Wilson* | 8 |
| 86 | Ginuwine | 11 | | 121 | Mase | 8 |
| 87 | Aaliyah* | 10 | | 122 | Michelle Williams | 8 |
| 88 | Al Green | 10 | | 123 | Musiq Soulchild | 8 |
| 89 | B.B. King | 10 | | 124 | Omarion | 8 |
| 90 | Billy Ocean | 10 | | 125 | Otis Williams | 8 |
| 91 | Chris Ivery | 10 | | 126 | Ralph Tresvant | 8 |
| 92 | Chuck Berry | 10 | | 127 | Tameka Cottle | 8 |
| 93 | Datari Turner | 10 | | 128 | Wayman Tisdale | 8 |
| 94 | Debra Anthony | 10 | | 129 | Ce Ce Winans | 7 |
| 95 | Dionne Warwick | 10 | | 130 | Levi Stubbs | 7 |
| 96 | Ella Fitzgerald* | 10 | | 131 | Regina Belle | 7 |
| 97 | Harvey Mason | 10 | | 132 | Evelyn Champagne | 6 |
| 98 | Johnny Gill | 10 | | 133 | Ben Tankard | 5 |
| 99 | Lalah Hathaway | 10 | | 134 | Black Francis | 5 |
| 100 | Lou Rawls* | 10 | | 135 | Blu Cantrell | 5 |
| 101 | Louis Armstrong* | 10 | | 136 | Bobby Brown | 5 |
| 102 | Maxwell | 10 | | 137 | Booker T. Jones | 5 |
| 103 | Miles Davis* | 10 | | 138 | Branford Marsalis | 5 |
| 104 | Millie Jackson | 10 | | 139 | Cissy Houston | 5 |
| 105 | Otis Redding* | 10 | | 140 | Dawn Robinson | 5 |
| *Figures should not be held to be completely accurate. *RIP! | | | | | TOTAL | See IV |

230

# AFRICAN-AMERICAN WEALTHIEST MUSICIANS III

| Chart IXC | | | | African American Wealthiest Musicians III | | |
|---|---|---|---|---|---|---|
| # | NAME | $M | | # | NAME | $M |
| 141 | Donnie McClurklin | 5 | | 177 | Russ Carr | 4 |
| 142 | Donnie Simpson | 5 | | 178 | Willow Smith | 4 |
| 143 | Freda Payne | 5 | | 179 | Be-Be Winans | 3.5 |
| 144 | George Benson | 5 | | 180 | Alexander O'Neal | 3 |
| 145 | Gerald Levert | 5 | | 181 | Amerie | 3 |
| 146 | Kim Burrell | 5 | | 182 | Andrae Crouch | 3 |
| 147 | LaToya Luckett | 5 | | 183 | Bootsy Collins | 3 |
| 148 | Left Eye* | 5 | | 184 | Deniece Williams | 3 |
| 149 | Marcus Miller | 5 | | 185 | Faith Evans | 3 |
| 150 | Marvin Gaye* | 5 | | 186 | Fantasia | 3 |
| 151 | Marvin Winans | 5 | | 187 | Freddie Jackson | 3 |
| 152 | Mary J. Blige | 5 | | 188 | Larry Graham | 3 |
| 153 | Montell Jordan | 5 | | 189 | Marvin Sapp | 3 |
| 154 | Natalie Cole* | 5 | | 190 | Morris Day | 3 |
| 155 | Nina Simone* | 5 | | 191 | Reuben Studdard | 3 |
| 156 | Rashida Jones | 5 | | 192 | Tamar Braxton | 3 |
| 157 | Ricky Minor | 5 | | 193 | Tamela Mann | 3 |
| 158 | Sheryl Lee Ralph | 5 | | 194 | Viola Davis | 3 |
| 160 | Solange Knowles | 5 | | 195 | Rebbie Jackson | 2.5 |
| 161 | Teddy Campbell | 5 | | 196 | Tracee Ellis Ross | 2.5 |
| 162 | Tim Witherspoon | 5 | | 197 | Aidina Howard | 2 |
| 163 | Yolanda Adams | 5 | | 198 | Amber Riley | 2 |
| 164 | Natalie Cole* | 5 | | 199 | D'Angelo | 2 |
| 165 | Monica Joseph-Taylor | 5 | | 200 | Kashif | 2 |
| 166 | Teyana Taylor | 5 | | 201 | Kenny Latimore | 2 |
| 167 | Jaheim | 4.5 | | 202 | LaTavia Roberson | 2 |
| 168 | Adrianne Archie | 4 | | 203 | Nathan East | 2 |
| 169 | Al B. Sure | 4 | | 204 | Raz-B | 2 |
| 170 | Christopher Williams | 4 | | 205 | Ronald Isley | 2 |
| 171 | Frankie Beverly | 4 | | 206 | Shirley Murdock | 2 |
| 172 | Jody Watley | 4 | | 207 | Stacy Lattisaw | 2 |
| 173 | Jonelle Monae | 4 | | 208 | Tevin Campbell | 2 |
| 174 | Kelis | 4 | | 209 | Tiffany Evans | 2 |
| 175 | Latoya Jackson | 4 | | 210 | Tito Jackson | 2 |
| 176 | Melanie Fiona | 4 | | 211 | George Clinton | 1.8 |
| *Figures should not be held to be completely accurate.  *RIP! | | | | | TOTAL | See IV |

# AFRICAN-AMERICAN WEALTHIEST MUSICIANS IV

| Chart IXD | | | | African American Wealthiest Musicians IV | | |
|---|---|---|---|---|---|---|
| # | NAME | $M | | # | NAME | $M |
| 212 | Chanta Moore | 1.5 | | 247 | Debra Laws | 0 |
| 213 | Miki Howard | 1.5 | | 248 | Dihann Carroll | 0 |
| 214 | Nia Peebles | 1.5 | | 249 | Donny Hathaway | 0 |
| 215 | Stephanie Mills | 1.5 | | 250 | Dorothy Dandridge* | 0 |
| 216 | Bobby Blue Bland | 1 | | 251 | Esther Phillips | 0 |
| 217 | Chrisette Michele | 1 | | 252 | Etterlene Debarge | 0 |
| 218 | Frankie Lymon* | 1 | | 253 | Gerald Albrght | 0 |
| 219 | Fred Hammond | 1 | | 254 | Glenn Jones | 0 |
| 220 | Jackie Jackson | 1 | | 255 | Goapele | 0 |
| 221 | Jermaine Jackson | 1 | | 256 | Melissa Morgan | 0 |
| 222 | Keith Sweat | 1 | | 257 | Mercedes | 0 |
| 223 | Kem | 1 | | 258 | Michel'le | 0 |
| 224 | Ledisi | 1 | | 259 | Minnie Riperton | 0 |
| 225 | Marlon Jackson | 1 | | 260 | Moses Tyson Jr. | 0 |
| 226 | Melba Moore | 1 | | 261 | Muddy Waters* | 0 |
| 227 | Shanice | 1 | | 262 | Najee | 0 |
| 228 | Slystone | 1 | | 263 | Nat King Cole* | 0 |
| 229 | T-Boz | 1 | | 264 | Roy Ayers | 0 |
| 230 | Teddy Riley | 1 | | 265 | Rufus | 0 |
| 231 | Angela Winbush | 0 | | 266 | Sam Cooke* | 0 |
| 232 | Barbara Morrison | 0 | | 267 | Tarralyn Ramsey | 0 |
| 233 | Betty Wright | 0 | | 268 | Tawatha Agee | 0 |
| 234 | Bo Diddley | 0 | | 269 | Tyrone Davis | 0 |
| 235 | Bob James | 0 | | 270 | Vanessa Armstrong | 0 |
| 236 | Bobby Caldwell | 0 | | 271 | Will Downing | 0 |
| 237 | Bobby Jones | 0 | | 272 | Whitney Houston*** | -20 |
| 238 | Brenda Russell | 0 | | 273 | | |
| 239 | Brian Culbertson | 0 | | 274 | | |
| 240 | Brian Doerksen | 0 | | 275 | | |
| 241 | Cherrelle | 0 | | 276 | | |
| 242 | Cheryl Lynn | 0 | | 277 | | |
| 243 | Curtis Mayfield | 0 | | 278 | | |
| 244 | Darwin Hobbs | 0 | | 279 | | |
| 245 | Daryl Coley | 0 | | 280 | | |
| 246 | Debra Killings | 0 | | 281 | | |
| *Figures should not be held to be completely accurate. *RIP! | | | | | TOTAL | $7.8B |

***Whitney Houston's net worth is offset by daughter, Bobby Christine; therefore, see Bobbi Kristina @ $20M.

# AFRICAN-AMERICAN WEALTHIEST *HIP HOP* ARTIST I

| Chart XA | | | | African American Wealthiest *Hip Hop* Artist I | | |
|---|---|---|---|---|---|---|
| # | NAME | $M | | # | NAME | $M |
| 1 | Dr. Dre | 810 | | 36 | Dennis Haysbert | 22 |
| 2 | Diddy | 730 | | 37 | Cee Lo Green | 22 |
| 3 | Jay-Z | 650 | | 38 | Busta Rhymes | 20 |
| 4 | Master P | 250 | | 39 | DJ Premier | 20 |
| 5 | Notorious BIG* | 160 | | 40 | Juicy J | 20 |
| 6 | Lil Wayne | 140 | | 41 | Pras Michael | 20 |
| 7 | Kanye West | 135 | | 42 | Sir Mix-a-Lot | 20 |
| 8 | Snoop Lion | 135 | | 43 | Jazze Pha | 18 |
| 9 | Ice Cube | 120 | | 44 | RZA | 18 |
| 10 | LL Cool J | 80 | | 45 | Ghostface Killah | 17 |
| 11 | Drake | 75 | | 46 | DeVyne Stephens | 16 |
| 12 | Ludacris | 75 | | 47 | Questlove | 16 |
| 13 | Will.I.Am | 75 | | 48 | Raphael Saadiq | 16 |
| 14 | Nicki Minaj | 70 | | 49 | 50 Cent | 15 |
| 15 | Rev. Run | 70 | | 50 | Chamillionaire | 15 |
| 16 | Busta Rhymes | 65 | | 51 | Chuck D | 15 |
| 17 | Nelly | 60 | | 52 | DJ Paul | 15 |
| 18 | Afeni Shakur | 50 | | 53 | GZA | 15 |
| 19 | Missy Elliot | 50 | | 54 | Pusha T | 15 |
| 20 | Queen Latifah | 50 | | 55 | Sandra Denton | 15 |
| 21 | Darryl McDaniels | 45 | | 56 | Too Short | 15 |
| 22 | TI | 40 | | 57 | Cheryl James | 14 |
| 23 | Tupac* | 40 | | 58 | Funkmaster | 14 |
| 24 | Voletta Wallace | 40 | | 59 | Inspector Deck | 14 |
| 25 | Wiz Khalifa | 36 | | 60 | Kendrick Lamar | 14 |
| 26 | Common | 35 | | 61 | Lupe Fiasco | 14 |
| 27 | Ice -T | 35 | | 62 | Mack Maine | 13 |
| 28 | T-Pain | 35 | | 63 | TechN9ne | 13 |
| 29 | Chris Lighty | 30 | | 64 | Big Sean | 12 |
| 30 | Flo Rida | 30 | | 65 | David Banner | 12 |
| 31 | Method Man | 28 | | 66 | DJ Clue | 12 |
| 32 | Rick Ross | 28 | | 67 | RaeKwon | 12 |
| 33 | SoulJa Boy | 25 | | 68 | Afrika Bambaataa | 10 |
| 34 | Palaw-da Don | 25 | | 69 | Bambaataa | 10 |
| 35 | Andre Harrell | 22 | | 70 | Benzino | 10 |
| *Figures should not be held to be completely accurate.  *RIP! | | | | | TOTAL | See III |

233

# AFRICAN-AMERICAN WEALTHIEST *HIP HOP* ARTIST II

| # | NAME | $M | | # | NAME | $M |
|---|------|-----|---|---|------|-----|
| **Chart XB** | | | | **African American Wealthiest *Hip Hop* Artist II** | | |
| 71 | Chingy | 10 | | 106 | Mike Jones | 6 |
| 72 | DJ Spinderella | 10 | | 107 | Nick Nervies | 6 |
| 73 | Jamal Edwards | 10 | | 108 | Rocky Williform | 6 |
| 74 | Jim Jones | 10 | | 109 | Trina | 6 |
| 75 | Kareem Biggs Burke | 10 | | 110 | Wale | 6 |
| 76 | Redman | 10 | | 111 | Acelfood | 5 |
| 77 | Russell Block Spencer | 10 | | 112 | Aloe Blace | 5 |
| 78 | The Dream | 10 | | 113 | Cassidy | 5 |
| 79 | Trey Songz | 10 | | 114 | Ed Lover | 5 |
| 80 | Tyga | 10 | | 115 | Fat Joe | 5 |
| 81 | Juele Santana | 9 | | 116 | Ja Rule | 5 |
| 82 | Lil Ronnie | 9 | | 117 | Kid Cudi | 5 |
| 83 | Jason Derulo | 8.5 | | 118 | Kurtis Blow | 5 |
| 84 | Camron | 8 | | 119 | Marley Marl | 5 |
| 85 | Cool and Dre | 8 | | 120 | Marques Houston | 5 |
| 86 | DJ Mustard | 8 | | 121 | Mike Will Make It | 5 |
| 87 | E-40 | 8 | | 122 | Mos Def | 5 |
| 88 | Easy E* | 8 | | 123 | Pastor Troy | 5 |
| 89 | Luther Campbell | 8 | | 124 | Phife Dawg | 5 |
| 90 | Mase | 8 | | 125 | Professor Griff | 5 |
| 91 | McLyte | 8 | | 126 | Sway Calloway | 5 |
| 92 | Obie Trice | 8 | | 127 | Tank | 5 |
| 93 | Q-Tip | 8 | | 128 | Dalvin DeGrante | 4.5 |
| 94 | Yung J | 8 | | 129 | Nipsey Hussle | 4.5 |
| 95 | Twista | 7 | | 130 | Chiddy Bang | 4 |
| 96 | Waka Flocka | 7 | | 131 | Diggy Simmons | 4 |
| 97 | 2 Chainz | 6 | | 132 | Kid Capri | 4 |
| 98 | Bobby V | 6 | | 133 | Lil Flip | 4 |
| 99 | DJ Envy | 6 | | 134 | Roscoe Dash | 4 |
| 100 | DJ Kayslay | 6 | | 135 | Sisqo | 4 |
| 101 | Dorwin Dorrough | 6 | | 136 | Talib Kweli | 4 |
| 102 | Grandmaster Flash | 6 | | 137 | Murphy Lee | 3.5 |
| 103 | KRS One | 6 | | 138 | 40 Glocc | 3 |
| 104 | Lil Mama Kirkland | 6 | | 139 | ASAP Rooky | 3 |
| 105 | Mack 10 | 6 | | 140 | Azealia Banks | 3 |
| *Figures should not be held to be completely accurate. *RIP! | | | | | **TOTAL** | See III |

234

# AFRICAN-AMERICAN WEALTHIEST *HIP HOP* ARTIST III

| Chart XC | | | | African American Wealthiest *Hip Hop* Artist III | | |
|---|---|---|---|---|---|---|
| # | NAME | $M | | # | NAME | $M |
| 141 | Flavor Flav | 3 | | 177 | Lil Twist | 2 |
| 142 | Frank Ocean | 3 | | 178 | Lord Jamar | 2 |
| 143 | Logic | 3 | | 179 | Maino | 2 |
| 144 | Mystikal | 3 | | 180 | MC Hammer | 2 |
| 145 | Phariahe Monch | 3 | | 181 | MC Shan | 2 |
| 146 | Ray J | 3 | | 182 | Melle Mel | 2 |
| 147 | Sheek Louch | 3 | | 183 | Memphis Black | 2 |
| 148 | Andre Nickatina | 2.5 | | 184 | Mick Mill | 2 |
| 149 | Biz Markie | 2.5 | | 185 | N.O.R.E | 2 |
| 150 | Lil Chuckee | 2.5 | | 186 | Nate Dogg | 2 |
| 151 | Lil Zane | 2.5 | | 187 | OJ Da Juiceman | 2 |
| 152 | Rich Dollaz | 2.5 | | 188 | Parrish Smith | 2 |
| 153 | Shawty Lo | 2.5 | | 189 | Pleasure P | 2 |
| 154 | Xzibit | 2.5 | | 190 | Rich Homie Quan | 2 |
| 155 | Anthiny Treach Criss | 2 | | 191 | Silkk the Shocker | 2 |
| 156 | BG Rapper | 2 | | 192 | Slick Rick | 2 |
| 157 | Brisco | 2 | | 193 | Slim Thug | 2 |
| 158 | Bushwick Bill | 2 | | 194 | Tone Loc | 2 |
| 160 | Charles Hamilton | 2 | | 195 | Travis Porter | 2 |
| 161 | Consequence | 2 | | 196 | Yo Gotti | 2 |
| 162 | Curren$y | 2 | | 197 | Young Noble | 2 |
| 163 | DaBrat | 2 | | 198 | Yung Berg | 2 |
| 164 | Daz Dillinger | 2 | | 199 | Joe Torrey | 1 |
| 165 | Devin the Dude | 2 | | 200 | Michael Elliot | 1 |
| 166 | Doug E. Fresh | 2 | | 201 | | |
| 167 | Dru Down | 2 | | 202 | | |
| 168 | Fetty Wrap | 2 | | 203 | | |
| 169 | Fontzworth Bentley | 2 | | 204 | | |
| 170 | Foxy Brown | 2 | | 205 | | |
| 171 | Fredro Starr | 2 | | 206 | | |
| 172 | Jae Millz | 2 | | 207 | | |
| 173 | Joe Budden | 2 | | 208 | | |
| 174 | JoJo Simmons | 2 | | 209 | | |
| 175 | Keith Murray | 2 | | 210 | | |
| 176 | Lil B | 2 | | 211 | | |
| *Figures should not be held to be completely accurate. *RIP! | | | | | TOTAL | $5.4B |

# AFRICAN-AMERICAN WEALTHIEST EXECUTIVES

| Chart XIA | | | African-American Wealthiest Executives I | | |
|---|---|---|---|---|---|
| # | NAME | $M | # | NAME | $M |
| 1 | R. Donahue Peebles | 700 | 36 | Fred Mwangaguhunga | 10 |
| 2 | Sheila Johnson | 700 | 37 | Jackie Christie | 10 |
| 3 | Janice Bryant | 620 | 38 | Jean-Michel Basquiat | 10 |
| 4 | Robert Johnson | 550 | 39 | Judge Kevin Ross | 10 |
| 5 | Quinto Primo III | 300 | 40 | Rich Paul | 10 |
| 6 | Daymond John | 250 | 41 | Rushion McDonald | 10 |
| 7 | John Thompson | 250 | 42 | Shaun Thompson | 10 |
| 8 | Herman J. Russell | 200 | 43 | Chaz Ebert | 9 |
| 9 | Ronald A. Williams | 170 | 44 | Kenneth C. Frazier | 8.3 |
| 10 | Kenneth I. Chenault | 125 | 45 | Johnnie Cochran* | 8 |
| 11 | Monica von | 100 | 46 | Lisa Nicole Cloud | 8 |
| 12 | Richard Dean Parson | 99 | 47 | Pam Veasey | 8 |
| 13 | Stanley O'Neal | 70 | 48 | Clarence Otis Jr. | 7.6 |
| 14 | Judge Joe Brown | 65 | 49 | Al Reynolds | 5 |
| 15 | Christopher Gardner | 60 | 50 | Charisse Jackson Jordan | 5 |
| 16 | Shondra Rhimes | 60 | 51 | Lance Crouther | 5 |
| 17 | Armstrong Williams | 50 | 52 | Mellody Hobson | 5 |
| 18 | Cookie Johnson | 50 | 53 | Oracene Price | 5 |
| 19 | Katherine Jackson | 50 | 54 | Shante Broadus | 5 |
| 20 | T'yanna Wallace | 50 | 55 | Tameka Raymond | 5 |
| 21 | Cynthia Stafford | 40 | 56 | Gizelle Bryant | 4 |
| 22 | Charles E. Phillips | 34 | 57 | Myron Gray | 4 |
| 23 | Dr. Ben Carson | 30 | 58 | Greg Leakes | 3.5 |
| 24 | Rosalind G. Brewer | 25 | 59 | Simone Whitmore | 3.5 |
| 25 | Al Rooker | 20 | 60 | Don Lemon | 3 |
| 26 | Camille Cosby | 20 | 61 | Jacqueline Walters | 3 |
| 27 | Daniel Simmone | 20 | 62 | Caesar Black | 2.5 |
| 28 | Donald Thompson | 20 | 63 | Kwame Jackson | 2.5 |
| 29 | Judge Greg Mathis | 20 | 64 | Christopher Darden | 2 |
| 30 | Ralo Wonder | 20 | 65 | Eugene Harris | 2 |
| 31 | Ursula M. Burns | 15.5 | 66 | Mally Roncall | 2 |
| 32 | Lynn Toler | 15 | 67 | Phaedra Parks | 2 |
| 33 | Rodney O'Neal | 14.2 | 68 | Toya Bush-Harris | 2 |
| 34 | Alec Monopoly | 12 | 69 | Walter Jackson | 2 |
| 35 | Charles Payne | 10 | 70 | Andre Leon-Talley | 1.5 |
| *Figures should not be held to be completely accurate.  *RIP! | | | | TOTAL | See II |

# AFRICAN-AMERICAN WEALTHIEST EXECUTIVES II

| Chart XIB | | | | African American Wealthiest Executives II | | |
|---|---|---|---|---|---|---|
| # | NAME | $M | | # | NAME | $M |
| 71 | Candace Smith | 1.5 | | 106 | | |
| 72 | Kim Kimble | 1.5 | | 107 | | |
| 73 | Aylwin Lewis | 1.3 | | 108 | | |
| 74 | Gregory Lunceford | 1 | | 109 | | |
| 75 | June Ambrose | 1 | | 110 | | |
| 76 | Sheree Buchanan | 1 | | 111 | | |
| 77 | | | | 112 | | |
| 78 | | | | 113 | | |
| 79 | | | | 114 | | |
| 80 | | | | 115 | | |
| 81 | | | | 116 | | |
| 82 | | | | 117 | | |
| 83 | | | | 118 | | |
| 84 | | | | 119 | | |
| 85 | | | | 120 | | |
| 86 | | | | 121 | | |
| 87 | | | | 122 | | |
| 88 | | | | 123 | | |
| 89 | | | | 124 | | |
| 90 | | | | 125 | | |
| 91 | | | | 126 | | |
| 92 | | | | 127 | | |
| 93 | | | | 128 | | |
| 94 | | | | 129 | | |
| 95 | | | | 130 | | |
| 96 | | | | 131 | | |
| 97 | | . | | 132 | | |
| 98 | | | | 133 | | |
| 99 | | | | 134 | | |
| 100 | | | | 135 | | |
| 101 | | | | 136 | | |
| 102 | | | | 137 | | |
| 103 | | | | 138 | | |
| 104 | | | | 139 | | |
| 105 | | | | 140 | | |
| *Figures should not be held to be completely accurate. *RIP! | | | | | TOTAL | $5.0B |

237

# AFRICAN-AMERICAN WEALTHIEST FILM ARTIST I

| # | NAME | $M | | # | NAME | $M |
|---|------|-----|---|---|------|-----|
| Chart XIIA | | | | African-American Wealthiest Film Artist I | | |
| 1 | Tyler Perry | 450 | | 36 | Ving Rhames | 16 |
| 2 | Bill Cosby | 400 | | 37 | Chadwick Boseman | 15 |
| 3 | Will Smith | 260 | | 38 | Cuba Gooding Jr. | 15 |
| 4 | Samuel Jackson | 170 | | 39 | Danny Glover | 15 |
| 5 | Denzel Washington | 140 | | 40 | Daphne Wayans | 15 |
| 6 | Morgan Freeman | 90 | | 41 | Forest Whitaker | 15 |
| 7 | Jamie Foxx | 85 | | 42 | Tim Story | 15 |
| 8 | Halle Berry | 70 | | 43 | Cuba Gooding Jr. | 15 |
| 9 | Wendy Williams | 60 | | 44 | Morris Chestnut | 14 |
| 10 | Phylicia Rashad | 55 | | 45 | Eriq La Salle | 14 |
| 11 | Chris Wallace Jr. | 50 | | 46 | Alfre Woodard | 13 |
| 12 | John Singleton | 50 | | 47 | Malcolm Lee | 13 |
| 13 | Nick Cannon | 50 | | 48 | Nia Long | 13 |
| 14 | James Earl Jones | 45 | | 49 | Dorien Brooks | 12 |
| 15 | Raven-Symone | 45 | | 50 | Dorien Wilson | 12 |
| 16 | Whoopi Goldberg | 45 | | 51 | Gabrielle Union | 12 |
| 17 | Spike Lee | 40 | | 52 | Idris Elba | 12 |
| 18 | Don Cheadle | 35 | | 53 | Benny Boom | 10 |
| 19 | Shaunie O'Neal | 35 | | 54 | Chi McBride | 10 |
| 20 | Laurence Fishburne | 30 | | 55 | Cicely Tyson | 10 |
| 21 | Terrence Howard | 30 | | 56 | Coko | 10 |
| 22 | Angela-Bassett | 28 | | 57 | F. Gary Gay | 10 |
| 23 | Harry Belafonte | 28 | | 58 | Jordin Sparks | 10 |
| 24 | Vanessa Williams | 27.5 | | 59 | Josie Harris | 10 |
| 25 | Eriq La Salle | 25 | | 60 | Lavan Davis | 10 |
| 26 | Sidney Poitier | 25 | | 61 | Lisa Bonet | 10 |
| 27 | Tyrese Gibson | 25 | | 62 | Lola Falana | 10 |
| 28 | Jada Pinkett-Smith | 20 | | 63 | Malcolm-Jamal | 10 |
| 29 | Malaak Rock | 20 | | 64 | Paris Barclay | 10 |
| 30 | Sammy Davis Jr.* | 20 | | 65 | Rashida Jones | 10 |
| 31 | William Packer | 20 | | 66 | Ron Glass | 10 |
| 32 | Antoine Faqua | 18 | | 67 | Stan Lathan | 10 |
| 33 | Thandie Newton | 17.5 | | 68 | Tony Todd | 10 |
| 34 | Rosario Dawson | 16 | | 69 | Wesley Snipes | 10 |
| 35 | Taye Diggs | 16 | | 70 | Datari Turner | 10 |
| *Figures should not be held to be completely accurate. *RIP! | | | | | TOTAL | See IV |

## AFRICAN-AMERICAN WEALTHIEST FILM ARTIST II

| Chart XIIB | | | | African American Wealthiest Film Artist II | | |
|---|---|---|---|---|---|---|
| # | NAME | $M | | # | NAME | $M |
| 71 | Devon Franklin | 10 | | 106 | Killer Mike | 5 |
| 72 | Roger M. Bobb | 10 | | 107 | Lee Daniels | 5 |
| 73 | Stan Lathan | 10 | | 108 | Monica Calhoun | 5 |
| 74 | Charles S. Dutton | 9 | | 109 | Peter Parros | 5 |
| 75 | Golden Brooks | 8 | | 110 | Reginald Vel Johnson | 5 |
| 76 | Jaden Smith | 8 | | 111 | Rodney Van Johnson | 5 |
| 77 | Kerry Washington | 8 | | 112 | S. Epatha Merkerson | 5 |
| 78 | Khandi Alexander | 8 | | 113 | Tichina Arnold | 5 |
| 79 | Pam Veasey | 8 | | 114 | Tyler James Williams | 5 |
| 80 | Regina King | 8 | | 115 | Yaphet Kotto | 5 |
| 81 | Tamaria Tunie | 8 | | 116 | A.J. Calloway | 4 |
| 82 | Zoe Saldana | 8 | | 117 | C.H. Pounder | 4 |
| 83 | Jerry LaMonte | 8 | | 118 | Christina Johnson | 4 |
| 84 | Billy Dee Williams | 7.5 | | 119 | Del Roy Lindo | 4 |
| 85 | Kevin Hunter | 7.5 | | 120 | Eartha Kitt | 4 |
| 86 | Harold Perrineau | 7 | | 121 | Gary Clark Jr. | 4 |
| 87 | Blair Underwood | 6 | | 122 | Gina Bythewood | 4 |
| 88 | Cassi Davis | 6 | | 123 | Henry Lennix | 4 |
| 89 | Judy Reyes | 6 | | 124 | Holly Robinson-Peete | 4 |
| 90 | Lauren London | 6 | | 125 | Jesse Williams | 4 |
| 91 | LeVar Burton | 6 | | 126 | Joe Morton | 4 |
| 92 | Meagan Good | 6 | | 127 | Larmone Morris | 4 |
| 93 | Sheree Fletcher | 6 | | 128 | Michael Dorn | 4 |
| 94 | Taraji P Henson | 6 | | 129 | Rae Dawn | 4 |
| 95 | Vivica Fox | 6 | | 130 | Rondell Sheridan | 4 |
| 96 | Garcelle Beauvais | 6 | | 131 | Rutina Wesley | 4 |
| 97 | Sheree Fletcher | 6 | | 132 | Sanaa Lathan | 4 |
| 98 | Ben Vereen | 5 | | 133 | Tamera Mowry | 4 |
| 99 | Clarence Gilyard | 5 | | 134 | Tessa Thompson | 4 |
| 100 | Essence Atkins | 5 | | 135 | Tia Mowery | 4 |
| 101 | Flex Alexander | 5 | | 136 | Tony Cox | 4 |
| 102 | George Benson | 5 | | 137 | Yvette Nicole Brown | 4 |
| 103 | Jeffery Wright | 5 | | 138 | Zoe Kravitz | 4 |
| 104 | John Ridley | 5 | | 139 | Mariah Hugh | 4 |
| 105 | Keith Powell | 5 | | 140 | Dule Hill | 3.5 |
| *Figures should not be held to be completely accurate.   *RIP! | | | | | TOTAL | See IV |

239

# AFRICAN-AMERICAN WEALTHIEST FILM ARTIST III

| Chart XIIC | | | | African American Wealthiest Film Artist III | | |
|---|---|---|---|---|---|---|
| # | NAME | $M | | # | NAME | $M |
| 141 | Petri Hawkins Byrd | 3.5 | | 177 | Torrei Hart | 3 |
| 142 | Amber Stevens | 3 | | 178 | Kim Whitley | 2.5 |
| 143 | Anika Noni Rose | 3 | | 179 | Lamman Rucker | 2.5 |
| 144 | Audrey Puente | 3 | | 180 | Laz Alonso | 2.5 |
| 145 | Ava DuVernay | 3 | | 181 | Sharin Leal | 2.5 |
| 146 | Chris Stokes | 3 | | 182 | Wesley Johnathan | 2.5 |
| 147 | Christopher Judge | 3 | | 183 | Adina Porter | 2 |
| 148 | Clifton Davis | 3 | | 184 | Ahmed Best | 2 |
| 149 | Curt Menefee | 3 | | 185 | Andre Royo | 2 |
| 150 | Debbie Allen | 3 | | 186 | Angell Conwell | 2 |
| 151 | Della Reese | 3 | | 187 | Anthony Mackie | 2 |
| 152 | Demetria McKinney | 3 | | 188 | Audra McDonald | 2 |
| 153 | James Avery | 3 | | 189 | Bianca Lawson | 2 |
| 154 | James Pickens Jr. | 3 | | 190 | Bill Nunn | 2 |
| 155 | Jascha Washington | 3 | | 191 | Bryshere Gray | 2 |
| 156 | John Amos | 3 | | 192 | Carl Lumbly | 2 |
| 157 | Lance Reddick | 3 | | 193 | Clarence Williams III | 2 |
| 158 | Leslie David Baker | 3 | | 194 | Crystal R. Fox | 2 |
| 160 | Malik Yoba | 3 | | 195 | Dennis Richmond | 2 |
| 161 | Margaret Avery | 3 | | 196 | Egypt Sherrod | 2 |
| 162 | Merrin Dungy | 3 | | 197 | Erika Alexander | 2 |
| 163 | Michael Beach | 3 | | 198 | Frankie Faison | 2 |
| 164 | Nelsan Ellis | 3 | | 199 | Gabrielle Dennis | 2 |
| 165 | Nicole Behavie | 3 | | 200 | Gene Chandler | 2 |
| 166 | Paula Patton | 3 | | 201 | Jayne Kennedy | 2 |
| 167 | Penny Johnson | 3 | | 202 | Juan Williams | 2 |
| 168 | Red Café | 3 | | 203 | K.D. Aubert | 2 |
| 169 | Roger E. Mosley | 3 | | 204 | Kadeem Hardison | 2 |
| 170 | Romany Malco | 3 | | 205 | Kellie Williams | 2 |
| 171 | Sherman Hemsley* | 3 | | 206 | Kevin Frazier | 2 |
| 172 | Stephen Bishop | 3 | | 207 | Kevin Grevioux | 2 |
| 173 | T.J. Holmes | 3 | | 208 | Kimberly Elise | 2 |
| 174 | Tanya Chisholm | 3 | | 209 | Lawrence Gillard Jr. | 2 |
| 175 | Torrei Hart | 3 | | 210 | Lil Fizz | 2 |
| 176 | Wendy Robinson | 3 | | 211 | Lisa Salters | 2 |
| *Figures should not be held to be completely accurate.  *RIP! | | | | | TOTAL | See IV |

## AFRICAN-AMERICAN WEALTHIEST FILM ARTIST IV

| Chart XIID | | | | African American Wealthiest Film Artist IV | | |
|---|---|---|---|---|---|---|
| # | NAME | $M | | # | NAME | $M |
| 212 | Mahershala Ali | 2 | | 247 | | |
| 213 | Marc John Jefferies | 2 | | 248 | | |
| 214 | Marietta Sirleaf | 2 | | 249 | | |
| 215 | Melissa Desousa | 2 | | 250 | | |
| 216 | Mia Frye | 2 | | 251 | | |
| 217 | Mike Colter | 2 | | 252 | | |
| 218 | Monique Coleman | 2 | | 253 | | |
| 219 | Monyetta Shaw | 2 | | 254 | | |
| 220 | Mykelti Williams | 2 | | 255 | | |
| 221 | Page Kennedy | 2 | | 256 | | |
| 222 | Regina Hall | 2 | | 257 | | |
| 223 | Richard Roundtree | 2 | | 258 | | |
| 224 | Rochelle Aytes | 2 | | 259 | | |
| 225 | Rockmund Dunbar | 2 | | 260 | | |
| 226 | Shari Headley | 2 | | 261 | | |
| 227 | Sharif Atkins | 2 | | 262 | | |
| 228 | Shaun Robinson | 2 | | 263 | | |
| 229 | Sonequa Martin | 2 | | 264 | | |
| 230 | Tamala Jones | 2 | | 265 | | |
| 231 | Teyonah Parris | 2 | | 266 | | |
| 232 | Tommy Sotomayer | 2 | | 267 | | |
| 233 | Vondie Curtis Hall | 2 | | 268 | | |
| 234 | Wendell Price | 2 | | 269 | | |
| 235 | Jeffre Phillips | 2 | | 270 | | |
| 236 | Ben Powers | 1.5 | | 271 | | |
| 237 | Karyn Parsons | 1.5 | | 272 | | |
| 238 | Lou Gossett Jr. | 1.5 | | 273 | | |
| 239 | Tasha Smith | 1.5 | | 274 | | |
| 240 | Bookland Tankard | 1 | | 275 | | |
| 241 | Gina Torres | 1 | | 276 | | |
| 242 | Isaiah Washington | 1 | | 277 | | |
| 243 | Kim Coles | 1 | | 278 | | |
| 244 | Tyra Ferrell | 1 | | 279 | | |
| 245 | Leslie Small | 1 | | 280 | | |
| 246 | | | | 281 | | |
| *Figures should not be held to be completely accurate. *RIP! | | | | | TOTAL | S3.6B |

241

# AFRICAN-AMERICAN WEALTHIEST COMEDIANS

| Chart XIII | | | | African American Wealthiest Comedians | | | |
|---|---|---|---|---|---|---|---|
| # | NAME | $M | | # | NAME | $M | |
| 1 | Byron Allen | 300 | | 36 | Bruce Bruce | 3 | |
| 2 | Martin Lawrence | 110 | | 37 | Orlando Jones | 3 | |
| 3 | Steve Harvey | 100 | | 38 | Tim Meadows | 3 | |
| 4 | Eddie Murphy | 85 | | 39 | Diane Thomas | 2.5 | |
| 5 | Chris Rock | 70 | | 40 | J.B. Smoove | 2.5 | |
| 6 | Keenan Ivory | 65 | | 41 | Mike Wayans | 2.5 | |
| 7 | Richard Pryor* | 40 | | 42 | Adele Givens | 2 | |
| 8 | Kevin Hart | 40 | | 43 | Deray Davis | 2 | |
| 9 | Marlon Wayans | 40 | | 44 | Jay Pharoah | 2 | |
| 10 | Shawn Wayans | 30 | | 45 | Lil Duval | 2 | |
| 11 | Tracy Morgan | 18 | | 46 | Michael Winslow | 2 | |
| 12 | Bernie Mac* | 15 | | 47 | Phill Lewis | 2 | |
| 13 | Cedric the Ent.... | 15 | | 48 | Robert Townsend | 2 | |
| 14 | Monique | 13 | | 49 | Rodney Perry | 2 | |
| 15 | Sinbad | 11 | | 50 | Sheryl Underwood | 2 | |
| 16 | George Wallace* | 10 | | 51 | Tommy Davidson | 2 | |
| 17 | Dave Chappelle | 10 | | 52 | Eddie Griffin | 1 | |
| 18 | Katt Williams | 10 | | 53 | Paul Mooney | 1 | |
| 19 | Wayne Brady | 10 | | 54 | Chris Tucker | -11 | |
| 20 | Kenan Thompson | 9 | | 55 | | | |
| 21 | Loretta Devine | 8 | | 56 | | | |
| 22 | Dick Gregory | 8 | | 57 | | | |
| 23 | Aries Spears | 8 | | 58 | | | |
| 24 | Aishe Tyler | 8 | | 59 | | | |
| 25 | Wanda Sykes | 6 | | 60 | | | |
| 26 | Mike Epps | 6 | | 61 | | | |
| 27 | H. Jon Benjamin | 6 | | 62 | | | |
| 28 | Flip Wilson* | 6 | | 63 | | | |
| 29 | Craig Robinson | 6 | | 64 | | | |
| 30 | Arsenio Hall | 5 | | 65 | | | |
| 31 | Damon Wayans | 5 | | 66 | | | |
| 32 | D.L. Hughley | 5 | | 67 | | | |
| 33 | Brandon T. Jackson | 4 | | 68 | | | |
| 34 | Tony Rock | 4 | | 69 | | | |
| 35 | Redd Foxx* | 3.5 | | 70 | | | |
| *Figures should not be held to be completely accurate. *RIP! | | | | | TOTAL | $1.1B | |

# AFRICAN AMERICAN WEALTHIEST MODELS

| CHART XIV | NAME | $M |
|---|---|---|
| 1 | Juanita Jordan | 170 |
| 2 | Tyra Banks | 90 |
| 3 | Andrea Kelly | 40 |
| 4 | Tracey Edmonds | 30 |
| 5 | Tyson Beckford | 14 |
| 6 | Nicole Murphy | 10 |
| 7 | Pilar Sanders | 10 |
| 8 | Chanel Iman | 8 |
| 9 | Jessica White | 5 |
| 10 | Shamicka Lawrence | 5 |
| 11 | Malaysia Pargo | 3.5 |
| 12 | Crystle Stewart | 3 |
| 13 | Eva Marcille | 3 |
| 14 | Nona Gaye | 3 |
| 15 | Shanigua Tompkins | 3 |
| 16 | Bria Murphy | 2.5 |
| 17 | Deshawn Snow | 2 |
| 18 | Mimi Faust | 2 |
| 19 | Royce Reed | 2 |
| 20 | Toccara Jones | 2 |
| 21 | Vanessa Blue | 2 |
| | **GRAND TOTAL** | $410,000,000 |

# AFRICAN-AMERICAN WEALTHIEST POLITICIANS

| CHART XV | NAME | $M |
|---|---|---|
| 1 | Jeh Johnson | 51.5 |
| 2 | Colin Powell | 45 |
| 3 | Willie Lewis Brown, Jr. | 26 |
| 4 | Alexis Herman | 20 |
| 5 | Roger W. Ferguson | 12.5 |
| 6 | Barack Obama | 12 |
| 7 | Jesse Jackson | 12 |
| 8 | Michelle Obama | 12 |
| 9 | Vernon Jordan | 12 |
| 10 | Franklin Delano Roosevelt | 11.6 |
| 11 | Eric Holder* | 11.5 |
| 12 | Deval Laurdine Patrick | 6 |
| 13 | William Thaddeus Coleman Jr. | 5 |
| 14 | Rodney E. Slater | 4.5 |
| 15 | Condoleezza Rice | 4 |
| 16 | Ron Brown* | 4 |
| 17 | Valerie Bowman Jarrett | 3.3 |
| 18 | Harold Eugene Ford, Jr. | 3 |
| 19 | Louis Farrakhan | 3 |
| 20 | Charles Bernard "Charlie" Rangel | 2.5 |
| 21 | Hazel R. O'Leary | 2.5 |
| 22 | Desirée Glapion Rogers | 2.1 |
| 23 | Jesse Brown | 2 |
| 24 | Togo D. West Jr. | 2 |
| 25 | Clarence Thomas | 1.8 |
| 26 | Alphonso Jackson | 1.4 |
| 27 | Loretta Lynch | 1.2 |
| 28 | Adrian Malik Fenty | 1 |
| 29 | Alexis Margaret Herman | 1 |
| 30 | Anthony Foxx | 1 |
| 31 | Anthony G. Brown | 1 |
| 32 | Bennie G. Thompson | 1 |
| 33 | David Alexander Paterson | 1 |
| 34 | John Conyers, Jr. | 1 |
| 35 | John Kenneth Blackwell | 1 |
| 36 | John King Jr. | 1 |
| 37 | Kamala Harris | 1 |
| 38 | Karen Bass | 1 |
| 39 | Kendrick Brett Meek | 1 |
| 40 | Leah D. Daughtry | 1 |
| 41 | Lisa Perez Jackson | 1 |
| 42 | Louis Wade Sullivan | 1 |
| 43 | Maxine Waters | 1 |
| 44 | Michael S. Steele | 1 |
| 45 | Mike Espy | 1 |
| 46 | Mona Sutphen | 1 |
| 47 | Patricia Roberts Harris | 1 |
| 48 | Reggie Love | 1 |
| 49 | Robert C. Weaver | 1 |
| 50 | Rod Paige | 1 |
| 51 | Roland Wallace Burris | 1 |
| 52 | Samuel Pierce | 1 |
| 53 | Thurgood Marshall | 1 |
| 54 | Yvette Diane Clarke | 1 |
| | GRAND TOTAL | $298,400,000 |

# AFRICAN-AMERICAN WEALTHIEST AUTHORS

| CHART XVI | NAME | $M |
|---|---|---|
| 1 | Terry McMillian | 40 |
| 2 | Dr. Cindy Trimn | 15 |
| 3 | Christopher Paul | 10 |
| 4 | Aaron McGruder | 10 |
| 5 | Justine Simmons | 10 |
| 6 | Bishop William Darryl | 5 |
| 7 | Jewel Tankard | 5 |
| 8 | Michael Baisden | 5 |
| 9 | Scott Tamron Hall | 5 |
| 10 | Shirley Tankard | 5 |
| 11 | Karrime Steffans | 3.5 |
| 12 | Aaron McCargo | 3 |
| 13 | Donna Brazile | 3 |
| 14 | Eric Jerome | 3 |
| 15 | Patricia Smith | 3 |
| 16 | Rolland Martin | 3 |
| 17 | Thomas Weeks | 3 |
| 18 | Tony Gaskins | 3 |
| 19 | Grady Demond Wilson | 2 |
| 20 | Judge Glenda Hatchett | 2 |
| 21 | Lisa Nichols | 2 |
| 22 | Stephanie Johnson | 2 |
| 23 | Byron Pitts | 1 |
| | **GRAND TOTAL** | $147,500,000 |

## AFRICAN-AMERICAN WEALTHIEST MEGA-CHURCH PASTORS

| CHART XVII | Mega-Church Pastoral Ministries >1,000 active members | | | | |
|---|---|---|---|---|---|
| # | NAME | MEMBERSHIP | CITY | ST | $ |
| 1 | Charles Blake | 20,000 | Los Angeles | CA | 0 |
| 2 | Cecil Murray | 19,000 | Los Angeles | CA | 0 |
| 3 | T.D. Jakes | 17,000 | Dallas | TX | 18 |
| 4 | William Sheals | 16,000 | Norcross | GA | 0 |
| 5 | Creflo Dollar | 15,000 | College Park | GA | 27 |
| 6 | I.V. Hilliard | 13,500 | Houston | TX | 0 |
| 7 | Eddie Long | 13,000 | Lithonia | GA | 5 |
| 8 | A.R. Bernard | 13,000 | New York | NY | 0 |
| 9 | Rudolph J. McKissick | 12,000 | Jacksonville | FL | 0 |
| 10 | Keith Butler | 11,000 | Southfield | MI | 0 |
| 11 | Joe Ratliff | 11,000 | Houston | TX | 0 |
| 12 | E. Dewey Smith | 11,000 | Decatur | GA | 0 |
| 13 | Byron Brazier | 10,500 | Chicago | IL | 0 |
| 14 | Noel Jones | 10.000 | Gardena | CA | 6 |
| 15 | Paul S. Morton | 10,000 | Atlanta | GA | 0 |
| 16 | Milton Dawkins | 10,000 | Memphis | TN | 0 |
| 17 | Joseph H. Walker III | 10,000 | Whites Creek | TN | 0 |
| 18 | John Hunter | 10,000 | Los Angeles | CA | 0 |
| 19 | Grainger Browning | 10,000 | Ft. Washington | MD | 0 |
| 20 | Debra Morton | 10,000 | New Orleans | LA | 0 |
| 21 | Claude Alexander | 10,000 | Charlotte | NC | 0 |
| 22 | Andro Landers | 10,000 | Jonesboro | GA | 0 |
| 23 | James T. Meeks | 9,800 | Chicago | IL | 0 |
| 24 | Vashti Murphy McKenzie | 9,250 | Baltimore | MD | 0 |
| 25 | Cecil Williams | 9,016 | San Francisco | CA | 0 |
| 26 | Tommy Curry | 9,000 | Miami | FL | 0 |
| 27 | Remus Wright | 9,000 | Houston | TX | 0 |
| 28 | Raymond Gordon | 9,000 | Williamstown | NJ | 0 |
| 29 | Jack Wallace | 9,000 | Redford | MI | 0 |
| 30 | Fredrick D. Haynes III | 9,000 | Dallas | TX | 0 |
| 31 | B.A. Gilbert | 9,000 | Redford | MI | 0 |
| 32 | Denny Davis | 8,800 | Grand Prairie | TX | 0 |
| 33 | Charles Jackson | 8,075 | West Columbia | SC | 0 |
| 34 | Charles Ellis | 8,000 | Detroit | MI | 0 |
| 35 | Rickie Rush | 8,000 | Dallas | TX | 0 |
| 36 | Kevin W. Cosby | 8,000 | Louisville | KY | 0 |
| 37 | Kenny Ulmer | 8,000 | Inglewood | CA | 0 |
| 38 | Dennis Williams | 8,000 | Greensboro | NC | 0 |
| 39 | Ricky Rush | 7,500 | Dallas | TX | 0 |
| 40 | Otis Moss | 7,500 | Chicago | IL | 0 |
| 41 | Jeremiah A. Wright Jr. | 7,500 | Chicago | IL | 0 |
| 42 | Floyd Flake | 7,500 | Jamaica | NY | 0 |
| 43 | Dale Bronner | 7,300 | East Point | GA | 0 |
| 44 | Jeffery Johnson | 7,200 | Indianapolis | IN | 0 |
| 45 | Tony Evans | 7,000 | Dallas | TX | 0 |
| 46 | Kirbyjon Caldwell | 7,000 | Houston | TX | 0 |
| 47 | Jamal Harrison Bryant | 7,000 | Baltimore | MD | 0 |
| 48 | Gilbert Johnson | 7,000 | Boston | MD | 0 |
| 49 | Darrell Jackson | 7,000 | Columbia | SC | 0 |
| 50 | Ralph Douglas West | 6,411 | Houston | TX | 0 |
| 51 | Lance Watson | 6,257 | Richmond | VA | 0 |
| 52 | William Watley | 6,000 | Atlanta | GA | 0 |
| 53 | Walter Thomas | 6,000 | Baltimore | MD | 0 |
| 54 | H.B. Charles Jr. | 6,000 | Jacksonville | FL | 0 |
| 55 | Carlton Pearson | 6,000 | Tulsa | OK | 2 |

| # | NAME | MEMBERSHIP | CITY | ST | $ |
|---|---|---|---|---|---|
| 56 | Bob Jackson | 6,000 | Oakland | CA | 0 |
| 57 | R.L. White | 5,500 | Atlanta | GA | 0 |
| 58 | J. Alfred Smith | 5,500 | Oakland | CA | 0 |
| 59 | Joseph Simmons | 5,300 | Oakland | CA | 0 |
| 60 | Thomas Weeks~ | 5,000 | Washington | DC | 3 |
| 61 | R.A. Vernon | 5,000 | Warrensville Hgts. | OH | 0 |
| 62 | Mike Freeman | 5,000 | Baltimore | MD | 0 |
| 63 | Keith Reed | 5,000 | Philadelphia | PA | 0 |
| 64 | Jerry D. Black | 5,000 | Decatur | GA | 0 |
| 65 | Frederick K.C. Price | 5,000 | Los Angeles | CA | 0 |
| 66 | Donald Hilliard Jr. | 5,000 | Perth Amboy | NJ | 0 |
| 67 | Deiman Coates | 5,000 | Clinton | MD | 0 |
| 66 | Charles Adams | 5,000 | Detroit | MI | 0 |
| 68 | William Curtis | 4,800 | Pittsburg | PA | 0 |
| 69 | Marvin Winans | 4,500 | Detroit | MI | 0 |
| 70 | Kenneth Marcus | 4,400 | Marietta | GA | 0 |
| 71 | William Flippin | 4,000 | Atlanta | GA | 0 |
| 72 | Smokie Norful | 4,000 | Bolingbrook | IL | 3 |
| 73 | Patrick Payton | 4,000 | Midland | TX | 0 |
| 74 | Mike Pender | 4,000 | Houston | TX | 0 |
| 75 | Larry Trotter | 4,000 | Chicago | IL | 0 |
| 76 | Fred Luter | 4,000 | New Orleans | LA | 0 |
| 77 | Calvin O Butts III | 4,000 | Harlem | NY | 0 |
| 78 | Ben Gilbert | 4,000 | Redford | MI | 0 |
| 80 | Claybon Lea Jr. | 3,800 | Fairfield | CA | 0 |
| 81 | Terrance Johnson | 3,700 | Houston | TX | 0 |
| 82 | Bryan Carter | 3,650 | Dallas | TX | 0 |
| 83 | Marshal Ausberry | 3,594 | Yorktown | VA | 0 |
| 84 | Norman Robinson | 3,500 | Arlington | TX | 0 |
| 85 | Michael Jones | 3,500 | St. Louis | MO | 0 |
| 86 | Marvin E. Wiley | 3,500 | Maywood | IL | 0 |
| 87 | Leroy Bailey | 3,500 | Bloomfield | CT | 0 |
| 88 | Frank Reid | 3,500 | Baltimore | MD | 0 |
| 89 | Bryan Pace | 3,500 | Phoenix | AZ | 0 |
| 90 | Alfred Owens | 3,500 | Washington | DC | 0 |
| 91 | Robert Fairley | 3,400 | San Bernardino | CA | 0 |
| 92 | Luke Torrian | 3,400 | Dumfries | VA | 0 |
| 93 | Gregg Patrick | 3,400 | Houston | TX | 0 |
| 94 | Bartholomew Orr | 3,257 | Southhaven | MS | 0 |
| 95 | James Gray | 3,200 | Hoover | AL | 0 |
| 96 | W. Darin Moore | 2,100 | Mount Vernon | NY | 0 |
| 97 | Jonathan Borders | 2,100 | Mattapan | MA | 0 |
| 98 | Fred Lowery | 2,100 | Bossier City | LA | 0 |
| 150 | Alvin Freeman | 2,100 | Atlanta | GA | 0 |
| 151 | Rudy Ramos | 2,044 | Houston | TX | 0 |
| 152 | Kenneth Blake | 2,001 | Lewisville | TX | 0 |
| 153 | Wilbert McKinley | 2,000 | Brooklyn | NY | 0 |
| 154 | Walter Richardson | 2,000 | Miami | FL | 0 |
| 155 | Walter August | 2,000 | Houston | TX | 0 |
| 156 | Wallace Smith | 2,000 | Washington | DC | 0 |
| 157 | Tony Chester | 2,000 | Dayton | OH | 0 |
| 158 | Tim White | 2,000 | Redmond | WA | 0 |
| 159 | Terry Carmichael | 2,000 | Raleigh | NC | 0 |
| 160 | Sammy Smith | 2,000 | Greensville | SC | 0 |
| 161 | Robert Fowler | 2,000 | Las Vegas | NV | 0 |
| 162 | Ralph Carter | 2,000 | Taylors | SC | 0 |
| 163 | Michael Phillips | 2,000 | Apopka | FL | 0 |
| 164 | Michael Benton | 2,000 | Lithonia | GA | 0 |

| # | NAME | MEMBERSHIP | CITY | ST | $ |
|---|---|---|---|---|---|
| 165 | Mary Minor | 2,000 | Los Angeles | CA | 0 |
| 166 | Lee Arthur Madison | 2,000 | Tacoma | WA | 0 |
| 167 | Kevin Johnson | 2,000 | Philadelphia | PA | 0 |
| 168 | Johnny Youngblood | 2,000 | Brooklyn | NY | 0 |
| 169 | Jawanza Colvin | 2,000 | Cleveland | OH | 0 |
| 170 | Jasper Williams | 2,000 | Atlanta | GA | 0 |
| 171 | James Adams | 2,000 | Memphis | TN | 0 |
| 172 | Horace Smith | 2,000 | Chicago | VA | 0 |
| 173 | Hezekiah Walker | 2,000 | Brooklyn | NY | 8 |
| 174 | Harold Carter | 2,000 | Baltimore | MD | 0 |
| 175 | Gary Simpson | 2,000 | Brooklyn | NY | 0 |
| 176 | Eric Wendel Lee | 2,000 | Conyers | GA | 0 |
| 177 | Ephraim Williams | 2,000 | Sacramento | CA | 0 |
| 178 | Edgar Vann | 2,000 | Detroit | MI | 0 |
| 179 | Douglas Brown | 2,000 | Ft. Worth | TX | 0 |
| 180 | Donnie McClurkin | 2,000 | Freeport | NY | 5 |
| 181 | Darlingston Johnson | 2,000 | Silver Spring | MD | 0 |
| 182 | Crawford Lorittts | 2,000 | Roswell | IL | 0 |
| 183 | Craig Newborn | 2,000 | Huntsville | AL | 0 |
| 184 | Clarence McClendon | 2,000 | Carson | CA | 5 |
| 185 | Clarence Glover | 2,000 | Ft. Lauderdale | FL | 0 |
| 186 | Chris Esteves | 2,000 | Rancho Cu... | CA | 0 |
| 187 | Charles Tapp | 2,000 | Tacoma Park | MD | 0 |
| 188 | C. Carl Smith | 2,000 | Pittsburg | CA | 0 |
| 189 | Al Sutton | 2,000 | Birmingham | AL | 0 |
| 190 | Adrian Brooks | 2,000 | Evansville | IN | 0 |
| 191 | A.L. Patterson | 2,000 | Houston | TX | 0 |
| 192 | Juanita Bynum~ | 2,000 | Chicago | IL | 10 |
| 193 | John P. Kee~ | 2,000 | Charlotte | NC | 0 |
| 194 | Deitrick Haddon~ | 2,000 | Los Angeles | CA | 10 |
| 195 | Al Sharpton~ | ? | New York | NY | 5 |
| 196 | Dr. Cindy Trimm | ? | Ft. Lauderdale | FL | 15 |
| | GRAND TOTAL | | | | $156M |

* See Footnotes 152 & 153.

## AFRICAN-AMERICAN WEALTHIEST MEGA-CHURCH PASTORS, by State
## (BONUS LIST)

| CHART XVIII | Mega-Church Pastoral Ministries > 1,000 active members | | | | |
|---|---|---|---|---|---|
| # | NAME | MEMBERSHIP | CITY | ST | $ |
| 1 | James Gray | 3,200 | Hoover | AL | N/A |
| 2 | Gregory Clarke | 3,000 | Birmingham | AL | N/A |
| 3 | Steve Green | 3,000 | Birmingham | AL | N/A |
| 4 | Al Sutton | 2,000 | Birmingham | AL | N/A |
| 5 | Craig Newborn | 2,000 | Huntsville | AL | N/A |
| 6 | Steve Arnold | 3,000 | Little Rock | AR | N/A |
| 7 | Bryan Pace | 3,500 | Phoenix | AZ | N/A |
| 8 | Alexis Thomas | 2,200 | Phoenix | AZ | N/A |
| 9 | Charles Blake | 20,000 | Los Angeles | CA | N/A |
| 10 | Cecil Murray | 19,000 | Los Angeles | CA | N/A |
| 11 | John Hunter | 10,000 | Los Angeles | CA | N/A |
| 12 | Noel Jones | 10.000 | Gardena | CA | N/A |
| 13 | Cecil Williams | 9,016 | San Francisco | CA | N/A |
| 14 | Kenny Ulmer | 8,000 | Inglewood | CA | N/A |
| 15 | Bob Jackson | 7,500 | Oakland | CA | N/A |
| 16 | J. Alfred Smith | 5,500 | Oakland | CA | N/A |
| 17 | Joseph Simmons | 5,300 | Oakland | CA | N/A |
| 18 | Frederick K.C. Price | 5,000 | Los Angeles | CA | N/A |
| 19 | Claybon Lea Jr. | 3,800 | Fairfield | CA | N/A |
| 20 | Robert Fairley | 3,400 | San Bernardino | CA | N/A |
| 21 | Wayne Chaney | 3,000 | Long Beach | CA | N/A |
| 22 | C. Carl Smith | 2,000 | Pittsburg | CA | N/A |
| 23 | Chris Esteves | 2,000 | Rancho Cu | CA | N/A |
| 24 | Clarence McClendon | 2,000 | Carson | CA | N/A |
| 25 | Ephraim Williams | 2,000 | Sacramento | CA | N/A |
| 26 | Mary Minor | 2,000 | Los Angeles | CA | N/A |
| 27 | Timothy Winters | 1,800 | San Diego | CA | N/A |
| 28 | Ticey Brown | 1,200 | Los Angeles | CA | N/A |
| 29 | Melvin Wade | 1,000 | Los Angeles | CA | N/A |
| 30 | R.A. Williams Jr. | 1,000 | Los Angeles | CA | N/A |
| 31 | Deitrick Haddon~ | 1,000 | Los Angeles | CA | N/A |
| 32 | Leroy Bailey | 3,500 | Bloomfield | CT | N/A |
| 33 | Thomas Weeks~ | 5,000 | Washington | DC | N/A |
| 34 | Alfred Owens | 3,500 | Washington | DC | N/A |
| 35 | Wallace Smith | 2,000 | Washington | DC | N/A |
| 36 | Rudolph J. McKissick | 12,000 | Jacksonville | FL | N/A |
| 37 | Tommy Curry | 9,000 | Miami | FL | N/A |
| 38 | H.B. Charles Jr. | 6,000 | Jacksonville | FL | N/A |
| 39 | Marcus Davidson | 3,000 | Ft. Lauderdale | FL | N/A |
| 40 | Vaughn McLaughlin | 3,000 | Jacksonville | FL | N/A |
| 41 | Ronald Kimble | 2,500 | Eatonville | FL | N/A |
| 42 | George Davis | 2,200 | Jacksonville | FL | N/A |
| 43 | Randolf Bracy | 2,200 | Orlando | FL | N/A |
| 44 | Clarence Glover | 2,000 | Ft. Lauderdale | FL | N/A |
| 45 | Michael Phillips | 2,000 | Apopka | FL | N/A |
| 46 | Walter Richardson | 2,000 | Miami | FL | N/A |
| 47 | Dr. Cindy Trimm | xxxx | Ft. Lauderdale | FL | N/A |
| 48 | William Sheals | 16,000 | Norcross | GA | N/A |
| 49 | Creflo Dollar | 15,000 | College Park | GA | N/A |
| 50 | Eddie Long | 13,000 | Lithonia | GA | N/A |
| 51 | E. Dewey Smith | 11,000 | Decatur | GA | N/A |
| 52 | Andro Landers | 10,000 | Jonesboro | GA | N/A |
| 53 | Paul S. Morton | 10,000 | Atlanta | GA | N/A |

| # | NAME | MEMBERSHIP | CITY | ST | $ |
|---|------|-----------|------|-----|---|
| 54 | Dale Bronner | 7,300 | East Point | GA | N/A |
| 55 | William Watley | 6,000 | Atlanta | GA | N/A |
| 56 | R.L. White | 5,500 | Atlanta | GA | N/A |
| 57 | Jerry D. Black | 5,000 | Decatur | GA | N/A |
| 58 | Kenneth Marcus | 4,400 | Marietta | GA | N/A |
| 59 | William Flippin | 4,000 | Atlanta | GA | N/A |
| 60 | Alvin Freeman | 2,100 | Atlanta | GA | N/A |
| 61 | Eric Wendel Lee | 2,000 | Conyers | GA | N/A |
| 62 | Jasper Williams | 2,000 | Atlanta | GA | N/A |
| 63 | Michael Benton | 2,000 | Lithonia | GA | N/A |
| 64 | Marvin Moss | 1,800 | Atlanta | GA | N/A |
| 65 | Richard Haynes | 1,800 | Lilburn | GA | N/A |
| 66 | Tyrone Barnett | 1,800 | Decatur | GA | N/A |
| 67 | Byron Brazier | 10,500 | Chicago | IL | N/A |
| 68 | James Meeks | 9,800 | Chicago | IL | N/A |
| 69 | Jeremiah A. Wright Jr. | 7,500 | Chicago | IL | N/A |
| 70 | Otis Moss | 7,500 | Chicago | IL | N/A |
| 71 | Larry Trotter | 4,000 | Chicago | IL | N/A |
| 72 | Smokie Norful | 4,000 | Bolingbrook | IL | N/A |
| 73 | Marvin E. Wiley | 3,500 | Maywood | IL | N/A |
| 74 | Charles Jenkins | 3,100 | Chicago | IL | N/A |
| 75 | John Hannah | 3,000 | Chicago | IL | N/A |
| 76 | Jerry Doss | 2,900 | Springfield | IL | N/A |
| 77 | Marvin Parker | 2,500 | Broadview | IL | N/A |
| 78 | Donald Parsons | 2,200 | Chicago | IL | N/A |
| 80 | Crawford Lorittts | 2,000 | Roswell | IL | N/A |
| 81 | Juanita Bynum~ | 1,000 | Chicago | IL | N/A |
| 82 | Jeffery Johnson | 7,200 | Indianapolis | IN | N/A |
| 83 | Adrian Brooks | 2,000 | Evansville | IN | N/A |
| 84 | Kevin W. Cosby | 8,000 | Louisville | KY | N/A |
| 85 | Walter Malone | 2,500 | Louisville | KY | N/A |
| 86 | Debra Morton | 10,000 | New Orleans | LA | N/A |
| 87 | Fred Luter | 4,000 | New Orleans | LA | N/A |
| 88 | Fred Lowery | 2,100 | Bossier City | LA | N/A |
| 89 | Jonathan Borders | 2,100 | Mattapan | MA | N/A |
| 90 | Grainger Browning | 10,000 | Ft. Washington | MD | N/A |
| 91 | Vashti Murphy McKenzie | 9,250 | Baltimore | MD | N/A |
| 92 | Gilbert Johnson | 7,000 | Boston | MD | N/A |
| 93 | Jamal Harrison Bryant | 7,000 | Baltimore | MD | N/A |
| 94 | Walter Thomas | 6,000 | Baltimore | MD | N/A |
| 95 | Deiman Coates | 5,000 | Clinton | MD | N/A |
| 96 | Mike Freeman | 5,000 | Baltimore | MD | N/A |
| 97 | Frank Reid | 3,500 | Baltimore | MD | N/A |
| 98 | Donte' Hickman | 2,500 | Baltimore | MD | N/A |
| 99 | Jerome Stokes | 2,500 | Baltimore | MD | N/A |
| 100 | Oscar Brown | 2,500 | Randallstown | MD | N/A |
| 101 | Charles Tapp | 2,000 | Tacoma Park | MD | N/A |
| 102 | Darlingston Johnson | 2,000 | Silver Spring | MD | N/A |
| 103 | Harold Carter | 2,000 | Baltimore | MD | N/A |
| 104 | Charles Ellis | 8,0000 | Detroit | MI | N/A |
| 105 | Keith Butler | 11,000 | Southfield | MI | N/A |
| 106 | B.A. Gilbert | 9,000 | Redford | MI | N/A |
| 107 | Jack Wallace | 9,000 | Redford | MI | N/A |
| 108 | Charles Adams | 5,000 | Detroit | MI | N/A |
| 109 | Marvin Winans | 4,500 | Detroit | MI | N/A |
| 110 | Ben Gilbert | 4,000 | Redford | MI | N/A |
| 111 | Edgar Vann | 2,000 | Detroit | MI | N/A |
| 112 | Michael Jones | 3,500 | St. Louis | MO | N/A |

| # | NAME | MEMBERSHIP | CITY | ST | $ |
|---|------|-----------|------|-----|-----|
| 113 | Bartholomew Orr | 3,257 | Southhaven | MS | N/A |
| 114 | Claude Alexander | 10,000 | Charlotte | NC | N/A |
| 115 | Dennis Williams | 8,000 | Greensboro | NC | N/A |
| 116 | George Brooks | 2,800 | Greensboro | NC | N/A |
| 117 | Clifford Jones | 2,700 | Charlotte | NC | N/A |
| 118 | Terry Carmichael | 2,000 | Raleigh | NC | N/A |
| 119 | John P. Kee~ | 1,000 | Charlotte | NC | N/A |
| 120 | Raymond Gordon | 9,000 | Williamstown | NJ | N/A |
| 121 | Deforest Soaries | 6,000 | Somerset | NJ | N/A |
| 122 | Donald Hilliard Jr. | 5,000 | Perth Amboy | NJ | N/A |
| 123 | David Jefferson | 2,500 | Newark | NJ | N/A |
| 124 | Dharius Daniels | 2,500 | Ewing | NJ | N/A |
| 125 | Jerry Carter | 1,800 | Morristown | NJ | N/A |
| 126 | Chris McRae | 1,800 | Las Cruces | NM | N/A |
| 127 | Robert Fowler | 2,000 | Las Vegas | NV | N/A |
| 128 | A.R. Bernard | 13,000 | New York | NY | N/A |
| 129 | Floyd Flake | 7,500 | Jamaica | NY | N/A |
| 130 | Calvin O Butts III | 4,000 | Harlem | NY | N/A |
| 131 | Wyatt Walker | 3,000 | New York | NY | N/A |
| 132 | David Cousins | 2,500 | Brooklyn | NY | N/A |
| 133 | Anthony Trufant | 2,200 | Brooklyn | NY | N/A |
| 134 | W. Darin Moore | 2,100 | Mount Vernon | NY | N/A |
| 135 | Donnie McClurkin | 2,000 | Freeport | NY | N/A |
| 136 | Gary Simpson | 2,000 | Brooklyn | NY | N/A |
| 137 | Hezekiah Walker | 2,000 | Brooklyn | NY | N/A |
| 138 | Johnny Youngblood | 2,000 | Brooklyn | NY | N/A |
| 139 | Wilbert McKinley | 2,000 | Brooklyn | NY | N/A |
| 140 | David Hampton | 1,800 | Brooklyn | NY | N/A |
| 141 | Al Sharpton~ | 0 | New York | NY | N/A |
| 142 | R.A. Vernon | 5,000 | Warrensville Hgts. | OH | N/A |
| 143 | Elliot Cuff | 3,200 | Cincinnati | OH | N/A |
| 144 | Larry Macon | 3,000 | Oakwood Village | OH | N/A |
| 145 | Isiah Joshua | 2,500 | Dayton | OH | N/A |
| 146 | Jawanza Colvin | 2,000 | Cleveland | OH | N/A |
| 147 | Tony Chester | 2,000 | Dayton | OH | N/A |
| 148 | Carlton Pearson | 6,000 | Tulsa | OK | N/A |
| 149 | Keith Reed | 5,000 | Philadelphia | PA | N/A |
| 150 | William Curtis | 4,800 | Pittsburg | PA | N/A |
| 151 | Willie Richardson | 2,500 | Philadelphia | PA | N/A |
| 152 | Philip Davis | 2,300 | Easton | PA | N/A |
| 153 | Kevin Johnson | 2,000 | Philadelphia | PA | N/A |
| 154 | Charles Jackson | 8,075 | West Columbia | SC | N/A |
| 155 | Darrell Jackson | 7,000 | Columbia | SC | N/A |
| 156 | Eric Davis | 2,200 | Columbia | SC | N/A |
| 157 | Conrad Brown | 2,166 | Mt. Pleasant | SC | N/A |
| 158 | Ralph Carter | 2,000 | Taylors | SC | N/A |
| 159 | Sammy Smith | 2,000 | Greensville | SC | N/A |
| 160 | Joseph H. Walker III | 10,000 | Whites Creek | TN | N/A |
| 161 | Milton Dawkins | 10,000 | Memphis | TN | N/A |
| 162 | Frank Ray Sr. | 3,150 | Memphis | TN | N/A |
| 163 | Patrick Hood | 3,100 | Smyrna | TN | N/A |
| 164 | James Netters | 3,000 | Memphis | TN | N/A |
| 165 | William Owens | 2,500 | Chattanooga | TN | N/A |
| 166 | James Adams | 2,000 | Memphis | TN | N/A |
| 167 | Ron Philips | 1,750 | Hixson | TN | N/A |
| 168 | T.D. Jakes~ | 17,000 | Dallas | TX | N/A |
| 169 | I.V. Hilliard | 13,500 | Houston | TX | N/A |
| 170 | Joe Ratliff | 11,000 | Houston | TX | N/A |

| # | NAME | MEMBERSHIP | CITY | ST | $ |
|---|------|-----------|------|----|----|
| 171 | Fredrick D. Haynes III | 9,000 | Dallas | TX | N/A |
| 172 | Remus Wright | 9,000 | Houston | TX | N/A |
| 173 | Denny Davis | 8,800 | Grand Prairie | TX | N/A |
| 174 | Rickie Rush | 8,000 | Dallas | TX | N/A |
| 175 | Ricky Rush | 7,500 | Dallas | TX | N/A |
| 176 | Kirbyjon Caldwell | 7,000 | Houston | TX | N/A |
| 177 | Tony Evans | 7,000 | Dallas | TX | N/A |
| 178 | Ralph Douglas West | 6,411 | Houston | TX | N/A |
| 179 | Mike Pender | 4,000 | Houston | TX | N/A |
| 180 | Patrick Payton | 4,000 | Midland | TX | N/A |
| 181 | Terrance Johnson | 3,700 | Houston | TX | N/A |
| 182 | Bryan Carter | 3,650 | Dallas | TX | N/A |
| 183 | Norman Robinson | 3,500 | Arlington | TX | N/A |
| 184 | Gregg Patrick | 3,400 | Houston | TX | N/A |
| 185 | C.B.T. Smith | 3,000 | Dallas | TX | N/A |
| 186 | Gregory Foster | 3,000 | Richardson | TX | N/A |
| 187 | Alexander Kennedy | 2,800 | Katy | TX | N/A |
| 188 | Walter August Jr. | 2,700 | Houston | TX | N/A |
| 189 | Reginald DeVaughn | 2,675 | Pearland | TX | N/A |
| 190 | Anthony Murray | 2,500 | Dallas | TX | N/A |
| 191 | Curtis Wallace | 2,500 | Dallas | TX | N/A |
| 192 | Paul D. Landrew | 2,500 | Houston | TX | N/A |
| 193 | T.R. Williams | 2,500 | Houston | TX | N/A |
| 194 | Donald Burgs Jr. | 2,406 | Houston | TX | N/A |
| 195 | A.W. Mays | 2,200 | Austin | TX | N/A |
| 196 | Rudy Ramos | 2,044 | Houston | TX | N/A |
| 197 | Kenneth Blake | 2,001 | Lewisville | TX | N/A |
| 198 | A.L. Patterson | 2,000 | Houston | TX | N/A |
| 199 | Douglas Brown | 2,000 | Ft. Worth | TX | N/A |
| 200 | Walter August | 2,000 | Houston | TX | N/A |
| 201 | Terry Anderson | 1,900 | Houston | TX | N/A |
| 202 | Gaylon Clark | 1,800 | Austin | TX | N/A |
| 203 | Gene Moore | 1,800 | Houston | TX | N/A |
| 204 | Lance Watson | 6,257 | Richmond | VA | N/A |
| 205 | Marshal Ausberry | 3,594 | Yorktown | VA | N/A |
| 206 | Luke Torrian | 3,400 | Dumfries | VA | N/A |
| 207 | Howard-John Wesley | 2,800 | Alexandria | VA | N/A |
| 208 | William Darryl Scott | 2,500 | Tacoma | VA | N/A |
| 209 | Melvin Marriner | 2,363 | Redmond | VA | N/A |
| 210 | Horace Smith | 2,000 | Seattle | VA | N/A |
| 211 | Lee Arthur Madison | 2,000 | | WA | N/A |
| 212 | Tim White | 2,000 | | WA | N/A |
| 213 | Robert Manaway | 1,800 | | WA | N/A |
| | GRAND TOTAL | 1,028,675 | | | $156M |

```
1) Texas - 38
2) California - 23
3) Georgia - 18
4) Illinois - 14
5) Maryland - 13
6) New York - 13
7) Florida - 10
8) Michigan - 7
9) Tennessee - 7
10) New Jersey - 6
11) South Carolina - 6
12) Alabama - 5
13) North Carolina - 5
14) Ohio - 5
```

```
                          15) Virginia - 5
                          16) DC - 3
                          17) Washington - 3
                          18) Arizona - 2
                          19) Indiana - 2
                          20) Kentucky - 2
                          21) Louisiana - 2
                          22) Connecticut - 1
                          22) Massachusetts - 1
                          23) Missouri - 1
                          24) Mississippi - 1
                          25) New Mexico - 1
                          26) Nevada -1
                          27) Oklahoma - 1
                    Total Mega-Church Combined Membership(s) =
                    1,028,675
                              New York - 226,457
                              Texas - 170,787
                              California - 129,026
                              Georgia - 120,700
                              Illinois - 73,300
                              Maryland - 68,350
```

152  153

[152] "Mega-Church Statistics." Statistic Brain. http://www.statisticbrain.com/mega-church-statistics/ (accessed 2016).
[153] "Database of Mega-churches in the U.S." Hartford Seminary. http://hirr.hartsem.edu/cgi-bin/mega/db.pl?db=default&uid=default&view_records=1&ID=*&sb=5 (accessed 2000-2006).

## TOP 39 AFRICAN-AMERICAN WEALTHIEST INDIVIDUALS

| CHART XIX | TOP 39 AFRICAN-AMERICAN WEALTHIEST INDIVIDUALS (.0001% or 1/10,000) | |
|---|---|---|
| # | NAME | NET WORTH |
| 1 | Oprah Winfrey | $3,200,000,000.00 |
| 2 | Michael Jordan | $1,200,000,000.00 |
| 3 | Andre Young (Dr. Dre) | $810,000,000.00 |
| 4 | Sean Combs (Diddy) | $730,000,000.00 |
| 5 | R. Donahue Pebbles | $700,000,000.00 |
| 6 | Sheila Johnson | $700,000,000.00 |
| 7 | Tiger Woods | $700,000,000.00 |
| 8 | Shawn Carter (Jay-Z) | $650,000,000.00 |
| 9 | Janice Bryant Howroyd | $610,000,000.00 |
| 10 | Michael Jackson | $600,000,000.00 |
| 11 | Robert Johnson | $550,000,000.00 |
| 12 | Mariah Carey | $520,000,000.00 |
| 13 | Earvin Johnson | $500,000,000.00 |
| 14 | Beyonce Knowles | $450,000,000.00 |
| 15 | Tyler Perry | $450,000,000.00 |
| 16 | Bill Cosby | $400,000,000.00 |
| 17 | Floyd Mayweather | $400,000,000.00 |
| 18 | Ulysses Bridgeman Jr. | $400,000,000.00 |
| 19 | Shaquille O'Neal | $350,000,000.00 |
| 20 | Berry Gordy | $345,000,000.00 |
| 21 | Russell Simmons | $340,000,000.00 |
| 22 | Kobe Bryant | $320,000,000.00 |
| 23 | Quincy Jones | $310,000,000.00 |
| 24 | LeBron James | $300,000,000.00 |
| 25 | Prince | $300,000,000.00 |
| 26 | Quintin Primo III | $300,000,000.00 |
| 27 | Alex Rodriguez | $300,000,000.00 |
| 28 | Byron Allen | $300,000,000.00 |
| 29 | Will Smith | $260,000,000.00 |
| 30 | Dianna Ross | $250,000,000.00 |
| 31 | George Foreman | $250,000,000.00 |
| 32 | Percy Miller (Master-P) | $250,000,000.00 |
| 33 | Tina Turner | $250,000,000.00 |
| 34 | Daymond John | $250,000,000.00 |
| 35 | John Thompson | $250,000,000.00 |
| 36 | Herman J. Russell | $200,000,000.00 |
| 37 | Lionel Richie | $200,000,000.00 |
| 38 | Denzel Washington | $190,000,000.00 |
| 39 | Kevin Garnett | $190,000,000.00 |
| | GRAND TOTAL | $19,275,000,000.00 |

# TOTAL AFRICAN-AMERICAN CELEBRITY WEALTH

| Chart XX | TOTAL AFRICAN-AMERICAN CELEBRITY WEALTH | $$$ |
|---|---|---|
| 1 | Chart 8: African-American Wealthiest in Athletes, #1, (947 surveyed) | $21B |
| 2 | **African-American Musical Industry, #2,** (470 surveyed) | -$13.1B |
| 3 | Chart 9: African-American Wealthiest in Musicians, #2a, (272 surveyed) | $7.8B |
| 4 | Chart 10: African-American Wealthiest *Hip Hop* Artist, #2b, (198 surveyed) | $5.4B |
| 5 | Chart 11: African-American Wealthiest Executives, #3, (75 surveyed) | $5.0B |
| 6 | Combined Riches of Queen & King of African-American Wealth, *Winfrey & Jordan* (Their combined personal wealth exceeds 4 of 9 total African-American industries, more than 1/2). | **$4.3B** |
| 7 | Chart 12: African-American Wealthiest Film Artist, #4, (245 surveyed) | $3.6B |
| 8 | Queen of African-American Wealth: *Oprah Winfrey* (In a class alone, Oprah's personal wealth exceeds 5 of 9 total cultural industries, 3X the "King of Wealth"). | **$3.2B** |
| 9 | King of African-American Wealth: *Michael Jordan* (In a class alone, Jordan's personal single wealth exceeds 5 of 9 total cultural industries). | **$1.2B** |
| 10 | Chart 13: African-American Wealthiest Comedians, #5, (54 surveyed) | $1.1B |
| 11 | Chart 14: African-American Wealthiest Models, #6, (21 surveyed) | $410M |
| 12 | Chart 15: African-American Wealthiest in Politicians, #7, (53 surveyed) | $298.4M |
| 13 | Chart 17: African-American Wealthiest Pastors, #9, (212 surveyed) | $156M |
| 14 | Chart 16: African-American Wealthiest Authors, #8, (21 surveyed) | $147.5M |
| 15 | TOTAL (2,099 surveyed, Charts #8 – Charts #17) | **$45B** |
| 18 | Chart 19: TOP 39 **AFRICAN-AMERICAN** WEALTHIEST INDIVIDUALS (.0001% or 1/100%) | $19.3B |
| 19 | Chart 21: TOP 39 WEALTHIEST **AMERICANS** INDIVIDUALS (.00001% or 1/1000%) (The **WEALTHIEST** 39 general Americans literally make up ½ of the **TOTAL** African-American net worth). | $1.0T |
| 20 | TOTAL AFRICAN-AMERICAN NET WORTH | **$2.0T** |

## FORBES TOP 39 WEALTHIEST AMERICANS

| CHART XXI | FORBES TOP 39 WEALTHIEST AMERICANS | |
|---|---|---|
| 1 | Bill Gates | $76,100,000,000.00 |
| 2 | Warren Buffet | $62,000,000,000.00 |
| 3 | Larry Ellsion | $47,500,000,000.00 |
| 4 | Jeff Bezos | $47,000,000,000.00 |
| 5 | Charles Koch | $41,000,000,000.00 |
| 6 | David Koch | $41,000,000,000.00 |
| 7 | Mark Zuckerberg | $40,300,000,000.00 |
| 8 | Michael Bloomberg | $38,600,000,000.00 |
| 9 | Jim Walton | $33,700,000,000.00 |
| 10 | Larry Page | $33,300,000,000.00 |
| 11 | Sergey Brin | $32,600,000,000.00 |
| 12 | Alice Walton | $32,000,000,000.00 |
| 13 | S. Robson Walton | $31,700,000,000.00 |
| 14 | Christy Walton | $30,200,000,000.00 |
| 15 | Sheldon Adelson | $26,000,000,000.00 |
| 16 | George Soros | $24,500,000,000.00 |
| 17 | Phil Knight | $24,400,000,000.00 |
| 18 | Forest Mars Jr. | $23,400,000,000.00 |
| 19 | Jacqueline Mars | $23,400,000,000.00 |
| 20 | John Mars | $23,400,000,000.00 |
| 21 | Steve Balmer | $21,600,000,000.00 |
| 22 | Carl Icahn | $20,500,000,000.00 |
| 23 | Michael Dell | $19,100,000,000.00 |
| 24 | Laurene Powell Jobs | $19,100,000,000.00 |
| 25 | Alex Cox Chambers | $18,000,000,000.00 |
| 26 | Paul Allen | $17,800,000,000.00 |
| 27 | Len Blavatnik | $17,700,000,000.00 |
| 28 | Charles Ergen | $16,400,000,000.00 |
| 29 | Ray Dalio | $15,300,000,000.00 |
| 30 | Ronald Bren | $15,200,000,000.00 |
| 31 | Abigail Johnson | $14,200,000,000.00 |
| 32 | James Simons | $14,000,000,000.00 |
| 33 | Thomas Peterffy | $13,500,000,000.00 |
| 34 | Elon Musk | $13,300,000,000.00 |
| 35 | Patrick Soon-Shiong | $12,900,000,000.00 |
| 36 | Ronald Perelman | $12,500,000,000.00 |
| 37 | Steve Cohen | $12,000,000,000.00 |
| 38 | Robert Murdoch | $11,600,000,000.00 |
| 39 | Stephen Schwarzman | $11,600,000,000.00 |
| | **GRAND TOTAL** | **$1,028,400,000,000.00** |

154

---

[154] "Forbes 400." Forbes Magazine. http://www.forbes.com/forbes-400/list/#version:static (accessed 2016).

## GDP & GDP/DEBT RATIO BY COUNTRY

| CHART XXII | INTERNATIONAL MONETARY FUND | | | | |
|---|---|---|---|---|---|
| COUNTRY | RANK BY $ | DATE | GDP/DEBT % | GDP | CONTINENT |
| European Union | 0 | 2011 | 87% | $18.5t | Europe |
| United States | 1 | 2012 est. | 104% | $17.3t | North America |
| China | 2 | 2011 | 41% | $10.3t | Asia |
| Japan | 3 | 2011 est. | 229% | $4.6t | Asia |
| Germany | 4 | 2011 | 71% | $3.8t | Europe |
| United Kingdom | 5 | 2012 | 88% | $2.9t | Europe |
| France | 6 | 2011 | 95% | $2.9t | Europe |
| Italy | 8 | 2011 | 132% | $2.1t | Europe |
| Russia | 10 | 2011 est. | 17% | $1.8t | Asia/Europe |
| Canada | 11 | 2011 est. | 86% | $1.7t | North America |
| South Korea | 13 | 2011 est. | 35% | $1.4t | Asia |
| Spain | 14 | 2011 | 100% | $1.4t | Europe |
| Mexico | 15 | 2011 est. | 30% | $1.2t | North America |
| Switzerland | 20 | 2010 est. | 34% | $703b | Europe |
| South Africa | 33 | 2011 est. | 50% | $350b | Africa |
| Denmark | 34 | 2011 | 39% | $342b | Europe |
| Hong Kong | 37 | 2011 est. | 32% | $290b | Asia |
| Greece | 44 | 2011 est. | 179% | $237b | Europe |
| Cuba | 63 | 2011 est. | 17% | $78b | Asia |
| North Korea | 115 | 2007 est. | X% | $15b | Asia |

155 156 157

[155] "Country List Government Debt to GDP." Trading Economics.
http://www.tradingeconomics.com/country-list/government-debt-to-gdp (accessed 2016).
[156] "World Economic Outlook Database, October 2015." International Monetary Fund (IMF).
https://www.imf.org/external/pubs/ft/weo/2015/02/weodata/download.aspx (accessed 2016).
[157] "U.S. Debt Clock." United States Debt Clock. http://www.usdebtclock.org (accessed 2016).

"50 Cent Buries Hatchet With Mayweather "He's My Brother." TMZ. http://www.tmz.com/2015/04/23/50-cent-buries-the-hatchet-with-mayweather/ (accessed April 23, 2015).

"#569 Oprah Winfrey." Forbes. http://www.forbes.com/profile/oprah-winfrey/ (accessed April 7, 2016).

"African American Chairman & CEO's of Fortune 500 Companies." Black Profiles. http://www.blackentrepreneurprofile.com/fortune-500-ceos/ (accessed: January, 29, 2015).

Alchin, Linda. "Jim Crow Laws." Americana Historama. http://www.american-historama.org/1866-1881-reconstruction-era/jim-crow-laws.htm (accessed April 2016).

Alexander, Brian. "Jackson's Death: How Dangerous Is Propofol?" Time Magazine. http://content.time.com/time/arts/article/0,8599,1918363,00.html (accessed August 25, 2009).

"An Overview of the Governor's 1993-94 Budget." California's Legislative Analyst Office: Budget Brief. http://www.lao.ca.gov/1993/Overview_Gov_Budget_170_0193.pdf (accessed January 1993).

Barnes, Matt. Capitalism: *The Worst Economic System, Except for All The Others*. University of Pittsburg: The Pitt News. http://pittnews.com/article/5424/opinions/capitalism-the-worst-economic-system-except-for-all-the-others/ (accessed August 26, 2014).

"Biggest Athlete Endorsement Deals In Sports History." Total Sportek. http://www.totalsportek.com/money/biggest-endorsement-deals-sports-history/ (accessed January 27, 2016).

Bilbray, James, "Quote from James Bilbray." Liberty Tree. http://quotes.liberty-tree.ca/quote/james_bilbray_quote_6fe2 (accessed 2016).

Billinghurst, David. "Richard Wolff and Cornel West Talking About What's Wrong With Capitalism." You Tube. https://www.youtube.com/watch?v=gEOYVA0R1Tc (accessed July 28, 2015).

"Black America: Waking Life." The Economist. http://www.economist.com/news/briefing/21584003-his-i-have-dream-speech-martin-luther-king-threw-out-challenge-america-how-has-it (accessed August 24, 2013).

"Boomerang (1992) Movie Script." Springfield.
http://www.springfieldspringfield.co.uk/movie_script.php?movie
=boomerang (Accessed 1992).

Broder, Ken. "Record Number of Prison Lifers Released, but Few
Return." All Gov California.
http://www.allgov.com/usa/ca/news/top-stories/record-number-
of-prison-lifers-released-but-few-return-141230?news=855226
(accessed December 30, 2014).

Breunig, Matt. "The Racial Wealth Gap." The American Prospect.
http://prospect.org/article/racial-wealth-gap (accessed November
6, 2013).

Broder, John M. and Madigan, Nick. "Michael Jackson Cleared After 14
Week Child Molesting Trial." NY Times.
http://www.nytimes.com/2005/06/14/us/michael-jackson-
cleared-after-14week-child-molesting-trial.html?_r=0 (accessed
June 14, 2005).

Buckley, Cara. "Dr. Cornel West: Reviews, Heeding The Call, The
Places He Goes." Dr. Cornel West.
http://www.cornelwest.com/reviews.html#.Vxb2o6tX_zI
(Accessed January 22, 2010).

"CFR Backgrounders" Council on Foreign Relations.
http://www.cfr.org/financial-crises/credit-rating-
controversy/p22328 (accessed 2016).

Christensen, Jen. "Besting Ruth, Beating Hate, How Hank Aaron Made
Baseball History." CNN.
http://www.cnn.com/interactive/2014/04/us/hank-aaron-
anniversary/ (accessed April 2014).

Clymer, Adam. "When Presidential Words Led To Swift Actions." The
New York Times.
http://www.nytimes.com/2013/06/09/us/remembering-two-
seminal-kennedy-speeches.html?pagewanted=all&_r=0
(accessed June 8, 2013).

Colby C. "New Reality Show Spotlights Kids of Hip Hop Greats."
Uptown. http://uptownmagazine.com/2015/07/meet-cast-
growing-up-hip-hop/ (accessed July 8, 2015).

Colby, Sandra L. and Ortman, Jennifer M. "The Baby Boom Cohort in
the United States: 2012 to 2060: Population Estimates and
Projections, Table 1." U.S. Census Bureau. (Accessed May
2014) 11.

Collins, Chuck. "Wealth of 400 Billionaires = Wealth of All 41 Million African-Americans." Inequality. http://inequality.org/wealth-400-billionaires-wealth-41-million-africanamericans/ (accessed January 17, 2014).

Cone, James. *A Black Theology of Liberation.* Maryknoll, NY: Orbis Books, 1970.

Cooper, Alexia and Smith, Erica L. "Homicide Trends in the United States, 1980-2008: Annual Rates for 2009 and 2010." U.S. Department of Justice: Office of Justice Programs: Bureau of Justice Statistics. http://bjs.gov/content/pub/pdf/htus8008.pdf (accessed November 2011).

"Country List Government Debt to GDP." Trading Economics. http://www.tradingeconomics.com/country-list/government-debt-to-gdp (accessed 2016).

Cox, Kevin C."Atlanta Braves Get New Flood of Hank Aaron Hate Mail, Report Claims."CBSNews. http://www.cbsnews.com/news/atlanta-braves-get-new-flood-of-hank-aaron-hate-mail-report-claims/(accessed April 15, 2014).

Duke, Alan. "50 Cent pleads not guilty in domestic violence case". CNN. (accessed August 5, 2013).

"Database of Mega-churches in the U.S. "Hartford Seminary. http://hirr.hartsem.edu/cgibin/mega/db.pl?db=default&uid=default&view_records=1&ID=*&sb=5 (accessed 2000-2006).

"Deficit by President." About News. http://useconomy.about.com/od/people/fl/Deficit-by-President.htm (accessed March 1, 2016).

"Floyd Mayweather Released From Jail." ESPN and The Associated Press.http://espn.go.com/boxing/story/_/id/8228834/floyd-mayweather-jr-released-vegas-jail-serving-2-months (accessed August 3, 2012).

Foltz, Kim." Does Bo, Hurt, Know as Much?" NY Times. http://www.nytimes.com/1991/03/20/business/the-media-business-advertising-does-bo-hurt-know-as-much.html (accessed March 20, 1991).

"Forbes 400."ForbesMagazine.http://www.forbes.com/forbes-400/list/#version:static (accessed 2016).

Gibson, Campbell and Jung, Kay. "Historical Census Statistics On Population Totals By Race, 1790 to 1990, and By Hispanic Origin, 1970 to 1990, For Large Cities And Other Urban Places In The United States." United States Census Bureau. https://www.census.gov/population/www/documentation/twps0076/twps0076.html. (accessed February 2005).

Gilpin, Robert. *Global Political Economy*. Princeton, N.J: Princeton University Press, 2001; 70.

Giles, Matt and Jones, Nate. "A Timeline of the Abuse Charges Against Bill Cosby [Updated]." Vulture. http://www.vulture.com/2014/09/timeline-of-the-abuse-charges-against-cosby.html (accessed December 30, 2015).

Glick, Julia. "Black Leaders Blast Megachurches, Say They Ignore Social Justice." Religion News Blog. http://www.religionnewsblog.com/15084/black-leaders-blast-megachurches-say-they-ignore-social-justice (accessed June 29, 2006).

Graves, Scott. "Fewer State Prisons, Higher Cost Per Inmate." California Budget and Policy Center. http://calbudgetcenter.org/blog/fewer-state-prisoners-higher-cost-per-inmate/ (accessed April 7, 2013).

Greenspan, Alan. *The Age of Turbulence*. London, U.K: Penguin Group, 2007.

Harig, Bob. "'Tiger-proofing' Augusta Took a Toll on All." ESPN. http://espn.go.com/golf/masters11/columns/story?columnist=harig_bob&page=110329-RTTMasters (accessed April 1, 2011).

"Harrison Ford Reclaims Title of Highest Grossing Actor." The Telegraph. http://www.telegraph.co.uk/film/movie-news/harrison-ford-highest-grossing-actor/ (accessed January 16, 2016).

"Highest to Lowest - Prison Population Total." World Prison Brief: Institute for Criminal Policy Research. http://www.prisonstudies.org/highest-to-lowest/prison-population-total?field_region_taxonomy_tid=All (accessed April 2016).

Hill, Laura E., l and Johnson, Hans P. "How Fertility Changes Across Immigrant Generations." Public Policy Institute of California, Research Brief #58. http://www.ppic.org/content/pubs/rb/RB_402LHRB.pdf (accessed April 2002).

"Hitler Said, Even in His Death He Will Start World War 3. One Of His Soldiers Asked How? Hitler Replied....". FML. http://fmlgoneviral.com/hitler-said-even-death-will-start-world-war-3-one-soliders-asked-hitler-replied/ (accessed July 7, 2015).

"How Many Christian Denominations Worldwide?" Following Jesus in the 21st Century. https://theway21stcentury.wordpress.com/2012/11/23/how-many-christian-denominations-worldwide/ (accessed November 23, 2012).

Inaba, Dr. Darryl. *Uppers, Downers, All-Arounders 5ᵗʰ Edition*. Ashland, Oregon: CNS Publication, 2000; 101.

"Jesse Jackson Admits Affair, Illegitimate Child." ABC News. http://abcnews.go.com/Politics/story?id=122032 (accessed January 18, 2016).

Joyce, Joseph P. *The IMF and Global Financial Crisis*. New York: Cambridge University Press, 2013; 1, 195.

Jules, Marvin. "If All Goes To Plan, By 2020 Michael Jordan's Annual Nike Royalty Check Will Be RIDICULOUS!" Celebrity Net Worth. http://www.celebritynetworth.com/articles/billionaire-news/wont-believe-much-money-michael-jordan-may-make-royalties-year-2020/ (accessed October 22, 2015).

King Jr., Martin Luther. "I Have A Dream Speech." National Archives and Records Administration: United States Government. https://www.archives.gov/press/exhibits/dream-speech.pdf. (accessed August 28, 1963).

King, Peter . "Why Is This Man Smiling?" Sports Illustrated (accessed Aug. 12, 1991), pp. 13-14.

"Kobe Bryant." BrainyQuote.com, Xplore Inc, 2016. http://www.brainyquote.com/quotes/quotes/k/kobebryant167158.html, (accessed April 9, 2016).

"Kobe Bryant Charged With Sexual Assault." CNN. http://www.cnn.com/2003/LAW/07/18/kobe.bryant/ (accessed December 16, 2003).

Kreps, Daniel. "Prince Warns Young Artists: Record Contracts Are 'Slavery'." Rolling Stone. http://www.rollingstone.com/music/news/prince-warns-young-artists-record-contracts-are-slavery-20150809#ixzz476VdNN4j (accessed August 9, 2015).

Kwate, PhD., Naa Oyo A. and Meyer, PhD., Ilan H. "The Myth of Meritocracy and African American Health." National Center for Biotechnology Information: United States National Library of Medicine: National Institutes of Health. http://www.ncbi.nlm.nih.gov/pmc/articles/PMC2936997/ (accessed October 2010).

Lazarowitz, Elizabeth and Siemaszko, Corky. "Dr. Dre Sells Beats Electronics to Apple for $3 Billion." NY Daily News. http://www.nydailynews.com/entertainment/dr-dre-sells-beats-apple-3-billion-article-1.1808975 (accessed May 29, 2014).

Leiby, Richard. "The Ex-Spouse Who Roared: Shelia Johnson's Revelations." The Washington Post. http://www.washingtonpost.com/wp-dyn/articles/A1887-2004May30.html (accessed May 30, 2004).

Leod, Saul. "Erick Erickson". Simply Psychology. http://www.simplypsychology.org/Erik-Erikson.html (accessed 2008, updated 2013).

Lefton, Terry. "To 'Be Like Mike,' Gatorade Had To Poach Michael Jordan From Coke." Sports Business Daily. http://www.sportsbusinessdaily.com/Journal/Issues/2014/02/17/Champions/Schmidt-Jordan.aspx (accessed February 17, 2014).

Lynch, Willie, *The Willie Lynch Letter and the Making of a Slave*. New York, NY: Classic Books America; 2009.

"Magic Johnson Opens Up About His Promiscuous Past - Oprah's Next Chapter - Oprah Winfrey Network." You Tube. http://www.youtube.com/watch?v=S9pZd3Em6ag (accessed December 2, 2013).

Mars, Errol L. "Robert L. Johnson." Black Profiles. http://www.blackentrepreneurprofile.com/profile-full/article/robert-l-johnson/ (accessed 2016).

"Mega-Church Statistics." Statistic Brain. http://www.statisticbrain.com/mega-church-statistics/ (accessed 2016).

Mitchell, Corrie. "Ten Bible Verses Prosperity Gospel Preachers Need To Stop MisUsing." On Faith. http://www.faithstreet.com/onfaith/2014/05/09/ten-verses-prosperity-gospel-preachers-need-stop-misuising/32019 (accessed May 9, 2014).

Moore, Antonio. "The Decadent Veil: Black America's Wealth Illusion." Huffington Post. http://www.huffingtonpost.com/antonio-moore/the-decadent-veil-black-income-inequality_b_5646472.html (accessed August 5, 2014).

Morris, Charles. *The Two Million Dollar MeltDown*. New York, NY: Pubic Affairs, 2008; 62, 92-93, 111, 152-153.

*NAACP*. http://action.naacp.org/page/-/annual%20reports/2005ar.pdf (accessed May 29, 2005). http://action.naacp.org/page/-/annual%20reports/_NAACP_2013AR_WebFNL.pdf (accessed November 1, 2013).

Neighbor, Ralph & Jenkins, Lorna. *Where Do We Go from Here: A Guidebook for the Cell Group Church, 1ˢᵗ Ed.* Condell Park, Australia: Torch Publications Inc., 1990.

Noel, Peter. "Revenge of the Mad Rappers". The Village Voice. http://www.villagevoice.com/news/revenge-of-the-mad-rappers-6423066 (accessed December 1, 1998).

Nolan, Jonathan and Nolan, Christopher. "The Dark Knight Rises." https://alexcassun.files.wordpress.com/2012/08/tdkr.pdf, pg.90. United Kingdom: Faber and Faber LTD (accessed July 2012).

Norman, Tony. "The Big Difference Between 'Rich' and 'Wealthy'." Pittsburg Post-Gazette. http://www.post-gazette.com/opinion/tony-norman/2004/05/21/The-big-difference-between-rich-and-wealthy/stories/200405210167 (Accessed May 21, 2004).

Oliver, Roland and Fage, J.D. *A Short History of Africa.* New York: Penguin Group, Sixth Edition, 1988; 94-95.

"Out of State Prison Facilities." California Department of Corrections and Rehabilitations. http://www.cdcr.ca.gov/Visitors/CA_Out_Of_State_Facilities.html (accessed 2016).

Page, Clarence. "Thanks For Being Honest, Jimmy `The Greek`-too Honest." Chicago Tribune. http://articles.chicagotribune.com/1988-01-20/news/8803230751_1_thighs-black-professional-sports (accessed January 20, 1988).

Palmer, Louise D. The Boston Globe. This article includes information from the Seattle Post-Intelligencer Staff. This article appeared in the Seattle Post-Intelligencer, Pages A-1 & A-4. http://ronmull.tripod.com/racism.html (accessed March 2, 1999).

Parnass, Sarah. " The CNN Democratic Debate Transcript, Annotated." The Washington Post. https://www.washingtonpost.com/news/the-fix/wp/2015/10/13/the-oct-13-democratic-debate-who-said-what-and-what-it-means/ (accessed October 13, 2015).

Peet, Richard. *Unholy Trinity: The IMF, World Bank, and WTO, 2ⁿᵈ Ed.* London: Zed Books, 2008; 37, 42, 258-260.

Rampersad A, Roessel D. *The Collected Poems of Langston Hughes.* New York, NY: Knopf; 1994.

Rastogi, Sonya, Johnson, Tallase D., Hoeffel, Elizabeth M., and Drewery Jr., Malcolm P. "The Black Population 2010." U.S. Department of Commerce: Economics and Statistics Administration" United States Census Bureau. http://www.census.gov/prod/cen2010/briefs/c2010br-06.pdf (accessed September 2011).

"Sandra Davis Lawrence." Post Conviction Justice Project: University of Southern California. http://uscpcjp.com/meet-our-clients/sandra-davis-lawrence/ (accessed 2016).

Sands, Darren. "As He Soars, Sales of Tiger Woods PGA Tour 14 Steady." Black Enterprise. http://www.blackenterprise.com/lifestyle/tiger-woods-pga-tour-14-sales-steady-videogame/ (accessed May 14, 2013).

Sanyal, Sanyeev. "The End of Population Growth." Project Syndicate. http://www.project-syndicate.org/commentary/the-end-of-population-growth (accessed October 30, 2011).

Steed, Richard. Denmark. "Work/Life Balance - The Danish Way." The Official Website of Denmark. http://denmark.dk/en/meet-the-danes/work-life-balance-the-danish-way/ (accessed 2016).

Stephenson, Debbie. "When Did Athletes Start Getting Rich." The Deal Room. http://www.firmex.com/thedealroom/when-did-athletes-start-getting-rich/ (accessed June 24, 2014).

Sullivan, Arthur; Steven M. Sheffrin. *Economics: Principles in Action*. Upper Saddle River: Pearson Prentice Hall, 2003.

Tadena, Nathalie and Zhou, Momo. Divorce Has a Hefty Price Tag for Celebrities, Billionaires. ABC News. http://abcnews.go.com/Business/divorce-hefty-price-tag-celebrities-billionaires/story?id=8363063 (accessed August 20, 2009).

"The Cornerstone of California's Solution to Reduce Overcrowding, Costs, and Recidivism." California Department of Corrections and Rehabilitations. http://www.cdcr.ca.gov/realignment/ (accessed 2016).

*The Charters of Freedom*. Government Archives. http://www.archives.gov/exhibits/charters/bill_of_rights_transcript.html (accessed: 1776).

"The Future of California Corrections." California Department of Corrections and Rehabilitations. http://www.cdcr.ca.gov/2012plan/docs/plan/complete.pdf, pp. 15, Introduction 1, 3-4, 7, Population Projections 10.

*The Holy Bible, King James Version: Thompson Chain Reference*. Indianapolis, Indiana: B.B. Kirkbridge Bible Company, Inc., 1982.

"Tiger Woods' Affair: Has Golfer's Image Finally Recovered From Infidelity Scandal?" Huffington Post. http://www.huffingtonpost.com/2013/06/10/tiger-woods-reputation_n_3417137.html (accessed June 10, 2013).

Turner, Broderick. Eleven Years After Messy Breakup With Lakers, Kobe and Shaq Make Up On Podcast." L.A. Times. http://www.latimes.com/sports/lakers/la-sp-kobe-shaq-feud-20150830-story.html (Accessed August 30, 2015).

"UN Data: Total Fertility Rate (children per woman)." United Nations. esa.un.org (Retrieved 2012-09-17). [dead link].

*United Nations*. "World Population Policies 2011: Economic and Social Affairs." http://www.un.org/en/development/desa/population/publications/pdf/policy/WPP2011/w pp. 2011.pdf, pg.7 (accessed 2013).

"U.S. Debt Clock." United States Debt Clock. http://www.usdebtclock.org (accessed 2016).

Van Biema, David & Chu, Jeff. "Does God Want You to Be Rich?" Time Magazine. http://content.time.com/time/magazine/article/0,9171,1533448,00.html (accessed September 10, 2006).

Walker, Brenda. "California Releases Thousands of Lifers from Prison." V DARE. http://uscpcjp.com/meet-our-clients/sandra-davis-lawrence/ (accessed August 9, 2014).

Walter, John C. "The Changing Status of the Black Athlete in the 20th Century United States." Liverpool John Moores University: AR Net. http://www.americansc.org.uk/Online/walters.htm (accessed 1996).

Warner, Brian. "The Richest Celebrity Couples In The World – 2013." Celebrity Net Worth. http://www.celebritynetworth.com/articles/entertainment-articles/the-richest-celebrity-couples-in-the-world-2013/ (accessed June 4, 2013).

Warren, Rick. *The Purpose Driven Church*. Grand Rapids, MI: Zondervan, 1995.

Weisenfeld, Judith. "Religion in African American History." Oxford University Press. http://americanhistory.oxfordre.com/view/10.1093/acrefore/9780199329175.001.0001/acrefore-9780199329175-e-24 (accessed March 2015).

West Ph.D., Dr. Heather C. "Prison Inmates at Midyear 2009 - Statistical Tables." U.S. Department of Justice: Office of Justice Programs: Bureau of Justice Statistics. http://www.bjs.gov/content/pub/pdf/pim09st.pdf (accessed June 2010).

"What You Need to Know About Proposition 47." California Department of Corrections and Rehabilitations. http://www.cdcr.ca.gov/news/Proposition_47.html (accessed 2016).

"Who Are the Nouveau Riche." wiseGeek. http://www.wisegeek.com/who-are-the-nouveau-riche.htm <http://jetsetbabe.com/nouveau-riche-old-money/> (accessed 2013-2016).

Wolff, Richard. *Democracy at Work: A Cure for Capitalism*. Chicago, IL: Haymarket Books, 2012; 11-12, 17, 22.

Wojciechowski, Gene. "Jordan Hit On Gambling : Golf Bets: San Diego Man Says The Bulls' Star Played Him For Four Years, Once Owed Him $1.252 Million." L.A. Times. (accessed June 3, 1993).

"World Economic Outlook Database, October 2015." International Monetary Fund (IMF). https://www.imf.org/external/pubs/ft/weo/2015/02/weodata/download.aspx (accessed 2016).

Worthen M.Div., Carlton. "Slavery is Legal in America." http://carltonworthen.blogspot.com/2010_09_01_archive.html (Accessed September 10, 2010). Palmer, Louise D. The Boston Globe. This article includes information from the Seattle Post-Intelligencer Staff. This article appeared in the Seattle Post-Intelligencer, Pages A-1 & A-4. http://ronmull.tripod.com/racism.html (accessed March 2, 1999).

# INDEX

269

270

274

280

281

282